GEOGRAPHISCHE GESUNDHEITSFORSCHUNG

GEOGRAPHIC HEALTH RESEARCH

herausgegeben von

Thomas Kistemann und Jürgen Schweikart

Schriftenreihe des Vereins zur Förderung der Geographischen Gesundheitsforschung e.V.

Volume 7

Timo Falkenberg

Wastewater-Irrigated Urban Agriculture in the Context of WASH in Ahmedabad, India

The impact of irrigation water quality on the incidence of diarrhea

Umschlagabbildung: Cover illustration:
Ahmedabad 2012, Farmer placing pump into river. Picture taken approx. 250 meters downstream of sewage outlet. © Timo Falkenberg

Bibliografische Information der Deutschen Nationalbibliothek
Die Deutsche Nationalbibliothek verzeichnet diese Publikation in der Deutschen Nationalbibliografie; detaillierte bibliografische Daten sind im Internet über http://dnb.d-nb.de abrufbar.

Bibliographic information published by the Deutsche Nationalbibliothek
The Deutsche Nationalbibliothek lists this publication in the Deutsche Nationalbibliografie; detailed bibliographic data are available in the Internet at http://dnb.d-nb.de.

Diese Arbeit wurde unter dem Titel „Wastewater-Irrigated Urban Agriculture in the Context of WASH in Ahmedabad, India: the impact of of irrigation water quality on the incidence of diarrhea“ als Dissertation an der Mathematisch-Naturwissenschaftliche Fakultät der Rheinische Friedrich-Wilhelms-Universität Bonn online publiziert:

This work has been published online as a PhD thesis at the faculty of Natural Sciences of the Rheinische Friedrich-Wilhelms-Universität Bonn entitled: „Wastewater-Irrigated Urban Agriculture in the Context of WASH in Ahmedabad, India: the impact of of irrigation water quality on the incidence of diarrhea“:

http://hss.ulb.uni-bonn.de/2017/4656/4656.htm

Gedruckt auf säurefreiem, alterungsbeständigem Papier.

Printed on acid-free, age-resistant paper.

Printed in Germany.
ISBN 978-3-8440-9144-1
ISSN 2191-7213

Schriftenreihe des

Publication series of

Schriftenreihe des Vereins zur Förderung der Geographischen Gesundheitsforschung e. V.
www.VGGF.de

Schriftleitung

Editorial staff

Dr. Silvia Schäffer und Juliane Kemen-Wendt

Shaker Verlag GmbH, Düren
Internet: www.shaker.de • E-Mail: info@shaker.de

Editors' Preface

Medical Geography and Health Geography locate themselves at the interdisciplinary interface of medicine, public health and geography. Through crosscutting issues, they connect and combine human, physical and regional geographies in interdisciplinary ways. The *Geographical Health Research Series* offers an extensive and independent publication platform for a topic receiving increasing attention in modern research, teaching and practise in the German-speaking world. High-quality studies from all branches of Medical Geography and Health Geography are collated in this series. As well as disease ecology, this series will publish scientific papers dealing with space-related aspects of healthcare, health and development, salutogenesis and pathogenesis, spatial manifestations of social and cultural dimensions of health and disease, both in German and in English. All subjects in this series are bound by one specific characteristic: the geographical dimension in its widest sense, be that an Euclidean space or a meaningful place.

Thomas Kistemann, Bonn

Jürgen Schweikart, Berlin

Table of Contents

List of Figures

List of Tables

List of Abbreviations

AMC	Ahmedabad Municipal Cooperation
ATE	Average Treatment Effect
BMI	Body Mass Index
CFUs	Colony Forming Units
DALYs	Disability-Adjusted Life-Years
DFID	UK Department for International Development
EC	Escherichia Coli
HI	Hygiene Index
JMP	Joint Monitoring Programm for Water and Sanitation
l/c/d	liters per capita per day
MDGs	Millennium Development Goals
MPN	Most Probable Number
NaCl	Sodium Chloride
OLS	Ordinary Least Square
OR	Odds Ratio
ORS	Oral Rehydration Salts
PoS	Point-of-Source
PoU	Point-of-Use
RO	Reverse Osmosis Water Filter
SDGs	Sustainable Development Goals
SES	Socio-Economic Status
UA	Urban Agriculture
UNICEF	United Nations International Children's Emergency Fund
WASH	Water, Sanitation and Hygiene
WHO	World Health Organization
WSTR	Waste Storage and Treatment Reservoir

1 Introduction

The impact of 'WASH' (Water, Sanitation and Hygiene) on health is one of the key challenges of public health. The improvement of the water supply system coupled with adequate sanitation and hygiene is considered one of the greatest public health advances of 20th century Europe. John Snow's classic epidemiological study identified London's water pumps as the source of the cholera epidemic at the time (Snow, 1857). Improvements in the water supply quality, as well as improvements in sewage treatment and personal hygiene have resulted in the near-elimination of water-borne infections among developed nations. Nonetheless, poor water quality, lack of sanitation and inadequate hygiene remain key disease risks, with 88% of global diarrhea deaths still being attributed to WASH (UNICEF/WHO, 2009). Particularly developing and emerging countries are struggling to provide safe water and access to sanitation for their growing populations.

Rapid urbanization is a key phenomenon of the 21st century, providing opportunities but also presenting challenges. Growing urban agglomerations produce economic opportunities, largely arising from the advantages of economies of scale, resulting in development and potentially improvements of the quality of life of the inhabitants of the urban area (Quigley, 2008). However, the rate of urbanization exceeds development in many emerging countries, causing challenges for municipal governments (ibid; Ravallion, 2002). The large influx of largely unskilled rural people into urban areas results in a shortage of formal employment opportunities, in consequence fueling the informal economy (Gupta, 1993). The development of affordable housing lags behind demand leading to the formation of informal settlements. The spatial expansion of such cities also poses challenges for infrastructure development, as the extension of water supply and sewage treatment networks cannot keep up with the growth (Kundu & Roy, 2012). Additionally, spatial growth of the urban area increasingly encroaches on the agricultural land that feeds the urban population. Thus, a continuously increasing urban population is at the same time dependent on decreasing agricultural land resources. As a result, the food needs of the urban population are met through imports from other regions, states or countries. The transport costs increase and thus food prices rise, posing problems of food accessibility for people among the lower income quintiles and increases vulnerability to global market price fluctuations.

Urban agriculture has emerged as a mechanism to transform some of these challenges into opportunities. Particularly the issue of food accessibility is addressed through the cultivation of crops within the urban area. Perishable foods can be marketed fresh with low transportation cost, resulting in a lower price (De Zeeuw et al., 2011; Ensink et al., 2002). Furthermore, food produce may be consumed within the farming household itself or may be used for bartering. However, the cultivation of crops in the city has problems. The key challenge is presented by the availability of land, which is limited in the urban context. More value can be extracted from the land resource if it is used for the development of housing or industry, thus urban agriculture is usually situated in areas unsuitable for construction. Additionally, concerns about the food quality persist, as air, land and water contamination are common in the buzzing urban centers of emerging countries. These potential health problems of urban agriculture are the primary topic of this research study. The focus is, however, not on all forms of contamination but on the fecal contamination of irrigation water.

1.1 Research Question and Hypothesis

The key research question of this study is: "What is the effect of wastewater irrigation on the incidence of diarrhea among urban farming households in Ahmedabad, India", leading to the secondary question: "How does the effect of wastewater irrigation compare to the impact of drinking water, sanitation and hygiene (WASH)". In order for the primary research question to be answered a series of objectives needs to be fulfilled:

- Determine the incidence of disease
- Measure irrigation water quality

- Determine farming methods (irrigation method, crop varieties, treatment method, etc.)

To control for confounding effects and address the secondary research questions the following additional objectives need to be completed:

- Measure drinking water quality
- Assess the sanitation situation
- Determine household hygiene behavior
- Determine household characteristics (demographic, socio-economic and dietary information)

It is hypothesized that wastewater irrigation has significant adverse impacts on the incidence of diarrhea. The discharge of untreated wastewater represents a failure of the primary barrier, and forms the foundation for wastewater use. Once individuals come into contact with fecal pathogens, these are transmitted along the pathways depicted in the F-diagram (see Section 1.2.2). It is therefore hypothesized that wastewater irrigation forms an integral part of the WASH-nexus, where wastewater irrigation has adverse effects similar to those of open defecation.

To further assess how wastewater irrigation is integrated into the WASH nexus, three sub-questions are assessed:

- How does wastewater irrigation influence drinking water quality?
- How does wastewater irrigation influence hygiene behavior?
- How does wastewater irrigation influence child nutritional status?

It is hypothesized that the effect on drinking water quality is two-fold. On the one hand side, frequent irrigation with highly contaminated water can lead to the percolation of pathogens into ground water, which forms the drinking water source of the entire sample population. On the other handside, exposure to irrigation water may lead to the transfer of pathogens onto hands and clothes, thus contributing to in-household water contamination and cross-contamination. Overall, it is expected that irrigation water and drinking water quality are positively correlated.

Furthermore, it is hypothesized that farmers utilizing wastewater for irrigation engage in additional preventive and safety behaviors, especially in comparison with surface water users. Farmers relying on wastewater for irrigation are aware of the high contamination level due to its color and odor. This leads to the expectation that these farmers adopt preventive and safety behavior to reduce exposure. Farmers irrigating with surface water may not be aware that they essentially use diluted wastewater containing high pathogen densities. In consequence, it is hypothesized that wastewater farmers adopt additional preventive behavior, whilst surface water farmers do not.

1.2 Theoretical Background

'Health Geography' is a broad and interdisciplinary sub-discipline of human geography that has undergone transformation and popularization throughout the past three decades (Rosenberg, 2015; Giesbrecht et al., 2014; Kearns & Moon, 2002). The origins of the sub-discipline can be traced to the 1800's, when Leonhard Ludwig Finke coined the term 'Medical Geography' (1792–1795) and Friedrich Schnumer published the first global map of the distribution of disease in 1827 (Bleker, 2014). The traditional focus of medical geography on mapping of disease distributions and identification of spatial patterns has expanded both thematically and methodologically and in the process matured into health geography. Underlying the metamorphosis of the sub-discipline is a shift away from "the interests of the medical world" (Kearns & Moon, 2002:606) and the focus on disease towards the "holistic definition of health, where well-being and broader social models of health and health care" (ibid;606) become the object of study. Methodologically the sub-discipline has evolved, capitalizing on the interdisciplinary nature of health geography through adaptation of public health, epidemiological and sociological methodologies, drawing on social, political and economic theories and building on the understanding of ecological principals and processes. As a result, a wide range of methodological approaches are applied in health geographic research, ranging from traditional mapping approaches via quantitative assessments of environmental, social and health related factors to qualitative approaches that move the focus towards the subjective feelings that shape place and influence health status.

Despite the refocusing of health geography on health benefits and well-being, medical geography approaches remain an important component of the sub-discipline (Parr, 2002). Especially in the developing country context focus remains on infectious diseases, however, the approaches have advanced beyond mapping of disease distribution, now also assessing the complex interactions between the determinants of disease of a particular place and identifying the underlying systems shaping the place and its health determinants. This research follows the tradition of medical geography, adopting a public health perspective and utilizing an epidemiological methodology (see Chapter 2).

The central object of the study is urban agriculture, which essentially is agricultural production undertaken in an urban area. The urban context exerts external pressures on the places of food production that influence the impact of urban agriculture on health. Water, air and soil contamination are important negative externalities of urbanization and industrialization, which essentially shape the risk environment in and around the urban area. The focus of this study lies on the health impact of water contamination and its use for irrigation in particular.

In the following section (1.2.1), the concept of 'Urban Agriculture' is introduced and its theoretical underpinnings and rational are highlighted. The biomedical frameworks of disease transmission are discussed in section 1.2.2 that form the basis of the epidemiological methodology of this research. A vast variety of pathogenic organisms can survive in water, and their characteristics, infective doses and survival times are differentiated in section 1.2.3. The primary outcome variable of this study is the incidence of diarrhea. In section 1.2.4 the disease is defined and its biomedical processes explained followed by the recommended diarrhea treatment and prevention strategies (section 1.2.5). As dehydration is the key cause of diarrhea-related mortality, in section 1.2.6 the minimum water requirements per capita are explored. Finally, hygiene (section 1.2.7) and WASH (Water, Sanitation and Hygiene, section 1.2.8) interventions are reviewed highlighting the fact that a set of complex interactions between various determinants influences the incidence of diarrheal disease.

1.2.1 Urban Agriculture

Agricultural activities in and surrounding urban settlements have been practiced for centuries. An urban area cannot strive without a sufficient food supply for its inhabitants. In 1898, Ebenezer Howard introduced the concept of 'Garden Cities', and the term 'urban agriculture' was first coined by Shiro Aoskika in 1935 (Zhang et al., 2014). The concept was only popularized in academia in the late 1980's and early 1990's and since has gained growing interest among donors, development practioners and academics alike (Korth et al., 2014). Despite research efforts, the global scope of urban agriculture (UA) is not known (ibid); the only reliable estimation is outdated. In the UNDP Report 'Urban Agriculture: Food, Jobs and Sustainable Cities' it is estimated that in the early 1990's about 800 million people used urban agriculture as a livelihood strategy (Smit et al., 1996). During the global food price peak in 2008, the role of urban agriculture in stabilizing the local food market was highlighted (Holt-Giménez et al., 2009). Cities with a strong urban agriculture base were less likely to experience food insecurity (ibid). The positive impact of urban agriculture on urban food security is considered the primary benefit of urban agriculture.

The concept of urban agriculture is complex, as it is made up of a wide variety of farming systems and activities. Luc Mougeot coined the most commonly used definition:

"Urban agriculture is an industry located within (intra-urban) or on the fringe (peri-urban) of a town, a city or a metropolis, which grows and raises, processes and distributes a diversity of food and non-food products, (re-)using largely human and animal resources, products and services found in and around that urban area, and in turn supplying human and material resources, products and services largely to that urban area" (Mougeot, 2000:11).

This definition encompasses all elements of urban agriculture, without restricting its scope. The key criterion is geographic and restricted to agricultural activities undertaken in urban areas. The distinction between peri-urban and intra-urban is thus also of importance. Peri-urban areas usually have a more rural character, thus following more traditional farming systems; such systems are often unfeasible in urban areas. Riverbanks, road and rail sides, and backyards are common locations for urban agriculture, but also decommissioned industrial areas or vacant housing plots (Bellows et al., 2004). Mougeot's definition goes beyond the mere production of food to include the entire industry of urban agriculture, consisting of food production and processing, transport and sale. More importantly, it is not restricted to food but also entails non-food products, such as ornamental flowers or energy crops.

A key distinction can be made between subsistence or supplementary farming and commercial farming. Subsistence farming is, however, rather uncommon in the urban context; urban agriculture forms part of the people's livelihood strategy, providing supplementary food and income (Bellows et al., 2004; Lee-Smith & Prain, 2006). Commercial farming activities are often situated on the fringes of the city where sufficient land area is available.

The range of employment opportunities created through the urban agriculture industry is one of the reasons for its application as a coupled food security and poverty reduction strategy (Bellows et al., 2004; Brown & Jameton, 2000; Ruel et al., 1998). These strategies usually aim to formalize and regulate urban agriculture, as many urban authorities do not accept farming activities in the city due to zoning regulations. The informal and often illegal land use creates a high degree of uncertainty for urban farmers, affecting their ability to plan and their willingness to invest. The formalization of urban agriculture has led to great success stories in Latin America, for example in Rosario, Argentina (FAO, 2014). Urban produce can be bought in supermarkets, supplies restaurants and is recognized for its quality and freshness. After the economic collapse and industrial decline, Rosario was suffering high unemployment and widespread poverty when the national 'Pro-Huerta' programme was launched (ibid). An entire industry was created, consisting of the cultivation, processing, transport and sale of urban produce generating employment and livelihood opportunities (ibid). Rosario now is the prime example of successful urban agriculture, and through the formalization food security was improved, employment was created and the economy was revived.

Food security is a multidimensional concept, consisting of four pillars: availability, accessibility, utilization and stability (Clay, 2002; FAO, 2003; Tirado et al., 2010). The availability of food is in line with the traditional understanding of food security; if a sufficient quantity is available then food security is achieved. However, this does not take into account the distribution of food, thus accessibility also needs to be achieved. The low-income groups need to have access to sufficient food; mere availability at high prices does not ensure food security for the poor. Food utilization refers to nutrition, in particular micronutrients, which may be absent when the reliance is merely on staple foods. A balanced diet should hence also be achievable for the entire urban population. The fourth dimension refers to the stability of the food system and its ability to withstand environmental, economic and social shocks. Reliance on food imports makes urban markets vulnerable to price fluctuations and global market speculation. Urban agriculture is conceptualized to benefit food security in all four dimensions. Food production in the city undoubtedly increases the availability of food. Urban produce is rarely sold in supermarkets or formal markets, but more commonly through street vendors. Thus, food accessibility is improved through the development of an urban agriculture industry. Due to the close proximity of production and consumption, easily perishable yet highly nutritious foods, such as fruits and vegetables, can be cultivated. Food utilization improves as more diverse foods are accessible. The stability of the food system is also improved by urban agriculture, as it complements the existing food supply system and reduces reliance on food imports.

Urban agriculture also induces environmental benefits as the shorter transport distances not only reduce emissions but also require a shorter cooling chain. The dominant food supply system removes nutrients from the soil to produce food, which is ultimately consumed in distant regions or countries. These nutrients are replenished through chemical fertilizers, which are usually produced in yet another region. The consumed food naturally produces waste that needs to be safely disposed of, presenting a challenge to many rapidly urbanizing cities.

Urban agriculture diverges from this path and follows a more sustainable approach. Food is mainly produced close to where it is consumed. Furthermore, the nutrient cycle remains closed through the utilization of the urban waste stream. Organic waste forms a good basis for compost, potentially reducing the reliance on artificial fertilizers. Sewage water is not only rich in nutrients but also provides a continuous water source for irrigation (Drechsel & Evans, 2010; Drechsel et al., 2010; De Zeeuw et al., 2011). In this way, while nutrients are removed from the soil and consumed in the form of food, they are ultimately returned to the soil in form of compost, sewage or sludge. Thus, urban agriculture is often a low input system, relying on the urban waste stream to supply required resources. In turn, urban agriculture can be an integral part of the urban waste management strategy. However, in reality such waste recycling is often unplanned and uncontrolled.

Although such an organic waste recycling system is beneficial when adequately controlled, it can pose serious environmental and health hazards when operating unplanned. Urban wastewater is a mixture of sewage, residential, industrial and hospital wastewater, therefore hosting a multitude of pathogens and chemical substances (Hamilton et al., 2007; Srinivasan & Reddy, 2009; Hanjra et al., 2012). Particularly chemical contamination can be devastating to agriculture, leading to crop failure. Therefore, in a planned system, only sewage and residential wastewater should enter into the urban agriculture system. Although the utilization of sewage poses a health risk, its composition is beneficial for plant growth.

On-farm treatment systems, such as small sedimentation ponds or waste storage and treatment reservoirs (WSTR) could reduce the disease risk, particularly if coupled with the wearing of boots and gloves (Drechsel et al., 2010). Sedimentation ponds form the cheapest and simplest option to reduce the pathogen density of wastewater (Keraita et al., 2010). In the shallow ponds, usually around 1.5 m in depth, pathogens are effectively removed (Curtis et al., 1992). Sunlight penetrates the water and damages bacteria and viruses, whilst helminths and protozoa are removed by sedimentation (Keraita et al., 2010). The WSTR system essentially adds two tanks to the sedimentation pond, forming a three-chamber system (Mara, 2004). While the first tank is being filled, the water in the second tank rests, and the water from the third tank is available for use (ibid). The water quality can be improved to meet the standards for unrestricted irrigation; however, the depth of the sedimentation pond is negatively correlated with rate of pathogen die-off (Athayde Júnior et al., 2000). Thus, deeper ponds require longer retention times; in ponds 2-6 m in depth, retention time ranges from 15-25 days (ibid). Additionally, various secondary and tertiary treatment options are available, including oxidation ditches, trickling filters, sand filters, coagulation and flocculation (Drechsel et al., 2010). Unfortunately, most wastewater reuse is unplanned; thus, no risk mitigation strategies are in place. Wastewater is released untreated into waterways often leading to farmers unknowingly using diluted wastewater for irrigation purposes.

The health risks arising from urban agriculture form the basis of criticism of the concept. It is important to distinguish between two types of risk, i.e. the risk for the farmer and the consumer risk. The risk for the consumer arises from unsafe food produced in urban areas. A key concern is heavy metal contamination; urban soils are likely to accumulate heavy metals due to industrial residues, irrigation/flooding with industrial wastewater, or close proximity to major roads (Lee-Smith & Prain, 2006; Nabulo et al., 2008). Heavy metals are taken up by the plant and accumulate in the edible parts of the crop (Bellows et al., 2004; Hanjra et al., 2012), thus presenting a health risk. The consumption of even low doses of heavy metals over prolonged periods can have significant health impacts (Hanjra et al., 2012). Lead, for example, affects the mental development of children in low doses, while high concentrations of lead in the bloodstream cause permanent neurological, developmental, and behavioral disorders (Laidlaw et al., 2005). The utilization of the urban waste stream introduces chemical and biological contaminants into the farm system. Thus, urban produce can potentially be contaminated and cause adverse health effects on the consumer. However, adequate food hygiene can significantly reduce the biological health risks for consumers. Washing and peeling food before food preparation is essential to remove bacterial or chemical residues from the surface of the crop, and cooking the food at high temperature ensures the near-elimination of pathogens (Beuchat, 1998).

The farmer risk is higher compared to the consumer risk, as regular contact with soil, crops and irrigation water is inevitable. The risk can be divided into chemical, physical, biological and psycho-social (Lee-Smith & Prain, 2006). Chemical and biological risks arise from the direct and indirect contact with contaminated substances such as wastewater and soils. The physical risk refers to injuries obtained during agricultural work, whilst psycho-social risks are anxiety and stress that may be induced through insecure land tenure or uncertain weather conditions (ibid). Whilst such physical and psycho-social risks are important, these are not specific to wastewater use but occur in any agricultural setting. Chemical risks arising from fertilizer and pesticide application are also universally applicable to agriculture. However, direct exposure to wastewater poses additional chemical and biological risks to the farmers, inducing a variety of adverse health impacts. Prolonged skin contact, which occurs frequently during irrigation work, may lead to rashes and skin infection (Trang et al., 2007). Accidental ingestion of even small quantities of heavy metals can result in a variety of diseases, including cancer, liver failure and neurological disorders in the long term (Chang et al., 2002; Duruibe et al., 2007). Biological pathogens enter the body over various routes. Certain helminthes, hookworms for example, break the skin, whilst most bacteria and viruses enter the body orally. The specific symptoms and diseases depend upon the specific pathogens. Additionally, the farmer risk is compounded by the consumer risk, as most urban farmers consume part of their harvest themselves.

Similar to the consumer risk, adequate preventive behavior can greatly reduce the farmer risk. Safety wear, such as boots and gloves reduce direct exposure, while on-farm treatment systems have proven effective in the removal of pathogens (Drechsel et al., 2010). Adequate hygiene behavior after work reduces the potential of pathogen transfer and cross-contamination.

In 1998, Asano distinguished between three types of wastewater use: direct use of untreated wastewater, direct use of treated wastewater and indirect use of wastewater (Srinivasan & Reddy, 2009). Alternatively, three types of wastewater are defined: raw, diluted and treated (Costa-Pierce et al., 2005). Whilst the use of treated wastewater is certainly the desired option, direct and indirect use of untreated wastewater is widespread (Jamil et al., 2010). Over 80% of sewage generated in developing countries is released untreated (UNESCO, 2003). Consequently, most surface waterways are contaminated with wastewater, which leads to downstream farmers utilizing diluted wastewater, often unknowingly. Low awareness of the presence of wastewater and its adverse health impacts result in inadequate preventive behavior and thus increased health risks. In 1989, the World Health Organization (WHO) published their recommendation for the use of wastewater for agriculture, highlighting that the in water 1,000 *Escherichia coli* bacteria per 100 ml for unrestricted irrigation should not be exceeded (WHO, 1989). The guideline was revised in 2006, as the stringent standard was difficult to achieve in most developing countries. The updated recommendation is outcome-based; utilizing the calculation of DALYs (Disability-Adjusted Life Years) stating that wastewater use should not induce more than 10^{-6} DALYs per person per year (WHO, 2006). Despite these recommendations to protect health, untreated wastewater continues to be utilized raw and diluted, as urban farmers often do not have alternative options.

1.2.2 Transmission Routes

Water and wastewater in particular can host a multitude of pathogens from human as well as animal origin, including bacteria, viruses, protozoa and helminthes causing a wide array of symptoms and diseases (Bartram & Hunter, 2015). In 1972, White et al. proposed a classification of water-related diseases, which is now referred to as the Bradley Classification (ibid). It consists of four categories: water-borne, water-washed, water-based and water-related insect vector (White et al., 1972). Water-borne diseases are those caused by pathogens that are transported in water and ingested orally (Bartram & Hunter, 2015). *Vibrio cholerae* and *Salmonella typhi* are classical examples of the water-borne class. Fecal-oral pathogens can usually be water-borne as well as food-borne. Water-washed diseases are induced through the absence of sufficient water for personal hygiene, or "those whose incidence or severity can be reduced by augmenting the availability of water without improving its quality" (White et al., 1972:162).

Trachoma and skin sepsis are common water-washed diseases, as they are transferred person-to-person, and here hygiene forms a key preventive barrier (Bartram & Hunter, 2015). Fecal-oral diseases can also be classified as water-washed, as inadequate hygiene contributes to the spread of pathogens and person-to-person transmission (ibid). Water-based diseases are caused by pathogens that spend a necessary part of their life cycle in an aquatic host (White et al., 1972). These include helminthes and protozoa, and are divided into water multiplying and non-water multiplying pathogens (ibid). The latter category, i.e. water-related insect vectors, comprises diseases transferred by insects that bite or breed in or nearby water (ibid); malaria and dengue are classical examples.

All four disease types are relevant in regard to wastewater irrigation. However, the focus lies on water-borne diseases, as pathogens are introduced into the agricultural environment through wastewater. Most water-borne diseases are caused by fecal-oral pathogens, where the infective agent is transferred from the host's stool and then ingested by a new host. Wagner & Lanoix (1958) first conceptualized the fecal-oral transmission routes in what today is popularly referred to as the 'F-diagram' (see Figure 1). Feces form the pathogen stock from where these are transferred via water, hands, arthropods, soil and food to be eventually ingested by a susceptible host. Kawata (1978) renamed the individual components, changing water to fluids, hands to fingers, arthropods to flies and soil to fields, leading to the popular term 'F-Diagram'. Fomites are sometimes added to the transmission factors (Bartram & Hunter, 2015).

Apart from illustrating the multiple transmission routes of fecal-oral pathogens, the diagram highlights primary and secondary barriers. Primary barriers halt the release of fecal pathogens from feces into the environment (Curtis et al., 2000). These barriers are primarily infrastructural, focusing on safe and adequate disposal of feces through the construction of latrines, sewers and sewage treatment plants. Hand hygiene after defecation is also a key primary barrier. Secondary barriers halt the spread and multiplication of fecal pathogens that have entered the environment to stop them from reaching a susceptible host (Curtis et al., 2000). Drinking water treatment, both centrally and in-household, acts as a secondary barrier removing pathogens from water. Hygiene practice forms the key secondary barrier, as adequate hand, food and domestic hygiene reduce the pathogen load and cross-contamination (Curtis et al., 2000).

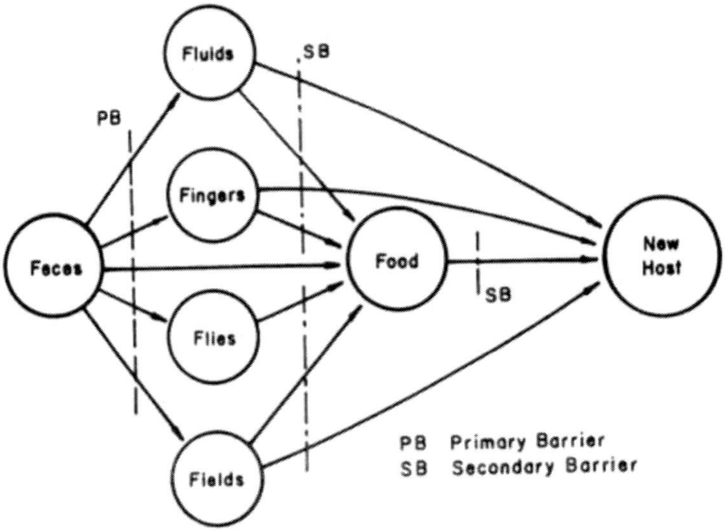

Figure 1: F-Diagram of disease transmission. Source: Kawata, 1978. Arrows represent transmission routes and dashed lines illustrate transmission barriers

The F-diagram indicates that when primary barriers operate adequately, secondary barriers are less important for disease risk reduction (Curtis et al., 2000). Although this appears logical and epidemiological evidence has confirmed the importance of adequate sanitation in the combat against fecal-oral diseases, the role of secondary barriers cannot be neglected. Even in areas where sanitation facilities exist, these may be poorly planned, constructed or maintained, potentially leading to pathogen transfer to the environment (Prüss et al., 2002). Furthermore, in most developing countries large volumes of untreated sewage are released into waterways, representing a failure of the key primary barrier (UNESCO, 2003). As fully functioning primary barriers cannot be achieved in the short term, it is essential to employ effective secondary barriers.

Fecal pathogens can be transmitted via multiple routes to reach a susceptible target. However, mere ingestion does not necessarily cause infection and disease.

In order to cause infection, pathogens have to reach the target site in the host's body, contact the target cell and start multiplying (Sobsey, 2015). Infections can be symptomatic or asymptomatic and may develop into diseases if the host's immune system cannot disable the pathogens (ibid). Thus, a set of pathogen properties and host characteristics mediate the outcome of infection and the severity of symptoms and disease (ibid). The minimum infective dose of various pathogens has been established in volunteer feeding studies (Buchanan et al., 2000). In such studies dose-response relationships are determined by describing the relationship between the intensity of exposure and the frequency of occurrence of certain symptoms within the population (Teunis et al., 1996). The intensity of exposure is the dosage of pathogens administered and is quantified in terms of colony-forming units (CFU), cysts or spores (ibid). Many protozoa, *Giardia lambia* for example, can cause infection with doses of only few cysts, whilst bacteria, such as S. *typhi*, require relatively high doses to cause infection (ibid; Leclerc et al., 2002). Thus, the probability of causing infection depends upon the pathogen's ability to survive in the environment in sufficiently large quantities.

1.2.3 Fecal-oral Pathogens

A vast number of fecal-oral pathogens exist, each with its own characteristics. Generally, three types of fecal pathogens can be distinguished, bacteria, viruses and protozoa (Leclerc et al., 2002). Viruses and enteric protozoa cannot multiply in water, whilst some bacteria, given the right conditions (sufficient nutrients and correct temperature) can (Leclerc et al., 2002). Protozoa are highly resistant in the environment and can even withstand disinfectants used in water treatment (Leclerc et al., 2002). Although bacteria can grow in water under favorable conditions it is generally assumed that bacteria exist under starving conditions in water. Thus, fecal pathogens generally "remain static in number or die off" (Leclerc et al., 2002:372). *E. coli* and *Salmonella spp*. can survive up to 60 days in water, whilst *Shigella spp*. and *V. cholerae* survive up to 30 days (Jamil et al., 2010). Viruses can survive even longer; enteroviruses for example can persist for 120 days in water (ibid). During irrigation, these pathogens are transferred to the soil and crops. As the water percolates into the soil, this acts as a barrier for pathogens leading to their accumulation in the topsoil (Bryan, 1974). Although the survival of pathogens in the soil depends on various factors, such as soil moisture, water holding capacity, pH and temperature, Feachem et al., 1983 found that enteroviruses, thermotolerant coliforms and *Salmonella spp.* survive less than 20 days, whereas *V. cholera* survives less than 10 days (Santamaría & Toranzos, 2003). Protozoa and helminthes are highly resistant to environmental factors and can survive several months in the soil (Santamaría & Toranzos, 2003; Leclerc et al., 2002). Many helminthes actually require soil in order to mature and develop their infectiousness. Although the range of pathogen survival times is wide, it is highly probable that some pathogens would "survive in the soil until harvest under some agricultural conditions" (Bryan, 1974:19). Similarly, pathogens can be transferred to crops during irrigation. Particularly crops that are grown in close proximity to the soil, such as vegetables or lettuce, are easily contaminated (Amahmid et al., 1999). Enteric pathogens can survive for similar time periods on crops and in soils. Usually, enteric bacteria, viruses, protozoa and helminthes do not "penetrate undamaged vegetables ... [but survive] ... in protected leafy folds, in deep stem depressions, and in cracks and flaws in the skin" (Shuval & Fattal, 2003: 242).

The type of infection and the resulting symptoms and disease depend upon the specific pathogen. Initially, it is important to distinguish between fecal-oral pathogens that penetrate the intestinal lining and those that cannot (Sobsey, 2015). These can also be differentiated between those remaining localized in the intestinal tract and those that spread to other tissues or organs (ibid). Pathogens that penetrate the intestinal lining but remain localized cause dysentery (bloody stool) (Mims et al., 2000). Pathogens that migrate to other tissues can cause a wide variety of diseases, e.g. hepatitis in the liver (Sobsey, 2015). Pathogens that multiply in the intestinal tract and remain localized cause infection of the intestines, which is referred to as acute gastroenteritis (ibid). The key symptom associated with acute gastrointestinal infections is diarrhea, often in combination with nausea, vomiting and fever (Baron, 1996).

1.2.4 Diarrheal Disease

Diarrheal disease remains one of the leading causes of morbidity and mortality worldwide (Schmidt et al., 2011; Guerrant et al., 2001). Disease transmission occurs primarily via the fecal-oral route (American Public Health Association, 2008; Ahs et al., 2010), thus rendering most morbidity and mortality induced by diarrhea preventable. Nonetheless, 760,000 children still die from diarrhea annually, with about 1.7 billion annual cases (WHO, 2013). Children under the age of five are most susceptible to and affected by diarrheal disease, making them the key risk group (UNICEF/WHO, 2009; Fischer Walker et al., 2012). In 2004, 17% of the global under-five mortality was attributed to diarrhea with the largest absolute number of diarrheal deaths occurring in India (UNICEF/WHO, 2009). Elderly people as well as immunocompromised individuals are also at high risk (Gerba et al., 1996; Krones & Högenauer, 2012).

Although commonly referred to as diarrheal disease, it is important to highlight that diarrhea is not a disease per se, but rather a disease symptom. As described earlier, a multitude of pathogens can cause infections leading to diarrhea. Gastroenteritis (infection of the gastrointestinal track) often leads to diarrhea in combination with other symptoms such as fever, vomiting and nausea; the specific disease depends upon the pathogen. Diarrhea is defined as "the passing of loose or watery stools three or more times per day" (UNICEF/WHO, 2009:9). Three forms of diarrhea can be distinguished: acute watery diarrhea, bloody diarrhea and persistent diarrhea (ibid).

'Acute watery diarrhea' is the common form of diarrhea and is associated with rapid fluid loss and dehydration (ibid). *V. Cholerae*, *E. coli* as well as rotaviruses cause acute watery diarrhea with symptoms persisting for hours or days. 'Bloody diarrhea', medically referred to as dysentery, is commonly caused by *Shigella* and is associated with severe cases of diarrhea (ibid). The key characteristic of dysentery is the presence of blood in the stool; consequently, it is linked to intestinal damage as well as nutrient loss in infected individuals (ibid). 'Persistent diarrhea', as the name suggests, is diarrhea with or without blood persisting for at least 14 days. It occurs primarily in immunocompromised and undernourished children with potentially detrimental effects.

Dehydration is the most immediate effect of diarrheal disease, as the frequent passing of loose stool induces the loss of large volumes of fluid. If infected people are not rehydrating, severe dehydration may occur resulting in the shut down of vital body functions and ultimately death (Howard & Bartram, 2003). In addition, nutrient absorption is disturbed during the acute phase of diarrhea, compounding the effect of reduced nutrient intake during episodes (Ahs et al., 2010). In consequence, frequent or persistent diarrhea can lead to malnutrition, which has a series of adverse health effects, including weakened immune system and slowing of cognitive development (Müller & Krawinkel, 2005). Malnutrition also forms a risk factor for diarrheal disease, as the weakened immune system renders individuals more susceptible to infections. This creates a vicious cycle, where children frequently suffering from diarrhea are more likely to develop malnutrition, which in turn places them at higher risk of frequent or persistent diarrhea further limiting nutrient absorption (ibid; UNICEF/WHO, 2009).

1.2.5 Diarrhea Treatment & Prevention

Oral rehydration forms the key treatment for diarrhea and has been practiced since the 1970's (UNICEF/WHO, 2009). The first controlled study was conducted in 1978 highlighting that rehydration during diarrheal episodes was successfully achieved by administering a sodium solution (Chatterjee et al., 1978). The treatment with 'ORS' (Oral Rehydration Salts) has been recommended by UNICEF/WHO since 1976 (ibid) and is considered one of the most important medical advances of the 20th century (UNICEF/WHO, 2009). A review by Munos et al. (2010) found that diarrhea mortality is reduced by 93% when treated with ORS. The effectiveness of ORS is based on a discovery made in 1955 by Fisher, who showed that glucose promotes intestinal ion transport (Farthing, 1994). It was also found that the sodium and glucose transport in the intestine are coupled (Curran, 1960). The high sodium concentration of ORS alters the salt balance in the intestines inducing reabsorption of fluids, whilst glucose is linked to reduced stool output during acute episodes (WHO, 2002). Thus, ORS treatment does not only rehydrate the infected individual but also reduces dehydration from diarrhea.

The secondary pillar of diarrhea treatment is zinc supplementation. Zinc is an important micronutrient influencing hundreds of enzymes, promoting immunity, restoring the mucosal barrier integrity, promoting antibody production and influencing ion channels (Lazzerini & Ronfani, 2013). Zinc deficiency is common in developing countries, as zinc cannot be stored in the body and is only present in high quantity in 'expensive foods', such as meat and fish (ibid). Excretion of zinc occurs primarily via the gastrointestinal track and is elevated during diarrheal episodes (ibid). The WHO recommends administering 10-20 mg of zinc per day for 10 to 14 days (UNICEF/WHO, 2004). A pooled analysis of clinical trials published by the Zinc Investigators' Collaboration Group in 2000 highlights that zinc supplementation "significantly reduces the duration of acute or persistent diarrhea" (Bhutta et al., 2000:1520).

The treatment package recommended by the WHO and UNICEF therefore consists of the ORS therapy to prevent dehydration as well as zinc supplementation to reduce the severity and duration of the diarrheal episode (UNICEF/WHO, 2009). It is also highly recommended to continue feeding during disease episodes; this also includes breast-feeding (ibid). Nutritional intake should be increased after diarrheal episodes. In the absence of ORS it is recommended to use homemade fluids and increase overall fluid intake during episodes (ibid). Although the treatment package is widely available and highly effective, a more sustainable solution is prevention.

The WHO recommends five components in their prevention package: rotavirus and measles vaccination, promotion of early and exclusive breast feeding with vitamin A supplementation, promotion of hand washing with soap, improved water supply quantity and quality, and community-wide sanitation promotion (UNICEF/WHO, 2009:2). The prevention strategy can, therefore, be divided into two approaches. The first aims to reduce susceptibility to severe diarrhea and dehydration through adequate nutrition and a well-functioning immune system, while the second attempts to reduce the exposure to pathogens by ensuring safe drinking water, adequate sanitation and a hygienic living environment (ibid). Whilst reducing susceptibility to contracting infection is an essential aspect of the prevention strategy, the focus of this review lies on exposure reduction.

It is estimated that 88% of the global diarrheal deaths are linked to unsafe drinking water, inadequate sanitation and poor hygiene (Black et al., 2003; UNICEF/WHO, 2009). Traditionally, interventions aiming to reduce diarrheal incidence have focused on the provision of safe drinking water and the adequate disposal of feces (Chen & Scrimshaw, 1983). Considering the fecal-oral transmission route, the provision of adequate sanitation coupled with avoidance of animal feces in the home environment should logically lead to a significant reduction in diarrheal incidences (Black, 1984). A systematic review by Clasen et al. (2010) highlights that most of the reviewed studies (11/13) consistently found some degree of protective effect from improving feces disposal. However, the overall quality of the studies is considered poor, preventing the estimation of the pooled effect size (ibid). Previous reviews have estimated the protective effect of improved sanitation in the range of 20% to 40% (Esrey et al., 1985; Esrey et al., 1991; Fewtrell et al., 2005; Waddington et al., 2009). This highlights that improving sanitation alone does not fully break the transmission route, implying the presence of additional exposure sources. Nonetheless, achieving total sanitation coverage remains an essential component of the fight against diarrhea. Whilst the millennium development goals (MDGs) called for halving the proportion of the population without access to basic sanitation (target 7c), the newly formulated sustainable development goals (SDGs) aim to achieve total sanitation coverage by 2030, thus aiming to end open defecation (goal 6) (WHO, 2015).

Improving access to sanitation is often coupled with efforts to ensure safe drinking water provision. In fact, both the MDG target 7c as well as the SDG goal 6 do not merely call for access to sanitation but also for the provision of safe drinking water. Contaminated drinking water has been responsible for major disease outbreaks in the past, including cholera epidemics (Snow, 1857; Taylor et al., 2015). The WHO recommends water provision through 'improved' water sources. These include piped water connections, tube or bore wells, protected dug wells, protected springs or rainwater (UNICEF/WHO, 2000). However, a recent systematic review concluded that insufficient evidence is available to assert that source-based improvements consistently reduce diarrheal incidence (Clasen et al., 2015). However, individual studies have found reductions of up to 50% through the provision of improved water sources (ibid). The effect of shifting from unimproved to improved water sources on diarrheal incidence is dependent on the difference of contamination level between the unimproved and improved water source in the given context. It is thus not surprising that the UNICEF/WHO's recommendation goes beyond mere access to improved water sources by also promoting safe in-household water storage, treatment and use (UNICEF/WHO, 2009). Clasen et al. (2015) emphasize that point-of-use (PoU) water quality interventions have protective effects regardless of the status of the water source and the sanitation facility. Filtration with ceramic filters and biosand filters appear to have the largest effect size, reducing diarrhea incidence by 50%, whilst PoU chlorination leads to a 25% reduction (ibid). Since 2011, the WHO strategy has strongly promoted PoU water quality interventions, even if this has not contributed to the achievement of the international water targets (WHO, 2011).

Access to safe drinking water forms a key preventive strategy for the reduction of diarrhea, however water quantity should not be neglected. Access to a sufficient quantity of water is essential to ensure adequate personal hygiene (Howard & Bartram, 2003). Particularly hand hygiene plays a crucial role in the transmission of diarrheal disease and is often neglected in the absence of sufficient water quantity (Cairncross & Feachem, 1993). Quantifying the volume of the domestic water requirement is challenging, as not only individual metabolic factors influence the hydration requirement but also environmental conditions and the activity level of the individual (Holliday & Segar, 1957; Grandjean, 2005). Moreover, water is required for cooking and hygiene as well as for other non-essential uses. White et al. (1972) suggest three types of domestic water uses: consumption, hygiene and amenity use. Here 'consumption' includes both water for hydration and for cooking, 'hygiene' encompasses all water needs for personal and domestic hygiene, and amenity uses refer to car washing and lawn watering. Thompson & Cairncross (2002) propose an additional domestic water-use type, i.e. 'productive' water uses, which include irrigation for horticulture, watering of animals and brewing. Such productive uses can be critical for sustaining livelihoods among the urban poor and thus have indirect effects on health (ibid). The only water use category that has no considerable effect on health is amenity use, while both consumption and hygiene uses have clear direct health implications.

1.2.6 Minimum Water Requirement

A minimum water uptake is required to sustain life, as throughout the day the body loses fluids via evaporation of the skin, excretion losses and insensible loss from the respiratory tract (Gleick, 1996). These losses need to be balanced with fluid intake or dehydration occurs (Howard & Bartram, 2003). Dehydration can severely impair body functions and can ultimately be fatal. White et al. (1972) suggest a minimum water requirement of about 3 liters per capita per day (l/c/d) in tropical climates. Gleick (1996) confirms that 3 l/c/d is the minimum requirement for adults in most situations. Howard & Bartram (2003) however stress the additional hydration requirements of pregnant (30 ml per day) and lactating women (1 l per day), therefore suggesting a minimum daily water requirement of 5.5 l per day. In addition to the water required for hydration, water is also needed for food preparation.

Estimating the minimum water quantity required for cooking is difficult as the types of food and modes of preparation differ between cultures and regions. Gleick (1996) found that 10 to 20 l/c/d are sufficient in most regions and suggests 10 l/c/d as a basic requirement. Howard & Bartram (2003) take a more pragmatic approach, and instead of relying on studies estimating the water volume used for cooking by the participants, they calculate the volume of water needed to cook the recommended daily serving of the most common staple, i.e. rice. Based on the assumption that 600 g rice are prepared using 1.6 l of water, a minimum water requirement of 2 l/c/d for cooking is suggested (ibid). The minimum water needed for consumption is not easily estimated, as different variables influence the amount required. Combining the hydration with the cooking water requirement, Howard & Bartram (2003) suggest 7.5 l/c/d, whilst Gleick (1996) estimates 13 l/c/d as the basic requirement.

Defining minimum water requirements for hygiene is also difficult, as specific hygiene practices and behavior are not solely dependent on water availability (Howard & Bartram, 2003). Various systematic reviews (e.g. Curtis & Cairncross, 2003 or Freeman et al., 2014) have demonstrated the importance of hand washing with soap in the prevention of diarrhea. Studies by Luby et al. (2011) and Hoque & Briend (1991) in Bangladesh demonstrated the effectiveness of other rubbing agents, such as mud or ash, as well as using water only, highlighting that an adequate hand washing technique is more important than the rubbing agent. Nonetheless, mere availability of water does not ensure adequate hygiene behavior. Gilman et al. (1993) found that the frequency of hand washing increases when higher water volumes are available in the home. Howard & Bartram highlight that "effective use of water and cleansing agents and the timing of hygiene practices … are more important than volumes of water used" (2003:16). In order for water to constrict hygiene, it must be available only in very small quantities, whilst hygiene improvement can only be expected at high service levels (ibid).

The WHO has refrained from providing recommendations for minimum domestic water requirements and instead defines service levels with corresponding water quantities likely to be used. This is based upon the assumption that the quantity of water used depends upon accessibility, which is determined by distance, time and reliability (ibid; Esrey et al., 1991). If water collection is more convenient and less time intensive, more water is likely to be used.

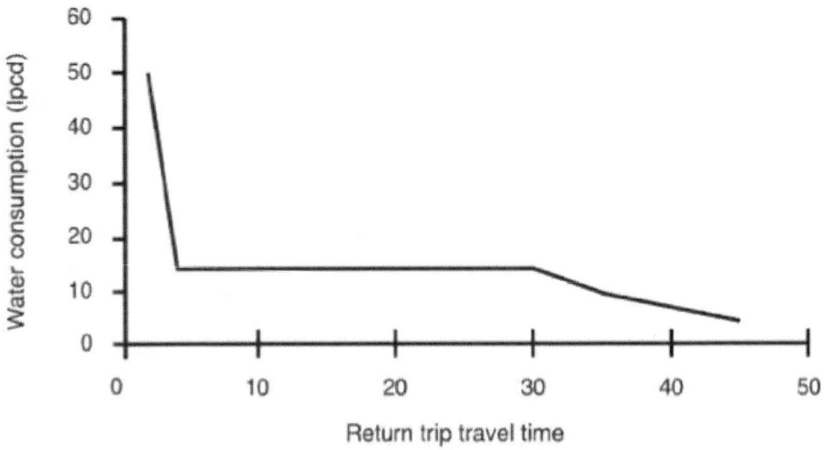

Figure 2: Bradley curve. Source: Cairncross, 1987. lpcd = liters per capita per day.

Underlying the distance and time measure, defining the water service levels, are studies conducted in the 1970's and 1980's by White et al. (1972), Feachem (1978) and Cairncross & Cliff (1987) (Evans et al., 2013). These studies found a clear relationship between time spent for water collection and the water quantity used in households, now referred to as the 'Bradley Curve' (see Figure 2). A steep decrease in the water quantity is observed if collection time exceeds 5 minutes, followed by a plateau between 5 and 30 minutes collection time and further declining water usage if collection time exceeds 30 minutes. It is estimated that during a round trip of 30 minutes a distance of 1 km can be covered (Cairncross, 1987). The 1-km boundary defines the 'basic access' service level (see Table 1), which represents the minimum water requirement for health (Howard & Bartram, 2003). While the water consumption requirements will be met through the 'basic access' level, "hygiene may be compromised [and] laundry may occur off-plot" (WHO, 2011:84). Gleick (1996) recommends a higher water quantity (50 l/c/d) as the minimum requirement corresponding with the 'intermediate access' service level. This water quantity is achieved when on-plot water provision is available and consequently "hygiene should not be compromised" (WHO, 2011:84).

Table 1: WHO service level descriptors for domestic water supplies. Adopted from WHO, 2011. l/c/d = liters per capita per day.

Service Level	Distance/Time measure	Likely Water Quantities Collected
No access	> 1000 m (> 30min collection time)	5 l/c/d
Basic access	< 1000 m (< 30min collection time)	Approx. 20 l/c/d
Intermediate access	On-plot (single tap in house or yard)	Approx. 50 l/c/d
Optimal access	Water supply through multiple taps within the house	100–250 l/c/d

To monitor the progress toward the achievement of MDG 7 target c (to halve the proportion of people without sustainable access to safe drinking water and sanitation), the Joint Monitoring Program for Water Supply and Sanitation (JMP) of the WHO and UNICEF defines 'reasonable access' "as the availability of at least 20 liters per person per day from a source within one kilometer of the user's dwelling" (UNICEF/WHO, 2000:77-8). The JMP Assessment 2000 moves away from the terms 'safe' drinking water and 'adequate' sanitation, as there is lacking information about the safety and adequacy of supplied water and sanitation (ibid). Instead, the terms 'improved' drinking water and sanitation were introduced, based on the finding that "certain technologies are safer or more adequate than others" (ibid:4) (see Table 2). Improved drinking water sources are assumed to provide safe drinking water with little health risks for the users, while unimproved sources are potentially contaminated and thus induce health risks. It must be noted, however, that this assumption is not true under all circumstances, as in some areas unprotected household wells may provide safer water than intermitted household connections (ibid). Bottled water is categorized as an unimproved water source although water quality may be superior to improved water sources. However, reliance on bottled water raises questions about sufficient water quantities used due to the high price. Despite the JMP's definition reflecting a minimum water quantity to be available per capita, the actual quantities used by households were not assessed. Instead the 1-km distance limit according to the Bradley curve is applied assuming that improved water sources within 1 km of the dwelling ensure that sufficient water quantities are withdrawn. The authors of the Assessment 2000 caution that "technology indicators do not provide information about the quality of the water provided or about its use" (ibid:4).

Table 2: Improved and unimproved drinking water sources. Adopted from WHO, 2011.

Improved Water Sources	Unimproved Water Sources
Household connection	Unprotected Well
Public standpipe	Unprotected Spring
Borehole	Vendor-provided water
Protected dug well	Bottled water
Protected spring	Tanker truck provision of water
Rainwater collection	

1.2.7 Hygiene Interventions

Whilst access to improved water sources and sanitation can be achieved through infrastructure development and quantified with technology indicators, hygiene improvement is more difficult to achieve and measure. Generally, there are two types of hygiene interventions: health and hygiene education and hand washing promotion (Fewtrell et al., 2005). The meta-analysis of 15 peer-reviewed articles conducted by Fewtrell et al. (2005) revealed a reduction in diarrheal incidence of 37% for all hygiene interventions. Separate calculations for both types of intervention showed slightly larger effect sizes for interventions specifically promoting hand washing (ibid). In a review by Ejemot-Nwadiaro et al. (2015), this finding was confirmed by studies only promoting hand washing achieving a diarrheal risk reduction of 37%, whilst those promoting multiple hygiene interventions reduced the diarrheal risk by only 19%. Curtis et al. (2000) highlight the necessity to target specific hygiene behaviors, as “too many messages confuses and exhausts the attention and goodwill of target populations” (Curtis et al., 2000:30). Therefore, it is necessary to focus on behaviors that break the transmission of fecal-oral diseases, particularly those serving as primary barriers. Hand washing after defecation and contact with child’s feces therefore forms the most critical time for hand washing behavior (ibid; Curtis et al., 2011). Birmingham et al. (1997), however, found that not washing hands before food preparation formed the key household risk factor for dysentery in their study in Burundi. Interestingly, the rates of secondary household transmission were low in the study, implying that hand washing reduced primary infections through the prevention of food contamination (Birmingham et al., 1997). Hand hygiene before contact with food is thus also a critical hand washing time (Curtis et al., 2011).

Several systematic reviews have been conducted assessing the effect of hygiene promotion and diarrheal disease (Curtis & Cairncross, 2003; Fewtrell & Colford, 2004; Fewtrell et al., 2005; Ejemot-Nwadiaro et al., 2008; Freeman et al., 2014; Ejemot-Nwadiaro et al., 2015). The most recent review by Ejemond-Nwasiaro et al. (2015) found a 27% reduction in diarrheal incidence from hygiene interventions, while Curtis & Cairncross (2003) and Fewtrell et al. (2005) found reductions of 47 and 44%, respectively. It should be noted that the older reviews of Curtis and Fewtrell included case control and cross-section trials, while the review of Ejemond-Nwasiaro was conducted according to the Cochrane standard, thus only including randomized control trials (Ejemot-Nwadiaro et al., 2015). Nonetheless, the evidence clearly indicates that hygiene interventions and hand washing promotion in particular reduce the incidence of diarrhea (ibid). Furthermore, adequate hand hygiene has been shown to induce reductions in trachoma, respiratory infections and skin infections (Bartram & Cairncross, 2010). However, assessing the effect of hand hygiene promotion on disease incidence only partially shows the effectiveness of the intervention. Inducing successful behavior change among the participants requires the behavior to be accepted, adopted and most importantly sustained over time in order for the full health benefit to manifest. Particularly the sustainability of hygiene interventions is increasingly debated (Ejemot-Nwadiaro et al., 2015; Curtis et al., 2011; Luby et al., 2009; Ejemot-Nwadiaro et al., 2008; Cairncross et al., 2005).

Hoque et al. (1996) published the first long-term study, evaluating the sustainability of a WASH intervention program in Bangladesh. The study found that hygiene practices were poorer during the 1993 follow-up than in 1987, however the intervention group remained significantly better compared to the control group (Hoque et al., 1996). The diarrheal prevalence also remained lower in the intervention group six years after the completion of the intervention (ibid). However, the sustained health impact of the intervention cannot be attributed to sustained improved hygiene behavior, as the provision of water and sanitation facilities also created health benefits. A study by Wilson & Chandler (1993) conducted in Indonesia shows that self-reported hand washing with soap remained higher than at pre-intervention levels 2 years after completion. However, the amount of soap used decreased from post-intervention levels and the diarrheal prevalence, although still lower than before the intervention, increased (ibid). Cairncross et al. (2005) also utilized self-reported hand washing behavior to evaluate the sustainability of hygiene interventions in Kerala, India. The study included 10 communities that had received interventions 2-9 years ago, finding no "association between handwashing prevalence and time elapsed since conclusion of the intervention" (ibid: 2219). They therefore concluded that the effects of hygiene interventions are sustained over long time periods. However, self-reported hygiene behavior has been criticized for overestimating the practice, indicating the knowledge of socially desirable behavior but not necessarily its practice (Curtis et al., 2011). Curtis et al. (2001) adopted an observational approach to assess hand-washing behavior 3 years after the intervention and highlight significant increases in hand washing behavior. Luby et al. (2009) evaluated the sustainability of a hand-washing promotion intervention in Pakistan, emphasizing that the quantity of soap purchased by households was similar between the intervention and non-intervention group. During the 14 months after the intervention the diarrheal prevalence was not significantly different from that of the control households, indicating that the behavior was not sustained (Luby et al., 2009). As the intervention provided free soap, the cost of soap is suggested as a barrier to the sustained up-take of hand hygiene behavior (ibid).

The evidence base evaluating the sustainability of hygiene interventions is rather limited (Waddington et al., 2009; Curtis et al., 2001), nonetheless it is accepted that well-designed hygiene interventions induce long-term health benefits (Cairncross & Shordt, 2004; Curtis et al., 2011). Generally, there are four channels for hygiene promotion: mass communication, group activities, formal training and personal communications (Cairncross & Shordt, 2004). The review found that group activities are sufficient to induce minor behavior changes such as keeping the courtyard swept, however greater behavior changes, including hand hygiene behavior, require intense personal communications (ibid). However, reliance on any single channel appears to be insufficient (ibid). It is underscored that hygiene behavior is not sustained through continued access to water, “thus hygiene promotion and education should not be low-visibility ‘add-ons’ to water and sanitation programming” (ibid:7).

1.2.8 WASH Interventions

The effectiveness of WASH interventions in reducing diarrhea and other infectious diseases is undisputed, and various reviews have found significant reductions in disease incidence for the components water, sanitation and hygiene (Esrey et al., 1985; Esrey et al., 1991; Black et al., 2003; Curtis & Cairncross, 2003; Fewtrell et al., 2005; Ejemot-Nwadiaro et al., 2008; Waddington et al., 2009; Wolf et al., 2014; Clasen et al., 2015; Ejemot-Nwadiaro et al., 2015). However, the relative importance of each component is contested. Whilst Esrey et al. (1991) highlight that water quantity is more important than water quality, Fewtrell et al. (2005) found water quality interventions, particularly at the point-of-use, to be highly effective. The use of multiple interventions did not produce additive effects in Fewtrell’s review (ibid), while Waddington et al. (2009) found evidence for additional impacts induced by combining sanitation and/or hygiene interventions with water quality improvements. Although both Esrey et al. (1991)

and Fewtrell et al. (2005) found no additional effect from combining interventions, they recommend complimenting hardware interventions with software (hygiene) interventions. It has been understood that WASH interventions need to induce behavior change and thus cannot merely focus on construction. It is necessary that newly constructed sanitation facilities or water supply are maintained and effectively utilized by the community in order for health benefits to be sustained.

The complexity of WASH lies in the multiple exposure pathways; improving one component may reduce exposure but does not eliminate it (Curtis et al., 2000). Furthermore, it is important to acknowledge the potential failure of certain barriers and the consequent effects. Prüss et al. (2002) conceptualized transmission pathways, additional to the F-diagram, based upon poorly managed sanitation. Essentially, the primary barrier is not functioning properly, thus fecal matter is potentially transferred to hands, surface and groundwater (Prüss et al., 2002). In the context of WASH, it is assumed that access to sanitation coupled with its adequate use acts as an effective primary barrier; however, sewage treatment is limited in most developing countries, leading to the discharge of untreated wastewater into surface waterways. In consequence, fecal matter is reintroduced into the community via the agricultural sector that relies on these water resources for irrigation. Wastewater irrigation, both planned and unplanned, therefore forms an additional transmission pathway, potentially undermining health benefits induced through access to sanitation and safe drinking water. Accordingly, it is important to acknowledge the role of wastewater irrigation in the context of WASH, as it is both affecting and affected by WASH factors. Adequate sanitation and sewage treatment are expected to reduce the relative importance of irrigation on the exposure level, whilst wastewater use can transfer pathogens onto hands, soil and food, forming an exposure source in its own right. The key health risks associated with wastewater use are induced by fecal-oral pathogens, the same causative agents whose transmission is tackled in WASH interventions. In order to develop sustainable primary and secondary barriers, the role of urban agriculture and wastewater irrigation in particular cannot be neglected in the context of WASH.

1.3 Resumé

Urban and peri-urban agriculture is being practiced in cities of all sizes around the globe. In some regions, the urban agriculture industry is well planned and highly developed, showing the immense potential of the practice. However, even in areas where no planned urban agriculture exists, cultivation often does take place. In addition, food cultivation in the urban fringe, although often of more rural character, is common world wide, particularly in light of urban growth and urbanization. The majority of farmers rely on surface water for irrigation, consequently engaging in wastewater use, although often unknowingly. Sewage treatment capacities are limited in most developing countries leading to the untreated discharge of wastewater into surface waterways. The use of wastewater for irrigation introduces a variety of pathogens into the agricultural system posing health risks to both the farmer and the consumers of the produce. Fecal-oral infections form a key health risk of wastewater irrigation, however, the transmission of fecal-oral diseases is complex, as depicted by the F-diagram. Unsafe drinking water, lack of sanitation and inadequate hygiene are all strongly associated with fecal-oral disease transmission. The theoretical basis of WASH interventions is the F-diagram, essentially aiming to erect primary and secondary barriers to halt transmission and in turn reduce disease incidence and improve health status. The evidence clearly shows the effectiveness of WASH interventions in reducing diarrhea incidence. However, the WASH concept does not consider the effect of urban agriculture and wastewater irrigation although it is interwoven with the other WASH factors. Essentially, urban agriculture forms an additional exposure source induced by malfunctioning primary barriers. The untreated discharge of sewage is common in most developing countries and this is unlikely to change in the short term. It is, therefore, essential to acknowledge this additional exposure source in the fight against fecal-oral diseases and understand its contribution to the disease burden.

The key research questions of this study are:

- What is the effect of wastewater irrigation on the incidence of diarrhea among urban farming households in Ahmedabad, India?

- How does the effect of wastewater irrigation compare to the impact of drinking water, sanitation and hygiene (WASH)?

1.4 Structure of the Dissertation

Chapter 2 introduces the research frame and methodological conceptualization of the research. The methodological framework and the specific methods of measurement are explained in detail and the data collection process is highlighted. In Chapter 3, the study area and sample population are described, outlining the demographic structure of the sample population as well as their key characteristics, including access to sanitation and improved water sources as well as the prevalence of wastewater use across the sample population. Chapter 4 forms the analytical chapter presenting the results of the study divided into four sections. In section 4.1, the results of the irrigation water sampling are presented, differentiating water quality by the source of irrigation water. Additionally, the farming system and preventive behaviors are compared, emphasizing the effect of irrigation water quality and choice on household hygiene. Section 4.2 addresses the first sub-question, assessing the extent of in-household water contamination and identifying the factors affecting the degree of contamination. In section 4.3 the key results are presented, providing an overview of the diarrhea incidence rates of the sample population and sub-groups. Both the primary and secondary research question are addressed in this section, assessing the impact of irrigation water quality on the incidence of disease as well as comparing the effects of unsafe irrigation water with those of the WASH variables. The following section 4.4 forms an excursus focusing exclusively on children, assessing how wastewater use influences their nutritional status and risk of disease. In the final Chapter 5, the results of the individual chapters are integrated and discussed to draw final conclusions and answer the research questions.

2 Study Design & Methodolgy

2.1 Research Frame

Research in health geography is centered around 'place', on the one hand assessing how the interactions of various systems shape the place, and on the other hand how place and its unique characteristics influence health. Such framing moves away from the differentiation between medical and health geography and towards a unified conceptualization of health geography. The overarching framework of place exerting health effects is applicable for both the study of health and disease, although different methodological approaches are required for its quantification. Similarly, for the study of the factors shaping a particular place, various socio-cultural, economic and political methodologies are necessary, which will differ significantly depending on the object of study, the wider context and its purpose. For example, policy-oriented research will inherently adopt different methodologies compared to theory-building or intervention studies. In an attempt to develop a common framing of the sub-discipline, a unified framework for health geography is proposed (Figure 3).

At the heart of the framework, 'place' forms the common focal point of health geography. The upper sphere, 'place shaping', illustrates the various overarching systems that all interact with each other to shape the unique characteristics of place. The 'health effects' of place are illustrated in the lower sphere, essentially differentiating between physiological and psychological processes that influence health status. The pathology and transmission routes of pathogens, the environmental fate and uptake of non-organic toxins as well as immune reactions and human physiology, make up the 'physiological processes' that influence health status. The 'psychological processes' include the subjective feelings towards a particular place and how these induce health benefits. The concept of therapeutic landscapes is a good example to demonstrate how psychological processes influence health status. Certain elements of a particular place, a lake for example, induce emotional responses, often subconsciously affecting the well-being of the individual. The mental processes affecting the emotional rcsponsc as well as the subconscious mechanisms affecting well-being are represented as 'psychological processes'.

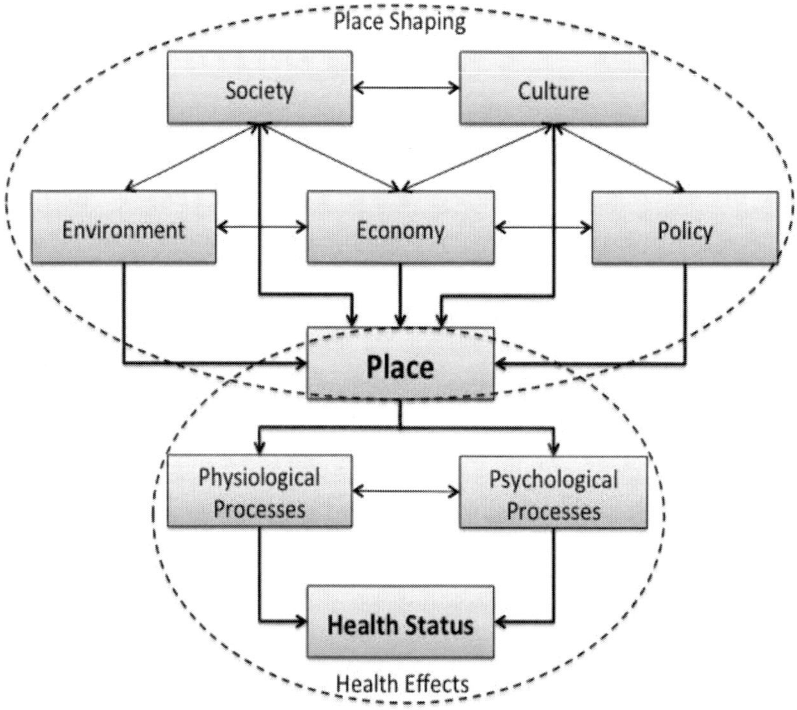

Figure 3: Framework of health geography. The central component of the framework is 'Place'. In the top circle systems influencing 'place shaping' are illustrated, in the bottom circle 'health effects' are situated.

The overarching framework aims to illustrate the interconnected processes that make-up the sub-discipline proposing a common perspective of health geography, where 'place' forms the intersection of the differing approaches to health geography. Each of the boxes of the framework requires individual conceptual and methodological frameworks depending on the specific object of study and the scope of the study. The unified framework does not restrict the methodological variety of the sub-discipline; on the contrary, it highlights the inherent requirement of interdisciplinarity in the study of health geography. Ideally, all health geographic studies would address the entirety of the interactions shaping place as well as accounting for its positive and negative health effects. However, given the complexity of interaction and the various disciplinary backgrounds needed, it is clear that single researchers cannot achieve such holistic analysis, but that coordinated interdisciplinary research teams are required. Nonetheless, the framework helps to put individual studies into perspective further promoting the holistic and interdisciplinary focus of health geography.

In this research, urban agriculture forms the key characteristic making up the place of study. Urban agriculture forms the land usage of the place, therefore forming the intersection between human behavior and the physical place. The underlying processes shaping the place are not assessed in this study, but their outcome, in form of water contamination, forms the primary object of the study. Therefore, the focus lies on the health effects sphere of the framework, requiring an epidemiological framework to disentangle the 'physiological processes' involved in the spread of disease and quantify the health effects.

As the primary aim of this research is to estimate the disease risk arising from the utilization of wastewater for irrigation among urban farmers in Ahmedabad, India, an epidemiological assessment is conducted with wastewater forming the exposure variable and the incidence of diarrhea the outcome variable. Multiple methods are employed in the design of the research. Longitudinal disease monitoring represents a primary component along with periodic microbiological water analysis. Additionally, various cross-sectional surveys are conducted to gain further insight and control for confounding factors.

The study investigates the impact of wastewater utilization and WASH (Water, Sanitation and Hygiene) factors on health outcomes, particularly diarrheal disease. It is expected that water quality and disease incidence vary throughout the year, thus a longitudinal study design was chosen. Participating households were followed up over the period from October 2013 until August 2014 during which disease information was collected on a bi-monthly basis. The study follows an epidemiological study design, thus splitting the cohort into control and exposure groups. Wastewater irrigation forms the primary exposure variable, accordingly farmers using groundwater for irrigation are classified as the control group. The exposure groups consist of a continuum of irrigation water sources, namely river, canal and wastewater. As WASH factors influence the risk of diarrheal disease, it is important to control these during analysis. To gain insight into these dynamics a set of interviews as well as a hygiene index are employed.

Four communities situated in the urban area of Ahmedabad were selected to participate in the study. During the pilot study conducted in September 2012, various communities that potentially fit the inclusion criteria were visited. The primary inclusion criteria were simple: situated within the AMC (Ahmedabad Municipal Cooperation) boundary and engaged in agriculture. The administrative boundary of the AMC was chosen to define 'urban' in the context of urban agriculture. Initially, a secondary focus was placed on non-commercial famers, as these are likely to consume a large portion of the harvest in the household. This was, however, abandoned, as all farmers pursue a primary commercial model. During the community visits, farmers were informally interviewed to gain insight into the community. The questions were number of households and farmers, irrigation source used, land ownership and if they permanently lived on the farm, and distance between farm and home. Ideally, communities would be identified with a large proportion of farmers living in close proximity to their farms with various irrigation water sources in use by different farmers. Unfortunately, no community was identified that utilized a good mix of irrigation water sources; consequently, one area was selected for each irrigation water type (ground, river, canal, waste). The selection was conducted purposive along the criteria, with some geographic consideration. All communities are situated along the river, the control group in the north (upstream) and the exposure groups in the south.

It was planned to sample 50 households in each of the four research areas, amounting to a total sample size of 200 households. There was no access to household lists or any form of population register, therefore a true random sampling technique could not be employed. Given the low information initially available, a snowball sampling approach was applied. This method allowed easy identification of farming households. A household was approached and asked whether they were engaged in agriculture, if yes, the enrollment process was initiated. During the process, the head of household was informed about the study, given time to ask questions and received an informed-consent form. Upon completion, the participant was asked to direct the researcher to another farming household nearby. Throughout the sampling process, attention was paid to the spatial spread of selected households avoiding clustering and ensuring good spatial coverage. This sampling process was undertaken in three of the four areas, the remaining area is the river exposure group (area II). In this area, an absolute sample was drawn, and all households were asked to participate in the study; four households denied participation. In total, 40 households were enrolled in the river exposure group (area II). The control group (area I) consists of 56 households, the canal exposure group (area III) has 48 participating households, and the wastewater group comprises 60 households (area IV). Thus, the total sample size is 204 households consisting of 1263 individuals.

The study was initiated in September 2013 with a cross-sectional survey, which served as baseline survey. The cohort phase started upon completion of the baseline survey. Each household was visited in bi-monthly intervals to collect health information. The visits were all structured similarly, i.e. the health diary was reviewed, additions or corrections were made as necessary, and upon leaving the hygiene index was completed (for further information on the instruments see below). Throughout the research period, 23 intervals were recorded from October 2013 to August 2014. These form the primary outcome variable, identifying cases of disease as well as establishing duration and severity. Simultaneously, four rounds of water testing were conducted. Each water-testing round consists of a three water samples, one from the drinking water source (source), one from the drinking water storage vessel (storage) and one from the irrigation water source (irrigation). The first rounds were conducted with one laboratory (GERMS Medial College & Laboratory, Sola), thus limiting the daily number of samples that could be processed. The first round of water testing was completed in January 2014; the second round lasted until April 2014. During the following two rounds, a second laboratory (Supratect Micropath Laboratory & Research Institute Pvt. Ltd) was employed; the third round was completed in June 2014. The final round was to capture the monsoon period. Therefore, the final round started after the monsoon rains had begun allowing a few days of heavy rain before initiating the sampling round. The fourth round started at the end of July 2014 and was completed by end August 2014. In total, 1200 water sample were tested throughout the research period

Additionally, two cross-sectional surveys were conducted. The farm survey began on 15th November 2013 and was completed in January 2014. A training session for the data collectors was conducted on 8th November 2013. In total, 161 farm surveys were completed amounting to 80% of the sample population. The low completion rate is caused by two factors. The first factor is farm laborers, who do not have land ownership and knowledge about specific farming practices. The farm laborers often work on more than one field and may not necessarily work on the same land several times. The second factor is canal restoration, which resulted in a dry irrigation canal from December 2013. In consequence, many farmers depending on canal water for irrigation stopped farming for the season. Many of these farmers were unwilling to complete the farm survey. The second cross-sectional survey is the hygiene survey, which was started on 27th January 2014 after two trainings sessions on 17th and 24th January. In February 2014, 198 surveys were completed. The surveys were quality checked and entered into the database RedCap.

2.2 Methodological Concept

The methodological framework is based on the F-diagram and the additional exposure sources conceptualized by (Prüss et al., 2002). Given the context of urban agriculture and wastewater irrigation, the primary barrier of the F-diagram is not fully functioning, thus giving rise to the additional exposure source. It is conceptualized that wastewater irrigation and (lacking) sanitation operate parallel in introducing pathogens into the living environment. The complexity of the problem arises from the overlap of transmission pathways of the exposure sources. Both exposure sources can lead to transfer of pathogens onto hands, water and food and thus potentially leading to ingestion. In addition, drinking water quality, although potentially affected by nonfunctional sanitation and wastewater irrigation, forms an important exposure factor in its own right. Hygiene behaviors and other secondary barriers can mediate the health effect of the exposure sources, therefore potentially acting as confounding factors. The framework highlights the key variables influencing the transmission of fecal-oral diseases, all of which need to be quantified for the estimation of the health impact of wastewater irrigation.

The framework follows the same structure as the F-diagram (see Figure 4); the main adaptation is the addition of the variable 'wastewater irrigation', which runs parallel to the traditional exposure source that is renamed 'sanitation'. The arrow from 'sanitation' to 'wastewater irrigation' indicates the systemic failure of wastewater treatment in many developing countries leading to wastewater discharge into surface waterways and its reuse in agriculture. Assuming such a failure of primary barriers on the metropolitan level exposes urban farming communities to fecal-oral pathogens regardless of their sanitation infrastructure. Communities without access to sanitation, therefore, suffer additional exposure from wastewater irrigation. The three primary exposure variables of this study, i.e. wastewater irrigation, sanitation and (drinking) water, are printed bold in the framework. The 'wastewater irrigation' and 'water' variables are quantified using microbiological water analysis, specifically the *E. coli* concentration per 100 ml sample. The cross-sectional surveys provide additional information about the frequency of exposure. Drinking water storage behavior and the water withdrawal method used can contribute to cross- or re-contamination, thus an additional water sample is quantified at point-of-use (PoU). This allows a more accurate quantification of the exposure load of drinking water, as well as serving as a proxy for in-household hygiene. The arrow from the 'hands' variable to the 'water' variable represents in-household water contamination measured by the difference in *E. coli* concentration between source and storage water.

Hygiene is an integral part of the fecal-oral transmission pathway and thus highly important in this research. The 'hands' variable is the outcome of hygiene behavior, i.e. if hands are not washed after defecation contamination is very likely, whilst sound hygiene behavior reduces the likelihood of hand contamination. Quantifying hand hygiene using microbiological techniques, such as hand swipes, certainly provides the most objective result. However, this method is unfeasible in the current research for financial and logistical reasons. Therefore, multiple methods are used to triangulate hygiene behavior. The primary method being an observational spot-check approach, which is complimented by the cross-sectional surveys.

The 'environment' variable is a minor adaptation of the F-diagram, combining the traditional factors 'flies' and 'fomites'. The cleanliness of the home environment influences the risk of cross-contamination. An unhygienic environment, such as open waste or feces, leftover food or unclean surfaces, often causes the presence of flies, which contribute to the transmission of pathogens. The 'environment' variable is quantified using the observational spot-check approach, similar to that of the 'hands' variable. High pathogen densities in the home environment are induced by inadequate hygiene behavior while forming an exposure source and contributing to cross-contamination.

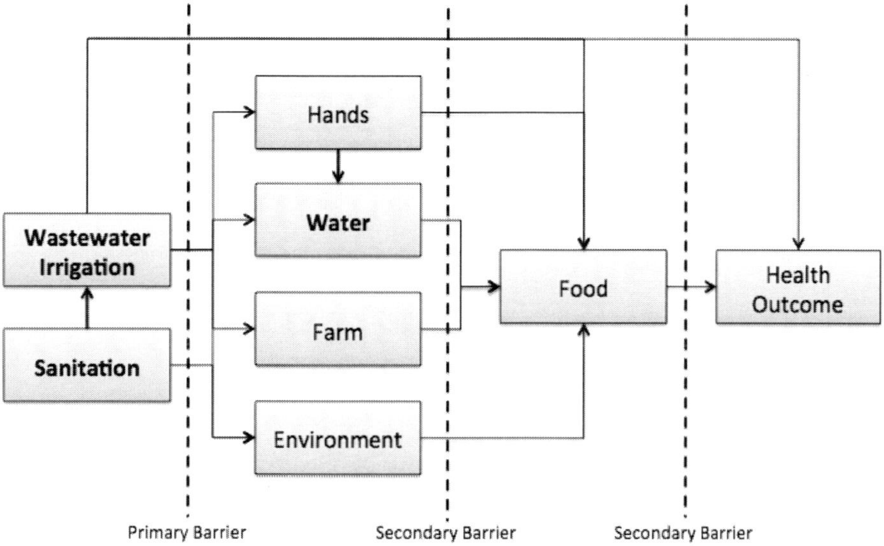

Figure 4: Conceptual framework. Adopted from Wagner & Lanoix, 1958. Boxes represent the variables quantified in the study; the key exposure variables are bold. Arrows represent transmission routes of fecal-oral pathogens. Dashed lines represent primary and secondary barriers.

The variable 'farm' represents the farming system and methods that contribute to or hinder the uptake of pathogens during agricultural work. Through wastewater irrigation, pathogens are introduced into the farming system that may be accidentally ingested by the farmers during agricultural work or transferred onto hands and clothing, thus contributing to the spread of pathogens into the home environment. Rather than quantifying the specific pathogen concentrations present in the soil of the farms, this variable classifies the farms according to the degree of exposure based upon the specific farming practices and the frequency of agricultural work. The variable is quantified using cross-sectional surveys, including data on irrigation method, crop selection, use of machinery and protective clothing.

The 'food' variable is potentially affected by all variables. On the one hand, there is a potential transfer of pathogens from hands, surfaces and water onto foods during food storage, preparation or consumption. On the other hand, there may be direct contamination of food during production due to wastewater use. The quantification is based upon the cross-sectional survey focusing on food storage and preparation, as well as the amount and type of food consumed raw and the proportion of self-produced food consumed. The behavioral component is viewed as more important than the specific pathogen concentration, as thorough cooking eliminates the majority of fecal pathogens. It is thus assumed that only households that often consume raw foods have a high probability of suffering adverse effects from high pathogen densities on food.

The primary outcome variable is quantified utilizing a health diary, essentially a prospective self-reported health method. All disease symptoms were captured including coughing and headaches to ensure that participants did not neglect mentioning 'minor' health problems. The definition of a 'minor' health problem can be very subjective and important information may be missed. Thus, households reported all health problems even though only relevant symptoms were used for analysis. The key disease outcome is diarrhea. The high prevalence of diarrhea ensures a sufficiently large number of cases thus allowing epidemiological analysis. Further symptoms that are considered relevant are stomach pain, fever and skin disease, but these were not analyzed in this study. Whilst stomach pain and fever are symptoms that are often associated with diarrhea, skin disease is not fecal-orally transmitted. Prolonged skin contact with contaminated water can lead to skin disease, thus following a fecal-dermal transmission route. Skin irritation may, however, also be caused by non-fecal pathogens or chemicals. Although irrigation water was not tested for these parameters it is still justified to consider the outcome variable, as it forms a direct health risk with respect to prolonged contact with wastewater.

The traditional exposure variable 'sanitation' is quantified in terms of access. Access to sanitation can be assessed quite easily, as answers from the cross-sectional surveys were cross-verified using the observational spot-check method. Thus, categorizing participating households according to access to sanitation forms a good control for this potentially confounding risk factor. Nonetheless, access to sanitation needs to also be understood in the larger community context. The absence of sanitation facilities in parts of the community directly leads to the unsafe disposal of excreta, creating potential contamination points. The larger the proportion of the community engaging in open defecation, the greater the risk of cross-contamination and infection. A particular risk arises from the absence of clean water for hand washing when practicing open defecation. Despite the apparent disadvantages associated with open defecation, some participants chose to follow this practice although having access to sanitation. The problem when assessing access to sanitation in terms of household disease risk is that only access is measured and not the actual use. Individual household members who opt for open defecation are still categorized as with access to sanitation. However, assessing the actual use of sanitation facilities is difficult. The cross-sectional surveys, especially the hygiene survey, were used to identify individuals that did not regularly use the household's facility.

Dashed lines represent the final components of the framework, illustrating primary and secondary barriers. Primary barriers are mechanisms that prevent the indiscriminate release of feces into the environment. Sanitation and hand washing after defecation are the traditional primary barriers. The adequacy of hand washing behavior is already included in the 'hands' variable, whilst access to sanitation is covered by the 'sanitation' variable. The community-level sanitation coverage indicates the degree of failure of the primary barrier, thus assuming higher exposure to fecal pathogens in communities with low sanitation coverage. Due to the introduction of the 'wastewater irrigation' variable, an additional primary barrier can be quantified, namely on-farm water treatment. Utilizing a simple sedimentation pond or three-chamber-system to treat irrigation water before applying it to the fields acts as a barrier for the transfer of pathogens onto the farms. The cross-sectional surveys are used to identify the use of such primary barriers among the farmers.

Secondary barriers include drinking water treatment as well as hygiene behavior. This component is included in the framework for completeness, as information about secondary barriers is included in other variables, namely 'water', 'environment', 'hands' 'food' and 'farm'. Secondary barriers are mechanisms that remove or reduce pathogens that have entered the community environment. Water treatment removes pathogens from drinking water, rendering it safe for consumption. The 'water' variable reflects the degree of in-household water contamination taking into account in-household water treatment. It should be noted that for the purpose of this research, centralized water treatment is not considered, but focus is placed on PoU water quality and thus only in-household water treatment is considered as a secondary barrier. The observational spot-check approach serves as a hygiene index in this study, and thus forms the primary input for the quantification of secondary barriers. The spot-check approach partially quantifies the 'environment', 'hands' and 'food' variables by identifying factors indicating inadequate hygiene behavior. This information is complimented by the cross-sectional surveys, providing deeper insight into water and food storage, frequency of specific hygiene behavior and food preparation practices. A further secondary barrier is related to agricultural work and is formed by the 'farm' variable. The use of protective clothing, adequate post-work hygiene as well as other preventive strategies reduces the exposure from wastewater irrigation. Overall, highlighting the role of secondary barriers is important as these factors influence the impact of exposure on the health outcome. It is thus important to control secondary barriers to avoid confounding effects.

In essence, five variables form the base of the study: irrigation water quality, drinking water quality, access to sanitation, hygiene behavior and disease outcome. It must be noted that hygiene behavior is a composite variable made up of personal hygiene, environmental hygiene, food hygiene and work hygiene. Additionally, demographic variables, including education level, socio-economic status and household composition are used to further control for confounding effects. Table 3 highlights the key variables of this study and indicates the type of each variable. In the following section the specific methods used to quantify the variables are presented

Table 3: Key variables used in the study. Three variable types are distinguished: continuous, binominal and categorical.

Category	Variable Name	Variable Type	Methodological Type
Outcome	**Disease Incidence**	Continuous	Epidemiological
Exposure	**Irrigation Water Quality**	Continuous	Microbiology
	Drinking Water Quality	Continuous	Microbiology
	Access to Sanitation	Binominal	Cross-Sectional
Irrigation	**Irrigation Method**	Categorical	Cross-Sectional
	Use of protective clothing	Binominal	Cross-Sectional
Drinking Water	**Water Storage**	Categorical	Cross-Sectional
	Water Treatment	Binominal	Cross-Sectional
Hygiene	**HI-Personal**	Categorical	Epidemiological /Cross-Sectional
	HI-Environment	Categorical	Epidemiological
	HI-Food	Categorical	Epidemiological
	Food Storage	Categorical	Cross-Sectional
Demographic Controls	**Household Composition**	Continuous / Categorical	Cross-Sectional
	Socio-Economic Status	Categorical	Cross-Sectional
	Education Level	Continuous / Categorical	Cross-Sectional

2.3 Methods of Measurement

The study has three major methodological components: epidemiological methods, cross-sectional methods and microbiological methods. Within each component multiple or differing methods are employed. Each method will be discussed below; the epidemiological methods: health diary and hygiene index; the cross-sectional methods include three surveys and anthropometric measurements and the microbiological methods are MPN (Most Probable Number) procedures for drinking water and surface water.

2.3.1 Epidemiological Methods

Health Diary

The cohort forms the heart of the research, as the primary outcome variable is assessed periodically throughout the research period. Capturing disease information poses various challenges all of which potentially influence the quality and validity of the data. Long recall periods are a key cause of error. Generally, two types of recall bias can be differentiated: omission and telescoping (Verbrugge, 1980). Whilst omission refers to a health event being entirely forgotten, telescoping means that a health event is placed in the wrong time period (ibid). Disease information, which is retrospectively self-reported, has a high risk of recall bias, consequently leading to underreporting and deflated rates (ibid). Additionally, the sensitive and private nature of the information can give rise to apprehension to share all relevant information.

To overcome the potential problem of recall bias, a prospective methodology was selected. The use of health diaries is not very common, yet its first application dates back to a study conducted by Downes & Collins between 1938 and 1943 (Verbrugge, 1980). However, these early applications of the health diary utilized it primarily as a memory aid rather than for principle data collection. Apart from strongly reducing recall bias, the prospective approach has further advantages, particularly in identifying minor symptoms and the high temporal resolution of the data. The key disadvantage of the health diary method is the high time requirement for both researcher and participants, as well as the high degree of cooperation necessary from the participants (Richardson, 1994). Although cooperation requires significantly more effort and time for respondents, (Verbrugge, 1980) highlights that attrition during diary phases was low and the survey response rate was similar to that of interview-based studies. However, conditioning effects were observed in health diary studies, particularly sensitization and fatigue (ibid). Through keeping a health diary, the participant may become more aware of his health and symptoms, thus being sensitized to health. As a result, the symptom count may increase. On the other hand, respondents may become fatigued of the process during longer diary studies. Reporting fatigue results in less thorough reporting of symptoms, thus causing artificial decreases in the symptom count.

The health diary utilized in this study was adopted from Herbst (2006) and comprised a single page containing a simple matrix consisting of rows representing family members, and columns representing days. Consequently, each family member had a box for each day. At the end of each day, the family member or his/her primary care-giver was to note, in the according box, any symptoms they may have encountered during the day or draw a diagonal line if no symptoms occurred. For simplifying, a set of simple symbols was used, e.g. 'X' represents diarrhea and 'O' stands for stomach pain. The use of simple symbols was to ease the process of completing the diary, while also counteracting (Richardson, 1994) concern that illiterate community members are excluded from participation. To avoid missing data and reduce potential fatigue, a bi-monthly health diary interval was chosen. Each household was visited every 14 days, and during the visits the health diary was reviewed and retrospectively completed if data was missing. In cases where a diarrhea episode was reported, a short follow-up questionnaire was administered providing additional information on the severity of the episode and the course of treatment. The diary was collected during each visit and a new diary page distributed. In order to relieve the potential of apprehension with respect to sharing sensitive information, the same data collector remained with the household throughout the research period. In addition, the data collectors were sensitized during training sessions highlighting the importance of building a trusting relationship with the participants.

Each household received training on how to complete the health diary, stressing that any symptom should be noted regardless of its severity. Stressing the importance of minor symptoms was to ensure that all diarrhea episodes were captured, as in some households, loose stool may not be viewed as a symptom worth reporting. Despite various training sessions with the participants, the majority of households failed to complete their health diary autonomously. This led to the retrospective completion of the diary during the visits with aid of the researcher. Although the prospective design has great advantages, particularly in regard to recall bias and temporal resolution, it was unfeasible in the given context. The great effort required from the participants made daily household visits necessary to ensure compliance, thus a retrospective approach was adopted. The bi-monthly interval was maintained, but to reduce recall bias a mid-cycle visit was introduced. The households were still instructed to complete their health diary on a daily basis. During the mid-cycle visits, the first 7 days of the health diary were reviewed and completed retrospectively if missing. During the bi-monthly visit, the second 7 days of the cycle were reviewed and retrospectively completed when necessary essentially transforming the method into a retrospective disease reporting with a 7-day recall period using the health diary as a memory aid. The mid-cycle visit was essential, as previous studies have shown that recall periods exceeding 7 days are prone to bias (Schmidt et al., 2011). Shorter recall periods of 2 to 3 days are considered more reliable but could not be realized given the temporal and financial constraints of the study. A 7-day recall period forms a compromise between the resource requirement and recall bias, ensuring reliability and achievability. In diarrhea trials, a 7-day recall period is most commonly chosen (Byass & Hanlon, 1994).

Hygiene Spot Check

A secondary method conducted during each bi-monthly visit was an observational spot-check approach, which assessed the hygienic situation of the households. Measuring hygiene is methodologically challenging. Relying on self-reported hygiene information from questionnaires or interviews consistently overestimates good hygiene behavior (Curtis et al., 1993; Biran et al., 2008). Microbiological indicators, such as hand-swipe cultures of fecal bacteria, are expensive and results are highly affected by time-of-day and day-to-day variations (Biran et al., 2008). Structured observation is considered the most accurate tool, however, it requires significant time and financial investment (Biran et al., 2008). Additionally, the presence of an observer in the home can lead to 'reactivity' problems, meaning that individuals modify their behavior due to being observed (Ruel & Arimond, 2002). The spot-check approach is an attempt to capitalize on the advantages of the structured observational approach while minimizing its disadvantages. Spot-checks are conduced rapidly and unobtrusively (ibid), thus making them much less labor intensive and costly than structured observations. In structured observations, specific hygiene behaviors are observed, thus requiring long observation periods in order to allow sufficient time for behaviors to occur. In the spot-check approach, however, the results of hygiene behaviors are observed. Thus, allowing observers to quickly and discretely assess the hygiene situation, reducing ‘reactivity’ compared to structured observations (ibid). For example, hand washing is not directly observed, but the presence of dirt on hands and nails serves as a proxy for the behavior. In order to overcome the problem of day-to-day variation, the spot-check approach was integrated into the cohort phase of this study. The spot-check was conducted during every bi-monthly visit providing two key advantages: first, temporal variations of the hygienic situation are captured and second, combining multiple observations into a single aggregate score eliminates issues of day-to-day variation.

The spot-check is essentially a list of factors that could potentially be observed, the score is then derived from the factors observed. The spot-check approach quantifies the hygiene index of this study. According to Boot & Cairncross (1993) hygiene behavior can differentiated into five domains: “disposal of human feces, use and protection of water sources, personal hygiene and domestic and environmental hygiene” (Boot & Cairncross, 1993:35). In consequence, the hygiene index is divided into five categories: environment, sanitation, water, food, and personal. A spot-check list for each category was developed, where the individual factors of the spot-check list were adopted from Webb et al. (2006). In each category a score of either +1, 0 or -1 was assigned according to the observations of the spot-check. For example, in the environment category piles of waste, feces and stagnant water are observations leading to a score of -1, whilst a significant number of flies and free-roaming animals lead to 0 scores. If none of the factors are observed, a score of +1 is assigned. The individual scores of each category are added to form the hygiene index score, consequently the maximum hygiene index score is +5 and the minimum score is -5.

Table 4: Overview Hygiene Index. The spot-check items of each category are listed in the columns.

Hygiene Index				
Enviornment	**Sanitation**	**Water**	**Food**	**Personal**
Fecal contamination	No sanitation / open defecation	Unimproved water source	Inadequate food storage	Dirt under finger nails
Waste piles	Unimproved sanitation	Storage container dirty	Significant number of flies	Dirty hands
Stagnant water	No water access	Containers not covered	Kitchen area contaminated	Dirty clothes
Free roaming animals	Fecal contamination	Inadequate withdrawal method	Food stored on the ground	Not wearing shoes
Significant number of flies			Food stored uncovered	Black or red teeth
			Dirty dishes	

The spot-check method is easy to apply and provides a good indication for some categories. Assessing 'environmental' hygiene works well with this observational approach, particularly when regularly repeating the spot-check. The category 'personal' also works well in this regard. The 'food' category was, however, more difficult to assess. Access to the kitchen may not be given during each visit and the presence or absence of dirty dishes may also be linked to the time of the visit. Similarly, the categories 'sanitation' and 'water' are challenging. On the one hand, these represent little variation (either an improved drinking water source or sanitation facticity exists or not), and on the other hand the time of the visit can have significant influence on the cleanliness of the facility. The primary weakness, however, is the very subjective nature of the observation itself.

It is advisable to avoid any sort of quantification, such as piles of waste or many flies, as different data collectors may interpret these differently. Instead an even simpler checklist should be created with yes and no answer options. Despite various shortcomings, the hygiene index provides a good indication of the overall hygienic situation of the household.

2.3.2 Cross-Sectional Methods

The cross-sectional component consists of three surveys: the initial household survey, which is referred to as baseline survey, and the farm and the hygiene survey. All three surveys were pilot tested; these tests consisted of two components. The data collection team was briefed about the specific survey and the data collectors instructed to interview each other. This has a dual advantage, as it serves as training as well as pilot testing. During the discussion, unclear questions were identified and some answer options adjusted to the local reality. After the initial pilot, an in-field pilot test was conducted, remaining issues were discussed in the following meeting, and adjustments were made if necessary.

Baseline Survey

The baseline survey was conducted with the head of household during the introduction of the study. It is made up of seven sections shedding light on all aspects of the household: general, diet and food, farming, drinking water, water and hygiene, sanitation and expenditure (Table 5).

Table 5: Overview Baseline Survey. Key variables captured in each of the 8 section is listed under each column heading (selected variables only).

Baseline Survey			
General Info	**Diet & Food**	**Farming**	**Drinking Water**
Demographics	Food preparation	Farm size	Drinking water source
Assets	Food variety	Irrigation method	Distance to source
Housing	Raw foods	Irrigation source	Time of availability
		Purpose of growing	Water treatment
		Proportion for own consumption	Water storage
Water & Hygiene	**Sanitation**	**Food Expenditure**	**Retrospective Disease Prevalence**
Source of general-purpose water	Access to sanitation	Food spending	Symptoms experienced during past days, week, month
Place of bathing	Type of facility	Non-food spending	Long-term / chronic conditions
Frequency of bathing	Water availability		
Critical hand wash times	Child defecation practice		

In the 'General' section of the survey, basic demographic information was captured, including gender, age and education status of each household member as well as household information, such as wall and flooring material, number of rooms and key assets (electricity, telephone, motorcycle). The section 'Diet & Food' focuses on dietary habits, the origin of the food and the place of food preparation. The 'Farming' section includes questions about the farm size, irrigation water source, fertilization method and the primary purpose for cultivation. The section 'Drinking Water' is concerned with quantifying the amount of water consumed, as well as the source and storage of drinking water. The section 'Water & Hygiene' focuses on the frequency of bathing, the place of bathing and the source of bathing and washing water. The section 'Sanitation' assesses the type of toilet facility available, the availability of water near the toilet, and the defecation practices of children. The section 'Food Expenditure' estimates the available household income by determining the average daily food expenditure as well as monthly non-food expenditures. An additional component of the baseline survey was 'Retrospective Disease Information'. This data serves as the baseline for the cohort phase of the research. The participant was asked to recall any symptoms of illness experienced in the past days, past months and past year. Any chronic diseases or ongoing treatment were also recorded at this time.

Farm Survey

The farm survey was conducted on the farm with the household member most frequently engaged in farming activities. The main reason for setting the interview location on the farm was to enable observations and cross-verification during the interview process. Confirming the irrigation water source, irrigation method and crop variety forms the basis for the exposure classification. Additional questions attempted to shed light upon the degree of exposure to irrigation water. Particularly important was the time spent working on the field, the frequency of irrigation and the degree of preventive behavior. Apart from the exposure classification, the farm survey also serves to classify the farming system. Size, ownership, number of workers, crop variety, fertilizer and pesticide use, as well as the output volume of the urban farm form key factors in the classification of the farming system.

Table 6: Overview Farm Survey. Under each category heading the key variables captured are listed (selected variables only)

Farm Survey

General	Irrigation	Crops	Exposure & Prevention
Farm size	Source	Crop selection	Use of protective clothing
Land ownership	Method	Crop rotation	Frequency of direct contact with water
Time spent on field	Alternative sources	Output	
Family member involvement	Costs	Fertilization frequency	Post-work hygiene behaviors
Farm labor employment	Frequency	Pesticide application	
Use of machinery			

Hygiene Survey

The hygiene survey was conducted with the female head of the household. It is assumed that the female head or primary caregiver of the family is most aware of the hygiene situation of the household. A set of questions was adopted from the baseline questionnaire and included in the hygiene survey. This serves as an internal verification process, whilst further questions provide deeper insight. Through the hygiene survey the household was classified into basic hygiene categories based on access to improved sanitation and drinking water, safe drinking water and food storage, place of food preparation and personal hygiene. The survey was also used to determine the risk of cross contamination. Determining the frequency of hand washing is particularly challenging (Curtis et al., 1993). Verbal questioning has been shown to produce inflated hand washing rates, as individuals are often aware of the socially desirable answer (Biran et al., 2008; Curtis et al., 1993). Consequently, the question was posed several times and with different wordings allowing the triangulation of the data and a more reliable result. Various questions were in open-ended format allowing more detailed and individual responses. The survey is divided into four sections: food, hygiene, drinking water and sanitation.

Table 7: Overview Hygiene Survey. Key information captured in each of the 4 section is listed under each column heading (selected variables only).

Hygiene Survey			
Food	**Hygiene**	**Drinking Water**	**Sanitation**
Food preparation	Frequency of hand washing	Drinking water source	Type of sanitation
Food variety	Frequency of bathing and laundry	Drinking water reliability	Frequency of cleaning
Raw food consumption	Bathing and laundry location	Drinking water storage	Water availability
Number of meals	Household cleaning	Size of storage container	Utilization of other facilities
Food origin	Daily routine	Drinking water treatment	Child open defecation practice
Food storage			

In the ‘food’ section, food preparation procedures and food hygiene is assessed. Additionally, the number of meals per day, food variety, frequency of consumption of raw/uncooked fruit or vegetables and origin of food are determined. The hygiene section focuses on the frequency of hand washing, bathing and laundry. As direct questions in regard to personal hygiene are prone to reporting bias, additional open-ended questions were used (Biran et al., 2008). Hence, the participant was asked to outline her daily routine with special attention to the triggers and frequency of hygienic behavior. In the drinking water section, the source and reliability of drinking water supply is assessed, as well as water safety measures such as boiling or filtering of water. It was attempted to quantify the amount of drinking water used in the household. For this purpose, the frequency of water collection and the size of the water collection container were determined. Lastly, in the sanitation section the sanitation situation was assessed. The type of toilet, frequency of cleaning, and availability of water near or at the toilet was measured. Special attention was paid to those situations when household members do not use the household's toilet and the defecation practices of children. The findings of the interview are complemented by the spot checks to provide a good indication of the households' overall hygiene behavior and the risk of cross contamination.

Anthropometric Measurements

Figure 5: BMI measurement BMI measuring event in Gyaspur (area IV) conducted at the school. Foto: Timo Falkenberg

Another method that was applied cross-sectionally was anthropometric measurements of children under the age of twelve. The anthropometric scores serve as a proxy for the nutritional status. Underweight can be as much a result of chronic disease as well as the cause for disease susceptibility, thus forming a vicious cycle particularly during child development (Dangour et al., 2013). The measurements were conducted only for children for practical reasons, as adults are more hesitant to partake. Moreover, local health authorities routinely conduct anthropometric measurements for children, thus the procedure is familiar to both mother and child. The measuring station was set up at a central location in each community, e.g. at the school or health center. Households with children were informed prior to the event and were reminded to partake on the day of the event. The WHO standard procedure for anthropometric measurements was applied (WHO, 2006). The child was weighed using a standard scale, which was calibrated on the day of the event. The weight was taken without shoes or heavy clothing. Height was measured using a non-stretch measuring tape fixed to a straight wall. A wooden board or book was placed on the child's head to mark the exact height. WHO growth charts for specific age groups were used to categorize the anthropometric data.

2.3.3 Microbiological Testing

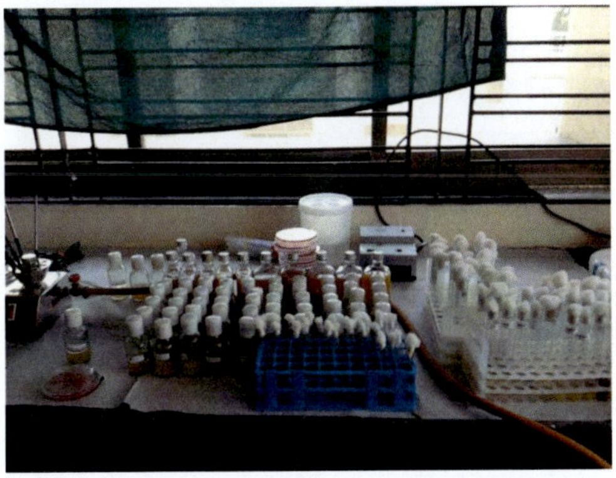

Figure 6: Water sample analysis. Test tubes after 48-hour incubation. Foto: Timo Falkenberg

The final major methodological component is the microbiological water assessment. It forms the counterpart to the health diary and makes up the primary exposure variable. The degree of fecal contamination was determined by the quantification of *E. coli*. This indicator bacterium was chosen as it is linked to fresh fecal contamination and the presence of other fecal pathogens (Moe et al., 1991; WHO, 2001; Bitton, 2005). The number of CFUs (Colony Forming Units) was determined using the multiple tube fermentation method, employing the MPN (most probable number) technique. Three different types of samples were collected during each water sampling round, i.e. two drinking water samples (from source and storage) and one irrigation water sample.

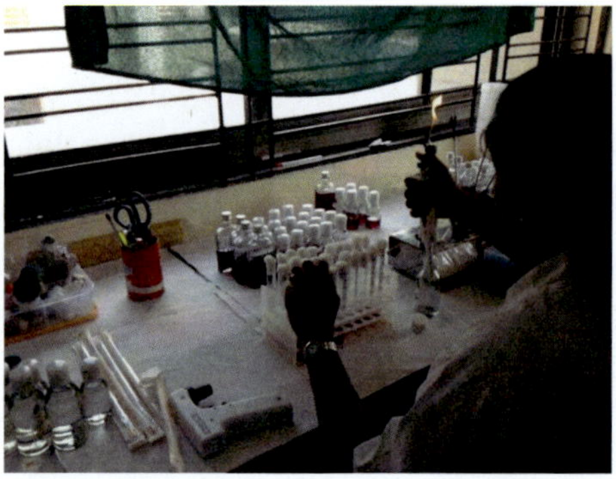

Figure 7: Water sample analysis Microbiologist at GERMS Medical College inoculating test tubes. Foto: Timo Falkenberg

The sample collection process was standardized to avoid error. Source drinking water samples were collected from the point of water collection of the particular household. The water was left running for one minute to allow any remaining water to leave the pipeline. The sample was collected in a sterile sampling container, capped, labeled and placed into a cool-box for transport to the laboratory.

Stored drinking water was collected in a similar manner. The household was asked to draw a cup of water from their water storage container; the water was then transferred to a sterile sampling container and processed as described above. Asking the household to draw a cup of water simulates the water quality situation at the point of consumption. Testing both source and stored drinking water allows the analysis of in-household water contamination providing insight into the hygienic situation and thus the risk of cross-contamination.

Irrigation water samples were collected from the irrigation source directly. During the sampling process, the entire bottle was submerged and pulled out towards the current of the waterway. If several farms used the same irrigation point, only one sample was collected representing all households utilizing that particular source. The samples were labeled and placed in a cool-box.

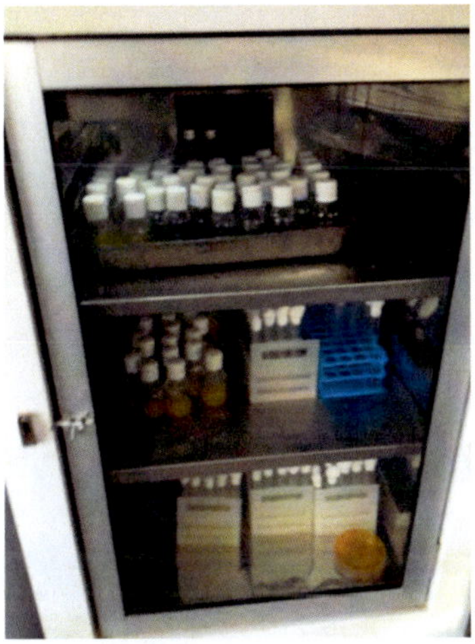

Figure 8: Designated incubator of this study. Top shelf: new samples. Middle shelf: samples of previous day. Bottom shelf: confirmation tubes. Foto: Timo Falkenberg

In the laboratory, drinking water and irrigation water samples were processed differently. The standard MPN procedure for drinking water was applied using 11 fermenting tubes. Each tube was filled with an agar solution, one tube with 50 ml MacConkey broth and five tubes with 10 ml MacConkey broth and five tubes with 1 ml MacConkey broth (WHO, 1958). The 50 ml tube was then inoculated with 50 ml of the sample, the 10 ml tubes with 10 ml of the sample, and the 1 ml tubes with 1 ml sample. Coliform bacteria ferment lactose, which is a primary component of the agar, releasing gas. The gas is captured in the inner vial of the tube and the resulting change in pH causes the color of the agar to change. Consequently, tubes showing gas production were categorized as preliminary positive. To allow fermentation to take place, the inoculated tubes were placed in an incubator at 36 °C for 24 h. Tubes without gas production were placed in the incubator for an additional 24 h. The preliminary test was completed after 48 h, at which point the total coliform concentration of the sample can be determined. In order to identify *E. coli,* a further confirmation step needs to be undertaken.

The confirmation procedure consisted of two steps, plating onto selective media and a series of biochemical tests. During the first step, samples of each positive tube were inoculated onto selective agar and placed in the incubator at 36 °C for 24 h. Due to the selective nature of the agar, *E. coli* can be easily identified by its color. Colonies that were identified as *E. coli* in the first confirmation step were further processed. First, a single colony was suspended in 0.5 ml trypton-tryptophan broth. This solution is then used to inoculate the biochemical tests. First, an oxidase-test was performed using a test strip. Only a negative oxidase test indicates *E. coli* and thus, a positive test renders the sample negative. Second, a test tube with citrate was inoculated with the initial trypton-tryptophan solution. Third, 3 ml trypton-tryptophan broth was inoculated. The tubes containing citrate and trypton-tryptophan were each incubated at 36 °C for 24 h. A positive reaction in the citrate test is indicated by a color change from green to blue. Only a negative test will indicate the presence of *E. coli*. Therefore, a positive citrate test will render the sample negative. The tubes with trypton-tryptophan test for indole formation; therefore 2–3 drops of indole-reactant were added to the broth. A color change towards red indicates a positive reaction, whereas no color change indicates a negative reaction. If *E. coli* is present, then the test will be positive. Thus, only when the oxidase and citrate tests were negative and the indole reaction positive was the initial MPN tube rendered positive for *E. coli*. The concentration of *E. coli* in the initial sample was estimated using probability. The MPN technique works on the basis of the probability of finding single bacteria in an ever-smaller volume of the initial sample. These probability calculations were first initiated in the 1920's and have since been validated and summarized in MPN index tables (Eisenhart & Wilson, 1943; Swaroop, 1956; EPA, 2002). The index table provides all probable combinations of positive and negative tubes with its according MPN index number. The same table is used for the determination of total coliform and *E. coli* concentration.

Irrigation water samples were analyzed in the same manner; however, very high bacterial concentrations were expected. When applying the same technique as for drinking water, it was very likely that all tubes would always be positive. The drinking water MPN technique has a high sensitivity and resolution for low bacterial concentrations, however concentrations in excess of 180 CFUs per 100 ml cannot be distinguished. Therefore, a dilution series was used to shift the spectrum of bacterial concentrations upwards. Essentially, the sample is diluted with sterile water, thus smaller quantities of the sample are tested, resulting in a lower probability of finding a bacterium. The key methodological difference is the number of fermentation tubes, whilst the drinking water MPN technique required 11 tubes; irrigation water was analyzed with 15 tubes. Three dilutions of each sample were analyzed using 5 tubes each (see Figure 9).

The 15 tubes were inoculated with 10 ml of MacConkey broth, and simultaneously a dilution series was prepared. The degree of dilution required depends upon the suspected coliform concentration of the sample. Table 8 shows the recommended dilutions levels for the various water sources. Accordingly, the samples from groundwater sources (control group) were diluted by a factor of 10^{-1}, 10^{-2} and 10^{-3}, surface water samples from the river and canal by a factor of 10^{-3}, 10^{-4} and 10^{-5}, and samples from the wastewater group by 10^{-5}, 10^{-6} and 10^{-7}. These dilution levels only serve as a guide, and the level of dilution may be adjusted if coliform densities strongly differ from the expectation. If all 15 tubes showed a positive result, the dilution series was increased by one level, whilst 15 negative tubes led to a downward adjustment of the dilution level.

The dilution series was prepared using multiple containers filled with 90 ml of 0.9% NaCl solution. Each container comprised one dilution, thus creating a dilution of 10^{-7} requires 7 containers of 90 ml NaCl solution. 10 ml of the original sample were added to the first container forming a 10^{-1} dilution. Transferring 10 ml of the newly created 10^{-1} dilution to the second container with 90 ml NaCl solution creates the next dilution level (see Figure 9). As a result, the second container contained a 10^{-2} dilution of the original sample. The 10^{-3} dilution level was obtained by adding 10 ml of the 10^{-2} dilution to the third container. This process was repeated until the desired dilution level was reached. For the MPN analysis only three dilutions were required, these were selected based on the above-mentioned guidelines. Each of the three dilutions was used to inoculate 5 fermentation tubes each prepared with 10 ml MacConkey broth. 10 ml of the first dilution level was added to each of the 5 tubes, the same was undertaken with the second and third dilution level. Thus, each dilution level was tested in 5 tubes simultaneously. All 15 tubes were placed in an incubator at 36 °C for 48 h, checking for gas production after 24 h and 48 h. Presumptive positive tubes were confirmed applying the same procedure as used for drinking water.

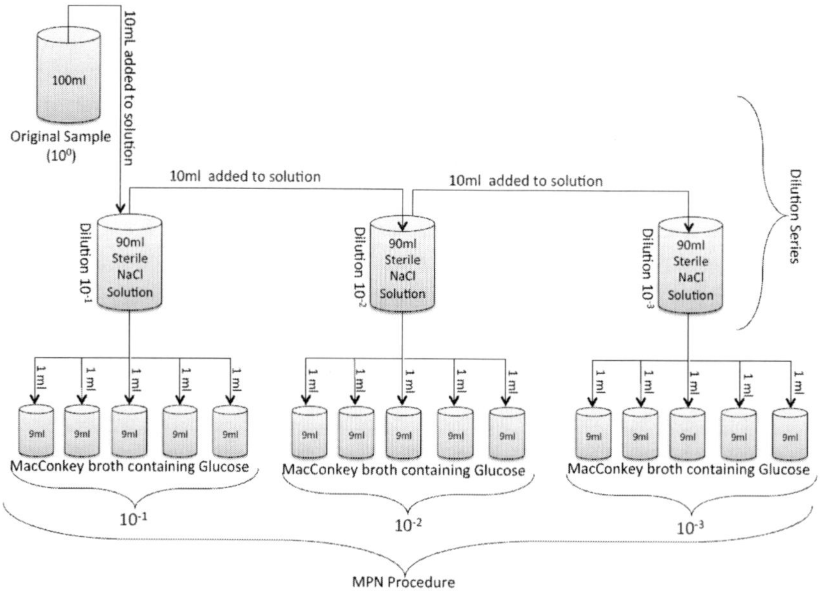

Figure 9: MPN procedure for irrigation water samples.

Table 8: Recommended dilution levels for different water sample types. Source: Hach (2012)

Sample type	Dilution 1	Dilution 2	Dilution 3
Swimming pool water, chlorinated	Undiluted (1x)	10x	100x
Bathing beach water	10x	100x	1,000x
Lake water	10x	100x	1,000x
Unpolluted river water	10x	100x	1,000x
Final effluent, chlorinated	100x	1,000x	10,000x
River water, polluted	1,000x	10,000x	100,000x
Strom water	10,000x	100,000x	1,000,000x
Unchlorinated final effluent	10,000x	100,000x	1,000,000x
Raw sewage	100,000x	1,000,000x	10,000,000x

The number of positive tubes was recorded for each dilution level. An MPN index table for 5 tubes and 3 dilutions was utilized to obtain the MPN index number. To calculate the 'most probable' *E. coli* concentration per ml sample, the MPN index number needs to be divided by the lowest dilution level used (EPA, 2002). This result is then multiplied by 100 to obtain the standard form *E. coli* per 100 ml.

$$MPN/\ 100\ ml = (MPN\ Index\ Number\ /\ lowest\ dilution\ level)\ x\ 100$$

For example, dilutions 10^{-4}, 10^{-5} and 10^{-6} were used; all 5 tubes of the first dilution were positive, three of the second dilution and none of the third dilution. Thus, the MPN index number for the combination 5-3-0 was derived from the MPN table: 7.9. Therefore $(7.9/10^{-4})$ x 100 = 7.9 x 10^{6}. In consequence, the original sample had a most probable *E. coli* concentration of 7.9 million CFU per

100 ml. The MPN reference table also provides the confidence limits of the MPN index number.

The microbiological analysis was conducted in two laboratories, initially all samples were processed in the state-accredited reference laboratory of GERMS Medical College; however, to allow more samples to be tested per day the private laboratory Supratech also received samples from May 2014. The samples were collected by the principal investigator and transported to the laboratories. There, the laboratory staff processed and analyzed the samples according to the previously described standardized process. A procedure guide was kept at each laboratory to ensure easy reference. At GERMS Medical College, the laboratory staff was supervised by the Head of Microbiology (Dr. Nidhi Sood) and supervision at Supratech Mircopath was undertaken by their Director, Dr. Bhavani Shah. During the daily sample deliveries, the fermentation tubes of the previous day were reviewed and the results recorded.

2.3.4 Mapping

In addition to the three main methodological components spatial data was also collected. All relevant points were geo-tagged, i.e. households, farms, drinking water and irrigation water sources. A series of maps were created using ArcGIS to illustrate the spatial dimension of the results. 'Open street maps' served as the initial base map, however the individual study communities were not included in the mapping. Satellite images, obtained from Google Earth, were geo-referenced and the missing roads of the study areas were traced resulting in a base map consisting of 'open street maps' extended by a self-created shape file of village and farm roads. The GPS coordinates of the households, water points and farms were added as individual layers to the map file and were linked to the data set. The disperse function of ArcGIS was used to avoid overlay of data points. In this way, maps of the research areas were created illustrating the distribution of selected households across the village and their key characteristics, i.e. access to sanitation and irrigation water quality.

Table 9: Overview of methods

Methodological Type	Method	Variable
Epidemiological	**Health Diary**	Disease Outcome
	Spot-Check	Hygiene Index
Cross-Sectional	**Baseline Survey**	Socio-Economic Status Education Level Household Composition Housing Type Access to Sanitation Type of Drinking Water Source
	Farm Survey	Irrigation Source Irrigation Method Crop Variety Number of Workers Time spent working Use of Safety Wear
	Hygiene Survey	Water Storage Vessel Water Quantity Used Food Storage Frequency of bathing Place of Child Stool Disposal Food Preparation Hand Hygiene Diet
	Anthropometric	Height Weight BMI
Microbiological	**Multiple Tube Fermentation**	Source Water Quality Drinking Water Quality (POU) Irrigation Water Quality
Spatial	**GIS**	Distance home to farm Sanitation coverage Distance to irrigation source

2.4 Data Collection

Data collection was conducted between September 2013 and August 2014. Prior to the initiation of the study ethical clearnance was sought from the University Bonn and the Indian Insititute of Public Health, Gandhinager. A team of data collectors was employed to conduct both the epidemiological methods (health diary and hygiene index) and cross-sectional surveys (baseline, farm and hygiene). Water samples were collected by the author and transported to laboratories where the microbiological staff of the laboratory conducted the analysis. During each week, the principal investigator for the purpose of cross-verification of survey responses as well as water sample collection, visited every research area at least once. The weekly visits were also used for geo-tagging households, farms and water collection points depending on the type of survey being cross-verified. The BMI measuring events were hosted in each research area individually, allowing the entire data collection team (including the research assistant and principal investigator) to be present during the event. In the following section (2.4.1) the data collection timeline is presented, followed by information regarding staffing (2.4.2), training (2.4.3) and language (2.4.4).

2.4.1 Data Collection Timeline

The research was initiated with the baseline survey in September 2013. Upon completion of the baseline in all households, the epidemiological methodology (health diary) was started (see Figure 10). Special attention was paid to the timing of the health diary interval ensuring that the 14-day cycle was maintained accurately. Particularly in the first round, the data collectors covered too many households on a single day, causing problems during the collection of the health diary. In consequence, a cohort cycle management system was introduced providing a structured guide for data collectors stating which households to visit on a particular day. On average, 6 households were visited on every working day, allowing 60 households to be covered over the 14-day period (10 working days). Although the health diary is illustrated as a single stream in Figure 10, it is actually quantified as 23 data points representing each 14-day interval. Parallel, the hygiene index was recorded during each household visit including the baseline survey, thus 24 data points were captured throughout the research period.

Simultaneously to the epidemiological method, the principal investigator along with the research assistant covered the microbiological stream. Ten water samples were collected daily during the first two rounds, while 20 and 30 water samples were collected during the third and fourth round, respectively. As the microbiological staff of the laboratory processed all samples, the daily number of samples was restricted by the processing capacity of the laboratory. To allow the rapid sampling required during the monsoon, the second laboratory was employed. Each of the water sampling rounds roughly represents one of the four seasons (winter, summer, monsoon and post-monsoon).

The epidemiological and microbiological methods make up the majority of the data collection workload, as the activities were conducted throughout the research period. In addition, two cross-sectional surveys as well as the BMI measuring events were undertaken. The farm survey was quantified by the data collection team between November 2013 and January 2014 and the hygiene survey between February and March 2014. The cross-sectional surveys were conducted in parallel to the regular bi-monthly household visits, essentially administering the survey after completing the health diary collection. Of the six households visited during any single day, two to three were selected to complete the survey, the other households were then covered in the subsequent round of household visits. The completion of the farm survey took longer than the hygiene survey because data collectors were instructed to conduct the farm survey on the field to allow immediate cross-verification of irrigation water source and crop selection. Consequently, the farm survey was not as easily combined with the regular household visits leading to less surveys completed per day and in consequence a longer completion time.

The BMI measuring events were hosted on a single day in each of the research areas individually. They were conducted at the weekend so as to not disturb the regular data collection procedure and to ensure that both child and caregiver were available at the time of the event. The first event was at an early stage of the research shortly after the induction of the study. Unfortunately, the turn up was low with many households not participating in the measuring event. As a consequence, a second BMI event was scheduled in each area at a later stage of the study. The household coverage of the second event was much better, which may be attributed to the building of trust between the participants and data collectors throughout the research period.

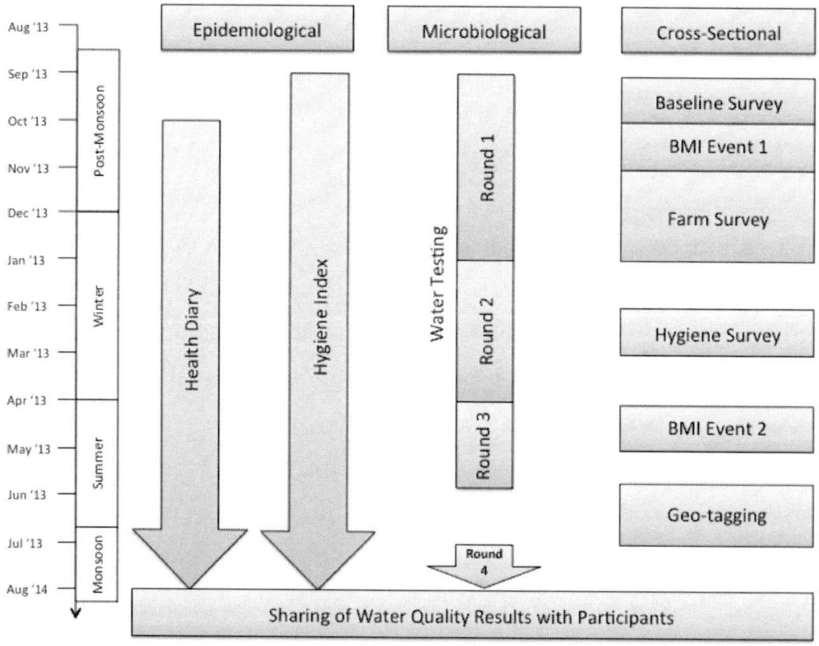

Figure 10: Data collection timeline. The three methodological streams of the research are presented (epidemiological, microbiological and cross-sectional).

Geo-tagging was done by the principal investigator during the cross-verification and water sample collection process. In Figure 10 geo-tagging is illustrated as a single block conducted between June and July 2014 although the activity was integrated into the daily sampling process. During the time period illustrated, the geo-tags were reviewed and missing locations were visited and their GPS coordinates recorded. Nonetheless, the geo-tagging activity was always combined with the cross-verification process.

Data collection was completed by the end of August 2014. The final field activity of the study was sharing of the results, particularly the drinking water quality results. An information sheet was developed for each household, highlighting the drinking and irrigation water quality using a simple color code (red = bad quality and green = good quality). Additionally, the key hygiene problems observed during data collection were explained to the participants and an information sheet illustrating adequate hygiene behavior was distributed. All households were visited individually by the principal investigator and the data collector of area sharing the above-mentioned information as well as distributing a small gift consisting of soap, a scoop with handle for water withdrawal, and educational coloring books for the children of the household.

2.4.2 Staffing

The research team consisted of four data collectors, each assigned to a specific research area and one research assistant, who provided administrative and linguistic support. In addition, one data entry operator and one quality assurance officer were part of the research team. The core team positions (research assistant and data collectors) were advertised through the regular channels of the local partner institution (IIPH-G) on 31.07.2013. Under the advice of the local supervisor Dr. Deepak Saxena, ten viable candidates were selected and invited to interviews on 13.08.2013. Key selection criteria included proficiency in both English and the local dialect Gujarati, as well as possession of a university degree, preferably in a health-related field.

The auxiliary staff was hired later, i.e. the data entry operator joined the research team on 01.10.13 and the data quality assurance officer on 01.05.14. This staff was selected from the IIPH-G network, with both individuals having successfully completed their respective tasks in previous IIPH-G projects. The selection was under guidance of the local supervisor and in accordance with IIPH-G procedural guidelines.

During the project period, two data collectors were replaced due to poor performance. The first data collector was dismissed after the initial trial period of

14 days and was replaced on 01.10.13. A second data collector was replaced on 14.10.13. As the staff turnover occurred at the early stage of the research, the consistency of the data was not affected. Each data collector was assigned to a specific research area throughout the entire research period to allow trusting relationships between data collector and participants to develop, ensuring sensitive information to be shared more freely. In order to ensure that data collected from different data collectors is comparable, the data collection process was standardized and extensive training was provided to the data collection team.

2.4.3 Training

The research was initiated with a team workshop held between 19.08.13 and 23.08.13, during which the project and its key theoretical and methodological basics were explained. Additionally, all research methods were introduced with particular emphasis on the baseline survey and the hygiene index. The standard procedure for the baseline survey was highlighted and each team member received a copy of the baseline survey to familiarize him- or herself with the format.

The individual questions of the baseline survey were discussed on the following day, allowing team members to clarify any uncertainties. A few answer options were adjusted to reflect the local realities. Conducting the survey was first practiced among the team members ensuring that each individual acted both as interviewer and interviewee. The exercise not only ensured that the team members gained practical experience with the baseline survey but also highlighted which questions were more sensitive and less easy to answer. Following the dry ractice, a farming village (not included in the research sample) was visited and each data collector administered at least two surveys. All surveys were checked for quality and consistency and any problems were discussed with the data collectors. Upon completion of the initial training, the data collectors were assigned to their research area and began data collection.

Figure 11: Weekly team meeting. Foto: Dr. Trupti Maitrak

A weekly team meeting was held at the IIPH-G office throughout the research period. The meetings served a triple purpose: quality control, communication and training. During each meeting, the data collectors submitted their data, 10% of which was immediately checked for completeness and quality. Surveys that were unsatisfactory were returned to the data collector and had to be repeated. The experiences of the data collectors were shared to allow common issues to be avoided and team members to learn from each other. During the meeting, all relevant problems were discussed and the next steps communicated.

Specific training sessions were conducted for each of the data collection methods. The individual training sessions all followed a similar structure. First, the research team was introduced to the specific method and the standard procedure and individual components highlighted. Unclarities or misunderstandings were discussed, followed by practical inter-team practice. Finally, in-field training was undertaken allowing each data collector to administer the particular instrument under real-life conditions.

2.4.4 Language

All surveys were originally developed in English and were professionally translated into Gujarati. The Gujarati survey was translated back into English and compared to the original survey. The translation was reviewed and minor changes were made where necessary. During the training sessions, the data collectors were first introduced to the English survey ensuring their understanding of the intended meaning of individual questions. Then they reviewed the Gujrati survey highlighting mismatching translations or suggesting alternative wordings. Although the literal translations may appear correct in the back-translation, implicit meanings of certain words may alter the intent of the question. In consequence, the feedback of the data collectors ensured a more accurate translation of the surveys.

All surveys were conducted in Gujarati and were administered orally by the data collectors. Although the language of data collection was Gujarati, the results were recorded in English to allow easy cross-verification and quality control of the principal investigator. The data collectors utilized the Gujarati survey to ask the questions but noted the answers in English. This system worked well especially for closed questions where specific answer options were available. Even some of the open-ended questions had pre-determined answer options, as these questions usually aimed at identifying hygiene behavior without directly asking whether certain hygiene behavior was practiced at a particular time. Qualitative information where no answer options were pre-defined was recorded in Guajarati and translated into English prior to data entry. Thus, all data entered into the database was in English allowing immediate quality control of the principal investigator.

2.5 Data Analysis

All data was crosschecked and entered into the online database RedCap (see Harris et al. 2009). The crosscheck procedure was conducted randomly at regular intervals. 10% of the completed surveys were checked for internal errors. A set of checking questions was inserted into each survey to simplify the crosscheck procedure. Errors were discussed during the team meeting and where necessary the households revisited. If the crosscheck revealed a large number of errors, a further 10% were reviewed. In case of a repeated high error rate, the entire survey was checked and selected questions repeated. Additionally, in-field cross-verification was conducted for 10% of the sample. These randomly selected households were revisited and a set of questions of the survey was asked again. Discrepancies between answers from the survey and the cross-verification were corrected. After the verified data was entered into the RedCap software, data entry quality checks were undertaken, where 10% of the data was checked for data entry quality and mistakes were corrected and recorded. The errors were shared with the data entry operator to ensure that similar errors did not occur again. Similar to the crosscheck procedure, an additional 10% were quality checked in cases were high error rates were observed in the initial 10% check. The systematic quality control system not only ensured that data was recorded accurately but also led to continuous improvements in data collection and entry quality.

The data set was then exported into the statistical software package STATA 12 for analysis (StataCorp., 2011). First, the baseline survey data was analyzed descriptively complemented by data of the farm and hygiene surveys. Simple description of the sample population was achieved using means, percentages and counts of several variables. Various categorical variables were observed in cross tables to gain a good understanding of the various communities and their key differences. An important classification arising from the descriptive analysis was the socio-economic status (SES) of the household. The linkage between SES and health is complex, as SES influences many factors, ranging from housing situation and education level to access to health services. SES can be quantified using income or expenditure information as well as assets based. Obtaining income information is prone to reporting bias; moreover, participants are often reluctant to share exact numbers. Utilizing an assets-based approach achieves a much more objective finding. Observations such as the wall material of the house, the presence of a fridge, TV or motorcycle provide robust indications for the SES of the houschold. Using the STATA 'pca' command, primary factor analysis was undertaken using a set of 32 variables. The Kaiser-Meyer-Olkin measure was used to test the sampling accuracy to ensure that factors did not show colinearity. The statistical software was then used to estimate a new variable based upon the selected factors. The new variable was converted into z-scores to allow classification into quintiles. It must be noted that the classification of SES is relative to the sample population, resulting in a balanced classification. The advantage of classifying SES based on the sample is a higher resolution of differences, as it is expected that all households fall into similar SES categories on the national level.

The outcome variable was collected bi-monthly and thus forms the bulk of the data set. For the incidence calculation, the data was restructured. The 14 daily binary scores were reduced to round-wise binary scores. A second variable was generated forming the count duration (number of days sick). The incidence rate was calculated by dividing the total number of cases by person-time and then multiplying the result by 1,000 to obtain the standard form: number of cases per 1,000 person-time (Rothman et al., 2008). Person-time is calculated by multiplying the number of people observed by the time of observation. In this study, person-weeks are used, therefore the number of household members was multiplied by 2 weeks to form the round-wise person-week variable. Adding the person-weeks of all rounds created the total number of person-weeks observed per household thus allowing the calculation of the incidence rate over the entire reporting period, as well as longitudinal comparison. This provided insight into the temporal variations.

To calculate the relative risk, a clear binary variable structure is required. The exposure variable, defining whether the subject is exposed or not, and the outcome variable, defining if the subject has the symptom, are essentially cross-tabulated (Rothman, 2012). The relative risk is thus derived from the difference in the proportion of sick people between the exposed and non-exposed population. The odds ratio is used similarly to the relative risk, there are however precise differences. Whilst the relative risk quantifies the risk of contracting the disease relative to a control group, the odds ratio describes the difference in the probability of contracting a disease between two groups (ibid). The exposure variable was thus converted into binary form; initially the categorization of the survey was used comparing wastewater farmers with non-wastewater farmers. Microbiological data forms the primary exposure variable, thus the continuous data had to be categorized. The WHO water standards and recommendations were used for this classification. Thus, water suitable for unrestricted irrigation is compared to water not suitable for irrigation. Similarly, the secondary exposure variable, drinking water, was transferred into binary form. Exposure to unsafe drinking water is defined as per WHO standard, i.e. $\geq$ 10 total coliforms per 100 ml or $\geq$ 1 *E. coli* per 100 ml. Relative risk and odds ratio were then calculated for each exposure variable. As the time dimension was especially important, it was necessary to match the appropriate water-sampling round to the correct cohort interval. In addition, the aggregate exposure and outcome variable were used to calculate the annual relative risk and odds ratio.

Quantifying household hygiene was essential for further analysis, and a multitude of variables needed to be combined to provide an accurate indication. The hygiene index was conducted during each household visit, thus corresponding to the cohort intervals of the outcome variable. Each of the five hygiene categories was scored at -1, 0 or +1, the scores then added to form the hygiene index score. The score was then converted into z-scores and divided into quintiles creating a hygiene classification. To generate the annual hygiene classification, the mean of the z-scores was calculated and used to classify households into quintiles. Another key dimension of hygiene is handwashing practice, which was assessed using the surveys. The most important times for hand washing are after defecation, after working on the farm, before food preparation and before eating. The critical handwashing times are in binary format, where '0' represents the absence of the particular hygiene behavior and '1' indicates that the behavior was practiced. The binary handwashing variables complement the hygiene index classification during analysis.

An additional hygiene indication was generated using an outcome-based approached, although it should be noted that the outcome in this case is not disease but water quality. As drinking water was tested both at the source and the storage level, the difference in contamination occurred in the household. As a consequence, in-household water contamination provides an indication of household hygiene. Negative values occurred when water quality improved inside the household, while positive values show increased contamination. Stratified T-tests and regression analysis were used to analyze the explanatory power of the hygiene index score.

An observational data set was produced as allocation to the exposure group was not random. Consequently, variations in characteristics and behaviors may be observed between the groups leading to confounding effects. Relying on bivariate analysis, such as odds ratios or incidence rate ratios, an observational study is thus prone to the effects of confounding. This is particularly true in this study, as it is well established that WASH factors influence the incidence of diarrhea. First, a stratified analysis was conducted in an attempt to overcome confounding effects. However, due to the large number of potentially confounding variables “there are too few subjects within each stratum to give useful estimates” (Rothman, 2012:219). Therefore, multivariable regression was applied to assess the unconfounded correlations between each independent variable and the outcome variable. The key advantage of regression analysis is that the estimated coefficients of the regression model are adjusted for all other variables included in the model, thus controlling for confounding effects (Rothman et al., 2008).

Two types of regression models were applied in this research, i.e. linear regression and logistic regression. In linear regression models, the coefficients are estimated using least square calculation, which means that the estimated values minimize the sum of squared deviations between the observed and predicted values of the dependent variable (Hosmer & Lemeshow, 2000). Thus, linear regression models are referred to as ordinary least square (OLS) regression in this research. Least square calculations do not reliably estimate the coefficients in logistic regressions, as the dichotomous variable structure induces different properties of the estimators (ibid). Whilst linear regression models are expressed as $E(Y|x) = \beta_0 + \beta_1 x_1 + \beta_n x_n$, thus implying that $E(Y|x)$ can take any value between negative and positive infinity, the logistic regression model is based on the formula $\pi(x) = [e^{g(x)}/(1+e^{g(x)})]$, where $g(x) = \beta_0 + \beta_1 x_1 + \beta_n x_n$, and the range of values is between zero and one (ibid). The key difference between linear and logistic regressions is the variable structure of the dependent variable; in OLS regressions continuous dependent variables are used, whilst the logistic regression uses binary dependent variables. Furthermore, the correlations between the independent and dependent variable are assumed to be linear in OLS regressions, thus the curve is characterized by a straight line, while in logistic regressions the curve is sigmoid shaped (Rothman, 2012).

The interpretation of the estimated coefficient also differs between the two regression model types. In linear regressions, the coefficient reflects the measuring scale of the dependent variable, illustrating the change in value of a one-unit change of the independent variable (Hosmer & Lemeshow, 2000). In logistic regressions, the coefficients are not given in the scale of the dependent variable but instead show the change of the logit given a unit change of the independent variable (ibid). In consequence, the coefficients can only be interpreted when applying a measure of association, thus placing the logit of the exposed population in relation to the logit of the unexposed population. As a result, the coefficient of the logistic regression is expressed as odds ratio, where $OR = [\pi(1) / (1- \pi(1))] / [\pi(0) / (1- \pi(0))]$. "This simple relationship between the coefficient and the odds ratio is the fundamental reason why logistic regression has proven to be such a powerful analytical research tool" (Hosmer & Lemeshow, 2000:50). The main advantage of the logistic regression is the coefficient output in form of odds ratios, which are easily compared to the results of the bivariate and stratified analysis.

In this study both OLS and logistic regression models were applied. Continuous dependent variables are fitted in OLS models, where the coefficient indicates the degree of change of the outcome variable, given a unit change of the independent variable. For example, the incidence rate forms the dependent variable and the natural logarithm of the *E. coli* concentration of irrigation water is the independent variable. The resulting coefficient of the linear regression illustrates the change in the incidence rate for one log-unit increase in the *E. coli* density. In the logistic regression, the dependent variablc is in binary form, thus the presence (1) or absence (0) of disease forms the outcome variable. Consequently, the resulting odds ratio represents the likelihood of disease to be present among those exposed to unsafe irrigation water in comparison to the unexposed population (Rothman, 2012). Therefore, linear regressions are used to analyze the degree of change in the outcome variable and logistics regressions inform of the likelihood of the outcome to occur.

The key challenge of observational data sets is the non-random assignment to the treatment group, resulting in the unbalanced distribution of independent variables. Consequently, to allow causal inference and confirm the effect size of the correlations, all independent variables need to be balanced across the exposure and control group. Thus, a quasi-experimental data set is created, where the differences in the outcome variable can only be induced by differences in the exposure variable. This allows the calculation of the average treatment effect (ATE) of the exposure variable. To balance the sample, propensity-score matching was conducted using the STATA commands pscore and psmatch2. "The basic idea behind propensity score matching is to match each participant with an identical nonparticipant and then measure the average difference in the outcome variable between the participants and the nonparticipants" (Khandker et al., 2009:181).

The propensity-score was estimated through regressing the exposure variable and the independent variables to assess to what extent group allocation was determined by the independent variables (Rothman et al., 2008). The propensity-score thus reflects all independent variables. According to the propensity-score, the sample was split into blocks, where the mean propensity-score was the same within each block and different between the blocks (Khandker et al., 2009). It was then tested that cases in the same block did not show significantly different mean scores across all independent variables. If the balancing property was satisfied, it could be assumed that cases with similar propensity-scores have similar characteristics across all independent variables (ibid). In the second step, exposed cases were matched to control cases based on their propensity score, ensuring that matched households were similar across all variables except exposure. The balancing property was retested after matching, comparing the mean scores of all independent variables between the exposure and control group. The balancing property was satisfied when no significant differences in the mean scores were found between the groups across all variables (Rothman et al., 2008). When the balancing property of the matched sample was satisfied, it could be assumed that the differences observed in the outcome variable was caused by the exposure variable (Khandker et al., 2009; Rothman et al., 2008). Propensity-score matching was conducted for exposure to unsafe irrigation water as well as the WASH factors to allow the comparison of the effect sizes and to gage the relative importance of each variable in regard to the disease outcome.

3 Study Area & Study Population

3.1 Ahmedabad

Ahmedabad is the largest city of Gujarat state, situated in the North-west of India (WaterAid, 2006). The city is located in the cotton belt of Gujarat, about 550 km North of Mumbai and 95 km of the Gulf of Combay (AMC, 2006). Historically, Ahmedabad was known as the 'Manchester of India', due to its large textile industry (ibid; Bhatt, 2003). Today, the city still serves as an important economic driver of Gujarat state, having evolved to a major industrial and service center (Mehta & Metha, 1993). In 2000, 19.3% of the factories and 27.7% of the workers of the state were in Ahmedabad (AMC, 2006). According to the results of the census 2011, the larger urban area of Ahmedabad has a population of 6.5 million people, whereas the city itself has a population of 5.6 million people (GoI, 2011). The area is characterized by its "tropical monsoon climate, which is hot and dry, except in the rainy season" (AMC, 2006:7). The region is classified as semi-arid with an average rainfall of 782 mm, which falls primarily during the monsoon season (ibid). Ahmedabad is divided by the Sabarmati River into west Ahmedabad and east Ahmedabad, which are connected by five bridges (Mahadevia, 2002). The historical walled city is situated in east Ahmedabad and has the highest density (ibid). The eastern part of the city was the first to industrialize due to the proximity to the railway line (ibid). Consequently, the working-class people primarily settled in east Ahmedabad and the eastern periphery (Mehta & Metha, 1993). West Ahmedabad, on the other hand, consists of middle and upper class residential areas, as well as slums housing the people providing services to the upper-class residents (ibid). About 40% of Ahmedabad's population lives in slums (WaterAid, 2006). Over the previous decades, population growth within the city has slowed down (Kundu & Roy, 2012). Particularly, the walled city has experienced negative growth rates, due to overcrowding and increasing commercialization. Consequently, the majority of population growth is occurring in the peripheral areas of the city (Mehta & Metha, 1993).

Although Ahmedabad is divided by the River Sabarmati, water supply has been a problem. The river practically dries-up during the summer, in consequence the city has been largely dependent on groundwater sources (AMC, 2006). Consequently, 58% of daily water demand is met by tube wells, 26% by radial wells and 16% from surface water (Ray, 1997). However, only 33% of the water released from the 'Dharoi' reservoir, located 150 km upstream from Ahmedabad actually reaches the city (AMC, 2006). An additional water source was constructed in 2000; the Raska Wier Project supplies the city with water from the River Mahi via an underground pipeline (ibid). This additional water source is highly important to avoid severe water crisis, especially when the monsoon fails (ibid). As groundwater has been the chief source of domestic, agricultural and industrial water, the groundwater table has been falling resulting in increasing failures of wells (ibid). The water supply was transformed over the previous decade, with 90% of irrigation water requirements now being met by surface water from the Narmada canal (Palrecha et al., 2012). A study by DFID found that 87% of non-slum urban households have individual water connection, however, only 23% of slum households have access to piped water supply (Fry et al., 2002). The city has a water treatment plant at Kotarpur, resultantly the drinking water quality of piped water is generally good (Ray, 1997). The level of water contamination is highest during the monsoon and post-monsoon period (ibid). Nonetheless, the urban poor and particularly the slum population often lack access to clean water; additionally, the average amount of water per person per day in slums is only 7.5 liters (WaterAid, 2006). It is estimated that the richest 25% of the population consumes about 90% of the available water, whereas the remaining 75% only have access to 10% of available water (Fry et al., 2002).

Ahmedabad installed its first underground sewer as early as 1893, and the entire walled city was sewered by 1930 (Tam, 2012). The sewerage system grew with the city, by 1939 the sewage network extended beyond the traditional walled city and in 1955 west Ahmedabad was also connected to the network (ibid). In 1958, Ahmedabad was proud to be the first Indian city to achieve a citywide underground sewerage system, "[h]owever, the quality of sanitation was far from ideal" (Tam, 2012:17). Especially, after the decline of the textile industry the expansion of the sewerage network slowed. The eastern peripheral areas remain under-serviced. Currently, about 75% of the municipal area is connected to the network (AMC, 2006). Although Ahmedabad has two wastewater treatment plants, with a capacity of 180 million liters per day (mld) and 75 mld respectively, a large portion of wastewater (168 mld) is discharged into River Sabarmati without treatment (ibid). "The quality of the river water is steadily seen to be deteriorating as it flows through the city" (Ray, 1997:2509). The sanitation situation is much worse in the peripheral areas, where no sewerage system exists and "sewage is left out in open through local drains" (AMC, 2006:38). Thus, flowing untreated to open fields, the Kharicut Canal or Khari River (ibid). "An estimated half a million people defecate in the open" (WaterAid, 2006:99). Especially during the monsoon months flooding can occur, leading to fecal contamination of the living environment.

The overall health infrastructure of Ahmedabad is good, with major hospitals in all zones of the city. The majority of hospitals are operated by the AMC, thus enabling access to healthcare for the low-income population. Nonetheless, 38% of urban children in Ahmedabad show signs of malnutrition and 37% of children reported diarrhea episodes over the past two weeks (Fry et al., 2002). The official infant mortality rate provided by the AMC was 27 per 1,000 infants in 2000, however this rate is suspiciously low as Lakdawala found the infant mortality rate to be 76 per 1,000 infants in 1997 for the whole city and 123 per 1,000 infants in the slum population (Fry et al., 2002). A study by Counterpart International in 2001 found that hygienic behavior is inadequate; only 9% of mothers "washed their hands before food preparation, before eating, before feeding children and after defecation" (ibid:12). A study by the World Health Organization found the most frequent causes of death among children under-five in Ahmedabad are diarrheal disease (28%), acute respirator infection (20%) and measles (11%) (ibid).

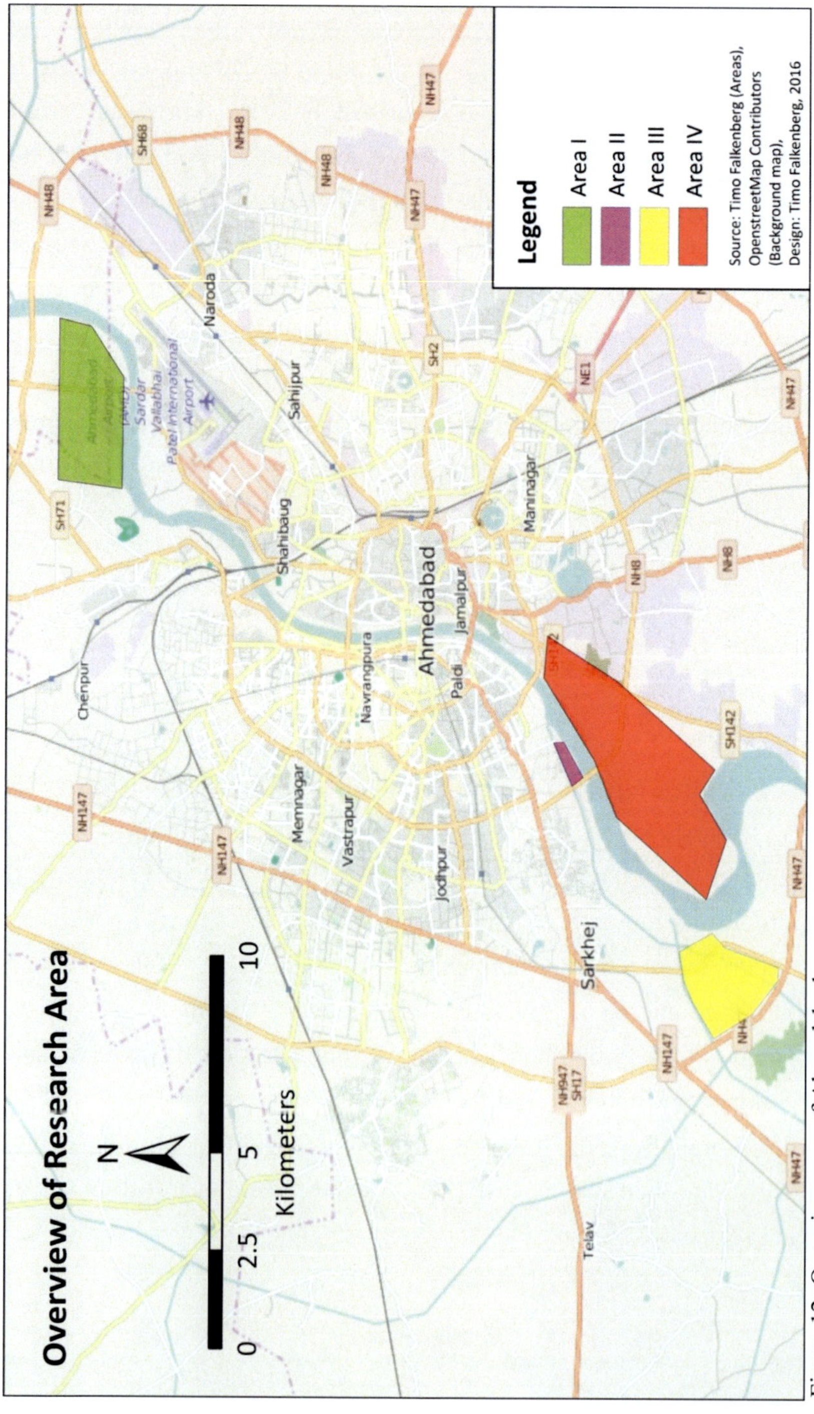

Figure 12: Overview map of Ahmedabad

3.2 Study Areas

The research was conducted in four urban areas of Ahmedabad; these were selected purposively on the basis of irrigation water choice. The control group (area I) primarily utilizes groundwater for irrigation and three exposure groups (area II, III and IV) irrigate with river, canal or wastewater. In the following section the situation of each area is described and the key characteristics of its inhabitants highlighted.

3.2.1 Area I

Figure 13: Koteshwar's farm area. Apartments encroaching farms. Foto: Timo Falkenberg

The control group is situated in the North of the city on the west bank of the river. The village is experiencing rapid change over the past few years, whilst most of the population was traditionally involved in agriculture, much of the farm land is giving way to housing developments. Many landowners have sold their agricultural land to developers and consequently have stopped cultivation. This trend is ongoing and it is expected that the farming population of the area will further decline over the coming years. Nonetheless, the primary occupation of population remains agriculture and animal husbandry, but an increasing proportion is involved in construction work. The village is serviced by the AMC and has good infrastructure. A public and a private primary school and a library are situated in the village, as well as a health care center, a bank branch and various vendors.

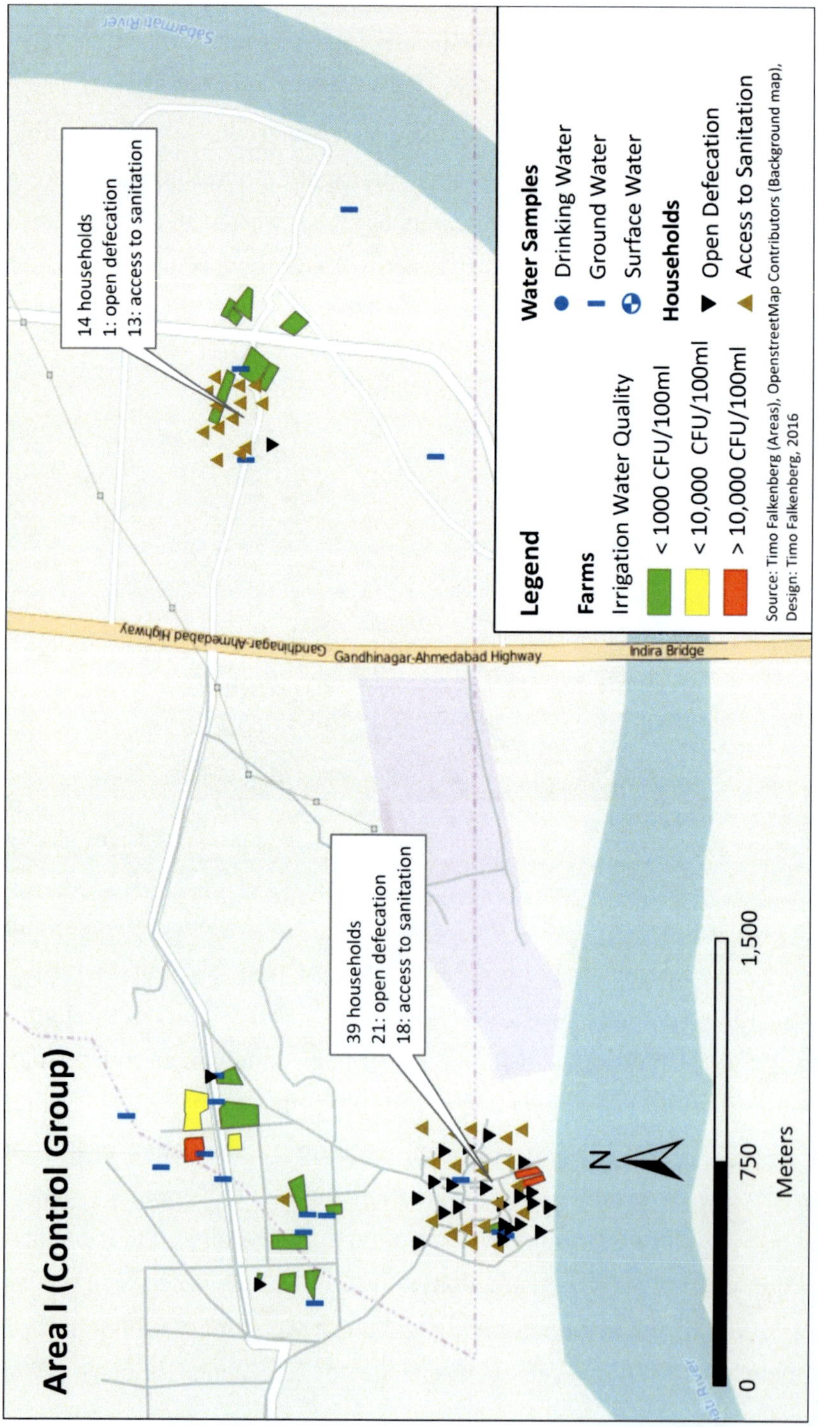

Figure 14: Map of Area I (Control Group)

Figure 15: Village water tank. Situated on the western village boundary. Foto: Timo Falkenberg

Drinking water is supplied through an AMC operated borewell located on the village boundary. Ground water from the borewell is pumped twice a day into the village water tank; from where it is distributed via underground pipelines to the individual households. An AMC appointed borewell operator is responsible for turning the pump on and off as well as adding chlorine to the water tank. Chlorine is provided free-of-charge by the AMC to ensure adequate chlorination of the drinking water supply. The village water tank is cleaned every three months and the quality of the borewell water is continuously tested in random intervals. The cleanliness of the water tank plays an important role, as water is stored for half a day. When the operator turns on the pumps in the morning, groundwater is pumped into the water tank while simultaneously releasing the stored water to the pipeline network. The individual households are thus required to store their water throughout the day, as piped water is only supplied in the morning and evening. Drinking water is stored in clay pots, called mataka, whilst general-purpose water is stored in plastic drums or cement basins. More prosperous households have a large water tank connected to in-household pipelines ensuring the 24-hour availability of tab water. Nonetheless, all households store their drinking water throughout the day.

Figure 16: Borewell for irrigation. Foto: Pankaj Yadav

The farmers of the area utilize groundwater to fulfill their irrigation requirements. Seven private borewells operate in the area and distribute water through underground pipelines to the individual farms. Farmers pay an hourly rate to receive irrigation water from the borewell owner. The average farm size is 3.8 bigha, converting to about 0.6 hectare. However, the farm sizes vary significantly, ranging from 0.5 bigha to 23 bigha. 54% of farmers own the land they cultivate and about 50% employ day laborers to aid during agricultural work, particularly during harvest. The primary crops cultivated in the area are wheat, millet and alfalfa as well as various vegetables including eggplant, potato, spinach and radish. The cultivation of herbs and spices, such as chili, coriander, garlic and fenugreek is also common. On average 4.5 people work on the farms, with 56% of farmers working alongside family members and 3% employing permanent workers. On all farms machinery is used, 73% utilize a tractor and 45% use a thresher during harvest. 72% of farmers fertilize their crops with chemical fertilizers, while 36% resort to compost to fulfill the fertilization requirement. Only 7% apply fertilizer using a shovel, the remainder simply uses their hands. There are no additional safety precautions during fertilizer application, 12%

indicated that they wear sandals as protective clothing. Similarly, all farmers apply pesticides to their fields without taking protective measures.

The control area consists of 56 households with 282 individuals, thus the average household size is 5.8 individuals. 46% of households have children with an average of 2.25 children per household (ranging from 1 to 7 children). Over half of the household heads are literate (55%), as defined by a minimum of six years schooling. In 85% of households at least one household member is considered literate. The population of the area is rather prosperous with the average socio-economic status reaching 3.4 on a five-point scale. This is reflected by over half of the population owning their farmland. 95% of households receive AMC water via pipeline on their premises, however, 33% of households resort to open defecation. The households with access to sanitation are not connected to the sewage network, but rely on septic tanks.

3.2.2 Area II

Figure 17: Vasna village (Area II). View from canal towards river. Foto: Timo Falkenberg

The area is a small informal settlement situated in the flood basin of the Sabarmati River. It is positioned in the south of the city along the west bank of the river and east of the irrigation canal. The settlement lays just downstream of the Vasna Barrage, opposite the first sewage inlets (situated on the east bank of the river).

As the area is situated in a flood prone zone, construction is formally prohibited and in consequently, no AMC operated services are provided to the community. Torrent Power is providing electricity to the area since 2009. Nonetheless, it is the only area in the sample not supplied by AMC monitored water sources. Shallow hand pumps that were privately constructed by the households supply the drinking water. Groups of three to five households share each hand pump. As the hand pumps are constructed and operated by the households themselves, the quality differs. 75% are covered, 40% have a platform and only 15% have drainage. The water is not filtered, boiled or chlorinated before consumption and the water quality is unmonitored. Drinking water is usually drawn in the morning and stored in matakas (clay vessels) throughout the day. Personal hygiene as well as washing and cleaning of clothes and cooking utensils are conducted directly at the hand pump site. The area is characterized by open defecation with none of the households having access to sanitation facilities. The bank of the river and canal serve as open defecation site for the entire village community.

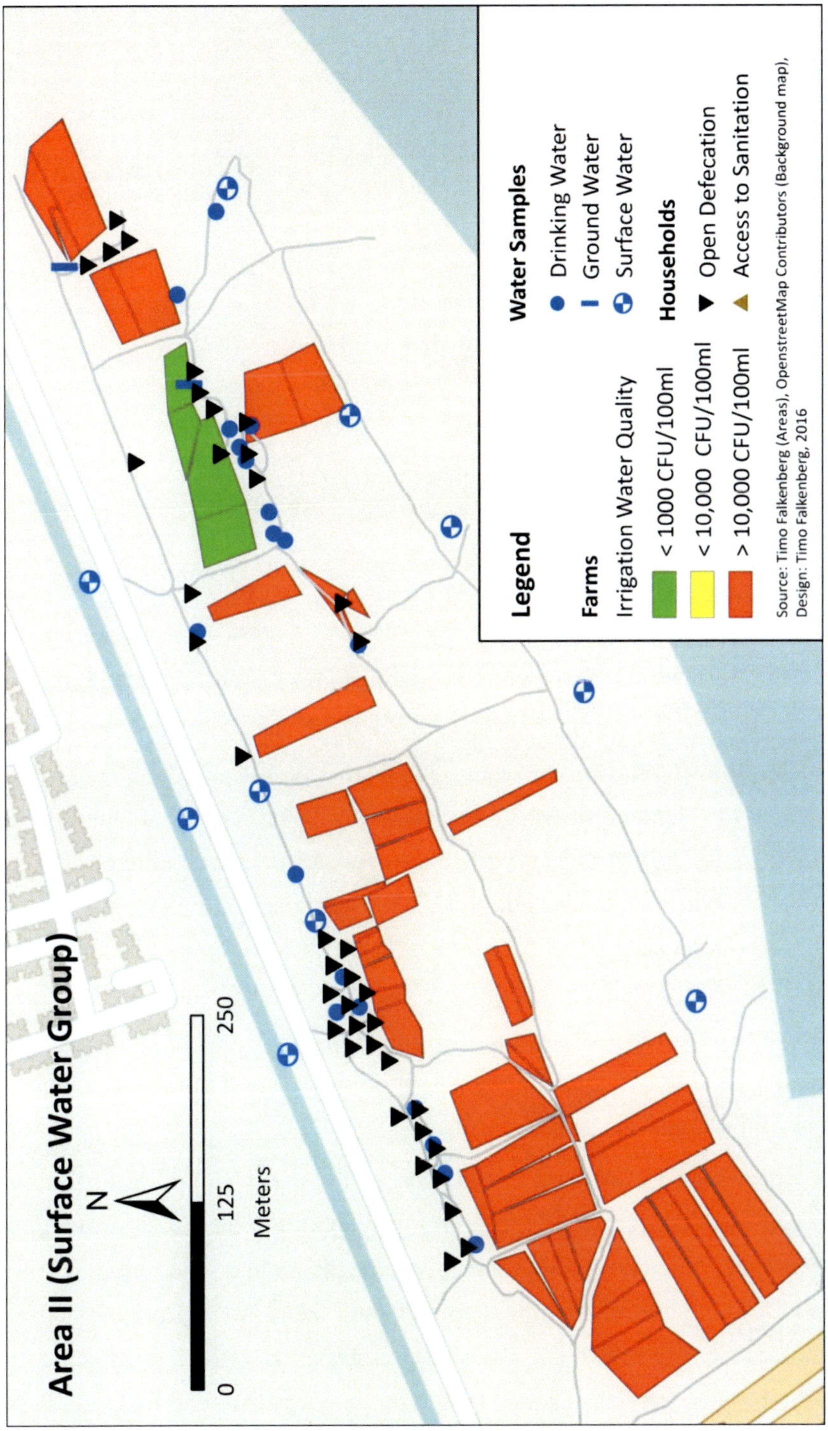

Figure 18: Map of Area II (Surface Water Group)

Figure 19: Hand pump / wash area. Shallow boreholes shared between two to four households. Foto: Timo Falkenberg

The farm sizes in the area are small, ranging from 0.5 to 4 bigha, with an average size of 1.2 bigha (approx. 0.2 ha). None of the households have ownership of the land they cultivate. The close proximity to both the river and the canal results in a mixed usage of surface water sources. 15% of farmers irrigate with river water, whilst 48% resort to canal water. Farmers utilize diesel pumps to draw the surface water and pump it via plastic hoses onto their respective field. Two borewells provide water for about 17% of farmers, who utilize ground water for their irrigation needs. Starting from December 2013 the irrigation canal was left dry until mid-June 2014, due to renovation work of the canal. As a result, farmers previously using canal water shifted their diesel pumps to the riverbank to satisfy their irrigation requirements.

Vegetables are primarily cultivated in the area, according to the farmers, other crops do not grow well due to the fertility of the land. All farmers practice furrow irrigation. The production of spinach, radish and eggplant is most common. During the hot summers spinach and beans are cultivated, while in the monsoon rains only radish is grown. The largest variety of crops is cultivated in the winter with spinach, radish, eggplant and cauliflower forming the bulk.

Additionally, the production of herbs, such as coriander and fenugreek are common as well as cultivation of chili, spring onion and green garlic. The bulk of produce is sold at the market, while the households consume a small proportion of the harvest themself.

Figure 20: River irrigation with diesel pump in Vasna village. Vasna barrage in the left background. Foto: Timo Falkenberg

On average 3.8 people are engaged in farm work, the majority (80%) being family members and 20% of households hire day laborers during harvest time. Despite the small farm sizes, use of machinery is common; 80% of farmers use a tractor during field preparation however no harvesting machinery is used. All farmers apply chemical fertilizers to their field using their hands without taken any protective precautions. Similarly, 98% of households apply pesticides to their field, none of which wear any form of protective clothing.

The sample consists of 40 households with 205 individuals. The average household size is 5.25, ranging from 3 to 10. 78% of households have children with an average of 2.25 children per household. The education level is low in the area with none of the head of households being classified as literate. Only 16% of households have at least one person with six or more years of education. The population has a low socio-economic status, averaging 1.8, with the highest socio-economic class found in the area being 3. The low socio-economic status of the area is reflected in the housing type, all houses are so-called kucha houses, meaning inferior building materials such as mud, thatch, plastic sheets and tin are used. Additionally, there are no services in the area, no school, no healthcare center and no water provision as well as the complete lack of sanitation facilities.

3.2.3 Area III

Figure 21: Narimanpura irrigation canal. Foto: Timo Falkenberg

Figure 22: Pakka house in Narimanpura with detached toilet (front right). Foto: Timo Falkenberg

The area is situated on the southern fringe of the city between two irrigation canals without direct access to the river. 48 households consisting of 326 individuals were sampled in the area. The average household size is 7.4 individuals. 67% of households have children with an average of 2.5 children per household. The area is well serviced, having a school, a healthcare center and various vendors. A key characteristic of the area is its large Muslim community, with only 20% of the sample being Hindu. Access to sanitation is good with 91% of households having access to sanitation. The population is the most prosperous among the entire sample with an average socio-economic status of 4. This is reflected in the education level, with 54% of the heads of household being literate and 96% of household having at least one literate member. In fact, the heads of household completed 6.2 years of schooling on average, showing that basic education achievement is common.

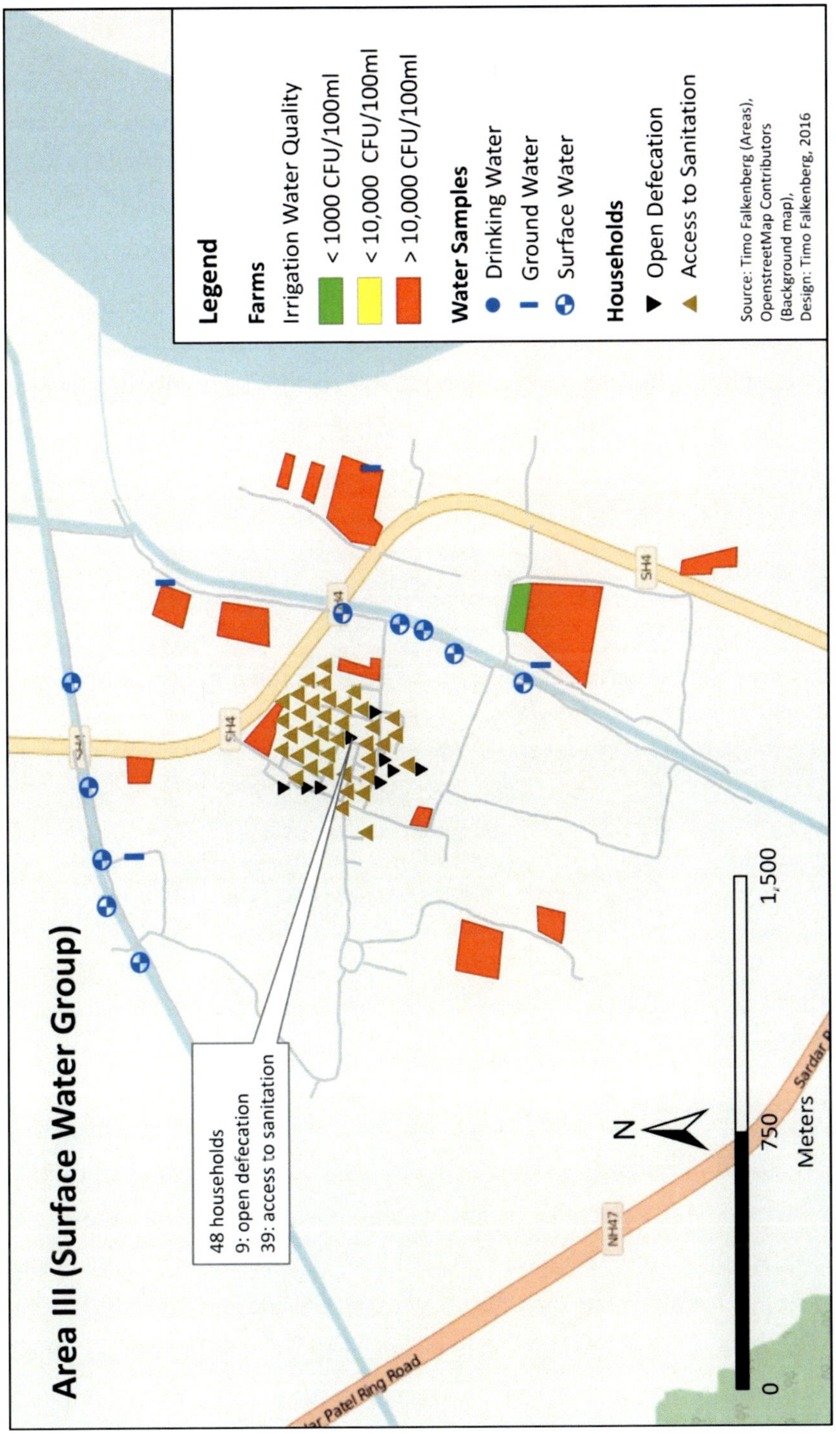

Figure 23: Map of Area III (Surface Water Group)

The water supply is provided and monitored by the AMC similar to area I. 97% of households are connected to the underground pipeline network. These receive water on their premises twice a-day, once in the morning and once in the evening. A village bore well situated on the outer edge of the village pumps water into the central water tank from where it is released into the pipeline network. It is noteworthy that water tank cleaning does not occur regularly, in fact it was reported that the tank has not been cleaned in years. This is important to note, as the *E. coli* concentrations measured in this study show the highest drinking water contamination in this area. Considering that the supply and monitoring system is the same as in area I, inadequate tank cleaning may form a key contamination point in area III.

Figure 24: Drinking water storage. Drinking water storage in matakas (clay vessel). Blue plastic drum stores general purpose water. Plastic sieve used for water filtration when filling the matakas. Foto: Timo Falkenberg

Regardless, all households require in-household water storage. Drinking water is stored in matakas as in the other areas, whilst general-purpose water is commonly stored in cement or plastic water tanks integrated into the house. The majority of houses are categorized as pakka (83%), meaning superior building materials, such as stone and concrete, make up the walls and flooring. The internal water tank does not only enable 24-hour tab water availability but also the use of the reverse osmosis filter system known as aquaguard®. 68% of households indicated filtering their water before consumption, however only one third of these utilize aquaguard®, with the remainder using a cloth or plastic sieve for filtration.

Figure 25: Dry irrigation canal between December 2013 and July 2014 due to renovation work. Foto: Timo Falkenberg

As the community is situated in between two irrigation canals, it is unsurprising that all farmers utilize it for irrigation. However, due to canal renovation work conducted by the AMC, the irrigation canal was dry from December 2013 until July 2014, similarly to area II. In consequence, many farmers discontinued cultivation for the season, while some resorted to bore wells to meet their irrigation needs. As the area was left without their primary irrigation source throughout most of the research period, farm information of the previous years was utilized for those unable to cultivate during this season. The primary crop grown in the area is rice, with all farmers engaging in rice cultivation from July until November. 53% of farmers produce solely for market sale, while 47% consume a small proportion of their harvest in household. Cultivating rice during monsoon time reduces irrigation requirements; nonetheless all farmers employ flood irrigation every 7–15 days. From November until February, wheat (40%), maize (30%) and safflower (17%) cultivation is common with only few farmers cultivating vegetables (9%). From March onwards, cultivation is reduced; maize, cucumber and alfalfa are most commonly grown during the hot and dry time of the year. Irrigation water is drawn from the irrigation canal using diesel pumps. Plastic hoses pump the water into the furrows of the field. Few farmers have private bore wells on their land for irrigation, due to the canal renovation work additional bore wells were privately constructed and the water sold to individual farmers on an hourly rate.

The farm sizes of the area are large, ranging from 2 to 50 bigha with an average of 10.8 bigha (approx. 1.7 ha). The majority of farmers (97%) own the land they cultivate with 68% employing day laborers. On average 5 people are involved in agricultural activities and 58% of farmers work alongside other family members. On all farms use of machinery is common, the majority using tractors (69%) and about 10% utilizing harvesting machinery. 73% of farmers apply chemical fertilizers to their field, while 27% use compost. 62% of those utilizing chemical fertilizers indicated wearing boots during fertilization. Whilst all farmers use their hands to apply fertilizer to their field, none indicated wearing gloves during application. The use of pesticides is also widespread (91%), with 21% not taking any protective measures. One third of farmers wear gloves during pesticide application and about 30% cover their face with a mask or cloth.

3.2.4 Area IV

The key exposure group is the wastewater area (area IV), situated on the west bank of the Sabarmati River, downstream of the sewage treatment plant. The wastewater area covers the village, where most farmers live as well as the surrounding farm area, where some farmers live directly on the farmland. The wastewater area borders the garbage dumpsite of Ahmedabad, as well as the sewage treatment plant. The area is situated in an industrial zone with predominantly textile coloring operations. The village is well serviced by the AMC, the village bore well was recently renewed and a fully automated chlorination mechanism installed. There is a school and a health center, as well as shops, a temple and an AMC extension office.

Figure 26: Gyaspur village square. Shiva Temple on the right, the central village water tank in the back left (blue). Foto: Timo Falkenberg

The water supply infrastructure operates in the same way as in area I and III, with a village borewell on the outer perimeter of the village, a central water tank and an underground pipeline network connecting the individual households. A new borewell was constructed by the AMC and went into operation in October 2013, simultaneously an automated chlorination mechanism was installed at the village water tank. A pre-determined volume of chlorine is pumped from a chlorine tank into the water tank, when the borewell is powered on. Similar to the other areas, water is released from the tank through the pipeline network to the individual houses, whilst the borewell water refills the water tank. In consequence, households receive water twice a day and need to store their drinking water throughout the day.

Drinking water is stored in clay matakas by the vast majority of the population (94%) with the remaining utilizing plastic or steel storage vessels. In-household water treatment is highly uncommon with only 8% of the population utilizing any filtration and none boiling their water before consumption. Among those filtering their water, only 20% utilize the modern aquaguard® system, whilst 60 and 20% resort to a cloth or plastic sieve, respectively. General-purpose water is stored in large plastic drums or integral cement tanks, as in the area I and III. Inside the village boundary most houses are pakka-type, with the more affluent population having general-purpose water tank integral in the house. Those living on the farmland usually constructed kucha houses, where general-purpose water is stored in plastic drums and withdrawn on demand. It should be noted that households outside of the village boundary do not receive water from the AMC bore well, but primarily collect water from the temple's borewell. Some households have constructed private hand pumps, similarly to area II, to satisfy their water requirement.

Figure 27: Kucha house in Gyaspur's farm area without access to sanitation. Foto: Timo Falkenberg

The area is characterized by the use of wastewater for irrigation (86%), with few farmers having private borewell on their farm for irrigating with groundwater (14%). In this area, the use of river water for irrigation is classified as wastewater use, as the area is located in close proximity of the sewage inlets (see figure 28). Along the east bank of the river, downstream of the Vasna Barrage, five sewage inlets essentially refill the river. The farmers use diesel engines to pump water onto their field just a couple hundred meters downstream of the sewage inlet. In consequence, the irrigation water source is classified as wastewater. Various diesel pumps are located along the bank of the river distributing water via underground pipelines and open furrows to the farms without direct access to the river. Farmers in close proximity to sewage pipelines attach their motor directly to the pipeline and pump the water onto their fields for irrigation.

Figure 28: Sewage inflow into Sabarmarti River. Picture taken from Narol-Sarkej Bridge facing southwest. Foto: Timo Falkenberg

Figure 29: Farmer placing pump into river. Picture taken approx. 250 meters downstream of sewage outlet. Foto: Timo Falkenberg

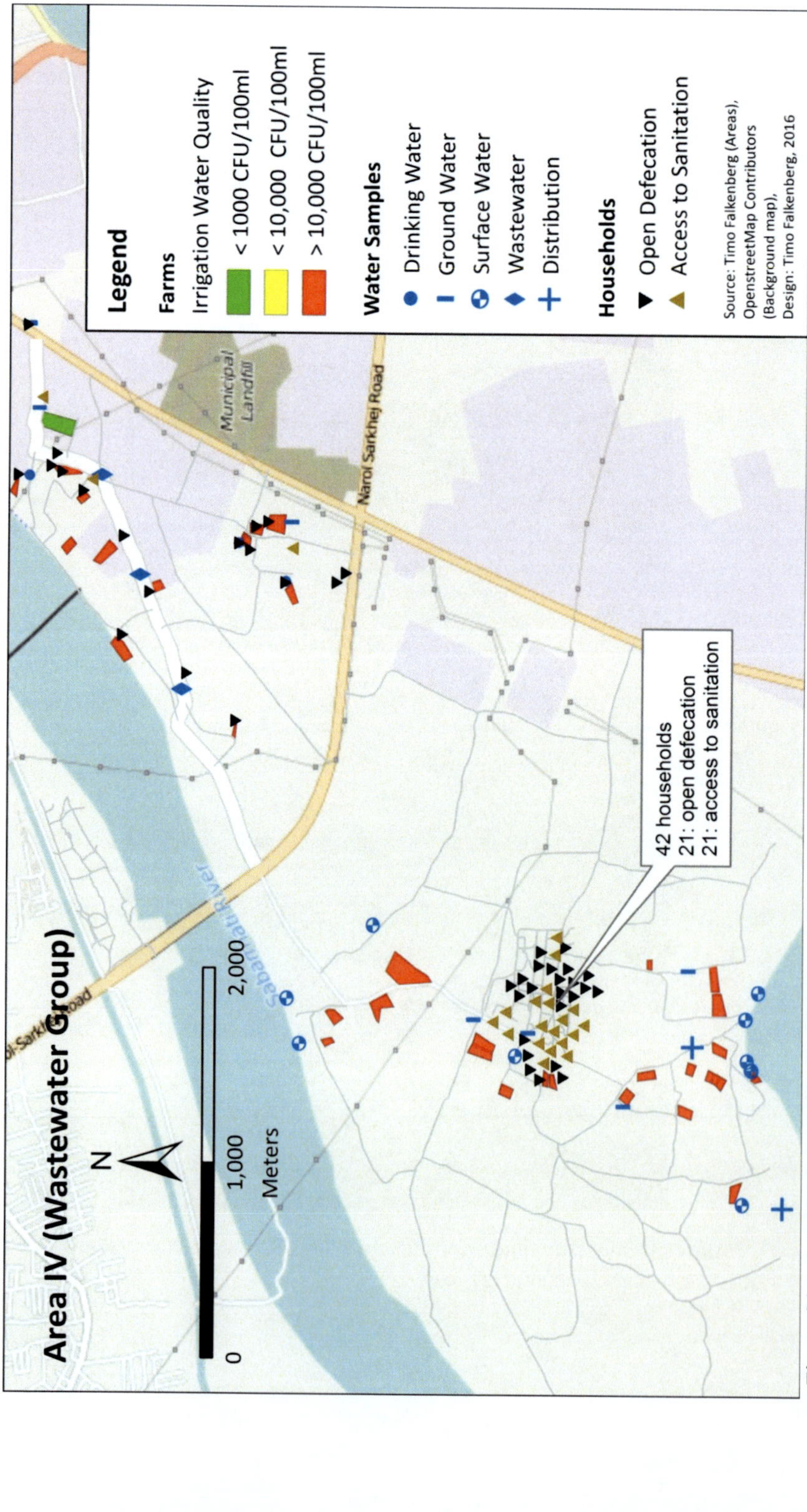

Figure 30: Map of Area IV (Wastewater Group)

The farm size differs significantly, ranging from 1 bigha to 100 bigha with an average of 5.6 bigha (0.9 ha). Cultivation is primarily done within the family, with 90% of farmers working alongside family members. On average only 2.7 people work on each farm, ranging from one to five individuals involved in agricultural work. The employment of permanent (6%) and day labor (3%) is uncommon in the area. Unlike the other areas use of machinery is not widespread with only 51% utilizing any form of machinery. Most commonly a tractor (45%) is employed during field preparation, while only 8% use a thresher during harvest. Despite using wastewater for irrigation, 95% of farmers apply chemical fertilizer to their field. It appears that farmers are unaware of the fertilization capacity of wastewater, which can result in over-fertilization and environmental damage. Although all farmers use their hands to apply fertilizer, none wear gloves during application. However, 30% and 10% indicated wearing boots or sandals during fertilization, respectively. Similarly, 91% utilize pesticides with only 10% taking preventive measures; 6% wear boots and 4% cover their face.

Figure 31: Ahmedabad landfill. Agricultural field in front, bordering the Ahmedabad Municipal Landfill (in the background). Foto: Timo Falkenberg

Wheat (48%), vegetables (32%), marigold (20%) and sorghum (13%) are most commonly cultivated in the area. Among the vegetables, spinach, cauliflower and eggplant are most frequently produced. Most farmers cultivate wheat or sorghum during the winter season and cultivate vegetables or ornamental flowers during the summer. During the rainy season sorghum is primarily cultivated but some vegetable cultivation persists throughout the year. The vast majority of farmers (95%) produce exclusively for market sale with only a small proportion of the sample eating some of their own produce.

The sample population of area IV consists of 60 households with 420 individuals. 68% of households have children, with 2.4 children per household on average. Half of the heads of household are categorized as literate, whilst 87% of households have at least one literate member. Despite 63% of farmers holding ownership of the land they cultivate, the average socio-economic status of the area is low, reaching 2.4 on average. Only 37% of households have access to sanitation, with the majority of the population utilizing the fringe of the village or the farm area as open defecation site. Access to sanitation is only present within the village boundary, households living on the farmland exclusively engage in open defecation.

3.3 Sample Population

The description of the individual research areas has revealed that the groups do not only differ in their choice of irrigation water source but also on other important risk factors such as access to sanitation as well as key characteristics such as socio-economic status and education achievement. Therefore, key descriptive statistics are presented, highlighting important differences beyond irrigation water choice. The exposure group is made up of wastewater and surface water farmers (essentially area II, III and IV), whilst the control group consists of groundwater farmers (area I). Additionally, distinctions between the wastewater and surface water exposure group are highlighted.

The entire sample population consists of 200 households with a total of 1286 individuals. The average household size is 6.4 individuals with 64% of households having at least one child. Households with children have 2.4 children on average, whilst the population average amounts to 1.5 children per household. 42% of the heads of household are classified as literate, on average five years of education were completed. In 75% of households at least one family member is literate, the average number of years of schooling of the most educated household member is 8.8 years. Table 10 highlights important differences between the study groups. The exposure group has the largest household size, which is reflected in the higher proportion of children, as well as the average number of children per household. Among the exposure groups, wastewater users have a larger average household size compared to surface water farmers; however, the proportion of children in the household is greater in the surface water group. As children are at the highest risk of suffering from diarrheal disease, it is important to control the variable in analysis. Similarly, the education level differs significantly between the exposure and control groups, with the control showing higher literacy rates for both the head of household and the highest educated family member. Interestingly, the wastewater group shows higher literacy rates compared to the control group, particularly among the highest educated family member. The low educational achievement in the surface water group therefore causes the large discrepancy between exposure and control group. Especially in area II, education achievement is very low resulting in the low literacy rate among the surface water group. Whilst literacy, is relatively well balanced between the wastewater and control group, analysis of the exposure effect, however, requires control of education achievement to avoid confounding effects.

The water supply system was previously presented for each research area. In general, the supply system is the same in all areas with the exception of area II. The key differences between water supply systems provided by the AMC is the chlorination mechanism and the water tank maintenance, yet the overall infrastructure is the same with a village borewell, a central water tank and an underground pipeline network connecting the households. Areas not serviced by the AMC, particularly area II but also some households living on the farmland in other areas; manage their water supply privately, by constructing shallow hand pumps. The majority of households (65%) receive piped water on their premises through the AMC supply system, while 32% utilize private hand pumps or borewells to satisfy their water requirement. The remaining 3% of households resort to unimproved water sources, utilizing public tabs, temple borewells or vendors to supply their water.

Table 10: Household composition among the study groups. Exposure group = irrigation water quality ≥ 1,000 E. coli/100 ml; Control group = irrigation water quality < 1,000 E. coli/100 ml; Wastewater group = farmers utilizing wastewater for irrigation; Surface water group = farmers utilizing river or canal water for irrigation

Variable	Exposure Group	Control Group	Wastewater Group	Surface Water Group	Total
Number of Households	129	58	52	77	200
Number of Individuals	842	444	361	481	1286
Average Household size	6.7	6.1	7.1	6.5	6.4
Proportion with children	71%	58%	67%	73%	64%
Average Number of children	2.4	2.3	2.5	2.4	2.4
Literacy (Head of HH)	36%	46%	47%	28%	42%
Literacy (Highest Educated)	70%	79%	86%	59%	75%

All households store drinking water throughout the day, as water is supplied only twice a day. Even households with private hand pumps collect their drinking water in the morning and store it for convenient use during the day. 92% of the sample population stores their drinking water in traditional clay vessels called mataka. About 5% of households indicated storing drinking water in plastic storage containers, another 5% utilize steel pitchers and 8% resort to buckets for drinking water storage. Most households use multiple storage vessels, although usually of the same type. More affluent households often use plastic storage containers to store the bulk of their drinking water, whilst steel pitchers are refilled from the storage container and placed in the fridge. A key advantage of the mataka is its cooling property, ensuring the availability of cold water even during the hot summers. As plastic storage containers tend to have the opposite effect, warming the water, households using such containers often place pitchers or bottles in the fridge to ensure cold-water availability for drinking.

As drinking water is stored in all households in some kind of vessel, water needs to be withdrawn on demand. Most commonly households draw water from their vessel directly with a cup (84%) or a scoop (4%). This withdrawal method can result in contact between hands and water and thus forms a potential point of in-household drinking water contamination. 12% of the sample population has an outflow valve for their storage vessel, thus allowing the withdrawal of water without contacting the stored water directly. It is therefore suspected that possession of an outflow valve reduces the risk of in-household water contamination.

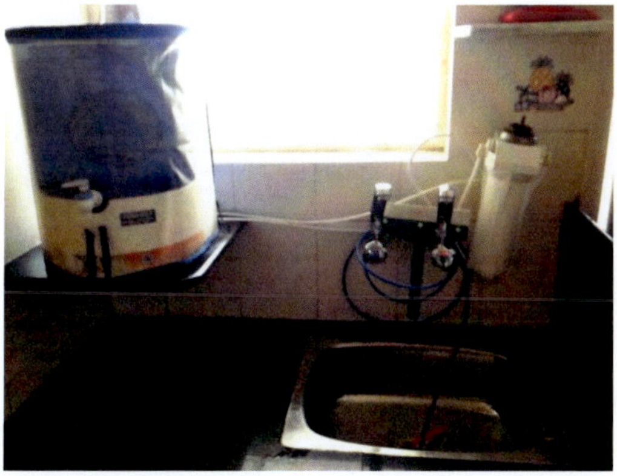

Figure 32: Reverse osmosis filter (white tube on the right) connected to a storage vessel (on left side). Foto: Timo Falkenberg

In-household drinking water treatment is not common among the sample population, despite 45% of households indicating filtering their water prior to consumption. Only 11% of the sample uses the modern reverse osmosis filter, aquaguard®(RO), with 18 and 16% resorting to plastic sieves and cloth, respectively. Only 1% of the households indicated boiling their water before consumption, whilst none of the households apply chlorine to the drinking water in household. It should be noted that the utilization of aquaguard® requires high initial investment as well as regular maintenance fees and is thus unaffordable for low-income houses. Aquaguard® is a reverse osmosis filter system and thus requires continuous water availability in order for sufficient pressure to be exerted onto the water. In reverse osmosis, water is separated from its solvents by forcing water through a semi-permeable membrane under pressure. As a result, the solvents get caught in the membrane, whilst the water passes through. In the aquaguard® system water is additionally passed through a carbon filter, which has the ability to absorb solvents, thus increasing the range of substances removed by the system. Aquaguard® does not only remove organic pathogens but also removes organic chemicals, chlorine, pesticides and herbicides.

Table 11 highlights important differences between the study groups in regard to drinking water. Whilst almost 80% of the control group receives water via the AMC supply system only 57% of the exposure group receive piped water on their premises. This situation is strongly impacted by area II, where the entire population resorts to hand pumps for drinking water supply. In consequence, the surface water group has the lowest proportion of households receiving piped water. In chapter 4.2, the water quality of the different water sources are compared; when assuming that AMC monitored water is of superior quality compared to hand pump water, it is important to control for drinking water source in further analysis. It should be noted, however, that drinking water quality is considered an additional exposure variable, thus controlling for the bacterial concentrations of drinking water is inevitable.

The primary storage vessel is the mataka in all areas, with similar percentages in all study groups. Only in the control group there are significant differences in the composition of storage vessels. 13% of control households have a plastic water storage container and 21% utilize other vessels in addition. It appears that only in the control population using multiple types of storage vessels is common. In all groups, the most common withdrawal method is by cup, with a small proportion utilizing scoops. The possession of an outflow valve is more common in the exposure group compared to the control group. However, when looking at the specific exposure groups, a large difference between wastewater and surface water farmers is noted. Whilst none in wastewater population have an outflow valve, 19% of the surface water group withdrawal water in this way. It should be noted that the high proportion of surface water farmers having an outflow valve, stem from area III as none of the households in area II possess an outflow valve. Similarly, filtration with aquaguard®, appears to be most common in the surface water group, however, none of the households in area II use this filtration system. Among the wastewater group, utilization of aquaguard® is uncommon with only 2% using the filtration system. The use of other filtration methods is common in the control group, whilst only 6% of wastewater farmers employing filtration. It is indicated that about one third of surface water farmers filter their water with plastic sieves or cloth, however, in area II none of the households use any filtration system. It is thus clear that there is a significant discrepancy within the surface water group, due the large differences between area II and III. Overall, the water treatment, storage and withdrawal variables are not balanced across the study groups; it is therefore necessary to control these in analysis.

Next to the drinking water quality, access to sanitation is closely linked to the incidence of diarrheal disease. It is therefore important to control the effect of sanitation, or better the lack of sanitation, when analyzing the impact of irrigation water quality on disease incidence. About half of the sample population has access to sanitation, with none of the toilets connected to city sewage network. In consequence, all sanitation facilities of the sample use a septic tank. Significant difference in access to sanitation was noted between the research areas, thus unsurprisingly differences are also observed between groups. Whilst 44% of the exposure group has access to sanitation, 54% of the control group uses sanitation facilitics. The difference is more pronounced between the wastewater and surface water group, with 32 and 53% of households having access to sanitation, respectively. It must be noted again that higher percentage among the surface water group is strongly influenced by area III (91% have access to sanitation), counterbalancing the complete absence of sanitation facilities in area II. Overall, access to sanitation is not balanced among the exposure groups and consequently needs to be controlled in analysis.

Table 11: Drinking water variables among the study groups.

Category	Variable	Exposure Group (n=129)	Control Group (n=58)	Wastewater Group (n=52)	Surface Water Group (n=77)	Total (n=200)
Water Source	**Piped Water**	57%	79%	67%	50%	65%
	Hand Pump	39%	19%	32%	45%	32%
	Unimproved	4%	2%	2%	5%	3%
Water Storage	**Mataka (clay)**	94%	92%	94%	93%	92%
	Plastic Storage	1%	13%	2%	0%	5%
	Other Vessel	7%	21%	4%	8%	18%
Water Withdrawal	**Cup**	84%	90%	98%	76%	84%
	Scoop	5%	4%	2%	5%	4%
	Outflow	11%	6%	0%	19%	12%
Water Treatment	**Aquaguard**	8%	10%	2%	12%	11%
	Other Filtration	12%	58%	6%	33%	34%
	Boiling	1%	0%	0%	1%	1%

Hygiene and hand hygiene in particular, form key preventive mechanisms and are thus expected to reduce the risk of diarrheal disease. The hygiene index forms the primary indicator for household hygiene; the critical hand washing times (after defecation, before eating, after work and before cooking) complement the indicator. The average hygiene index score of the entire sample population amounts to 1.42, on a scale of -5 to +5. Breaking down the hygiene index score into its component scores, highlights sanitation as most problematic with an average score of -0.07 on a scale of -1 to +1. The other components, water (0.55), food (0.33), environment (0.10) and personal (0.42) indicate a tendency to better hygiene practice among the sample population. The low average environment score suggests that a significant proportion of the sample have inadequate or neutral environmental hygiene. About half of the sample indicated washing their hands after defecation and before cooking. 56% wash their hands before eating, while 39% wash their hands after work. Table 12 presents the average hygiene index scores and critical hand washing times for the study groups.

The sample is highly unbalanced in terms of hygiene with the exposure group showing significantly lower hygiene index scores. The effect is more pronounced when comparing the wastewater and surface water groups, with the average index score being negative among wastewater farmers, while reaching 2 in the surface water group. The general trend is robust in all hygiene categories, clearly indicating lower hygiene among the exposure group and wastewater group in particular. The only exceptions are found in the sanitation and food category when comparing the exposure and control groups. Particularly, interesting is the sanitation score, as despite more people having access to sanitation in the control group compared to the exposure group, the sanitation hygiene score is lower among the control group. This indicates that the cleanliness of the sanitation facilities is inferior in the control group, as absent sanitation is scored as -1, unclean toilets as 0 and hygienic facilities as +1.

Farming practices influence the amount of direct contact with irrigation water, thus impacting the degree of exposure. It is therefore, essential to compare the general farming practices of the study groups. Farm sizes vary significantly among the sample, ranging from 0.5 bigha to 100 bigha with an average of

5.4 bigha. 55% of farmers own the land they cultivate with an average of 3.8 people working on each farm. 88% of farmers work alongside family members and 44% employ day labors. Most commonly the husband or wife of the farmer aids in farm work (61%), while 42% of farmers engage their children in agricultural work and 28% work alongside their siblings. 22% of farmers cultivate their land with aid of their parents and about 12% receive help from their daughter-, or sister-in-law.

Table 12: Hygiene and hand washing among the study groups. HI = Hygiene Index Component; HW = Hand Washing

Variable	Exposure Group (n=129)	Control Group (n=58)	Wastewater Group (n=52)	Surface Water Group (n=77)	Total (n=200)
Access to Sanitation	44%	54%	32%	53%	49%
Hygiene Index Score	1.14	1.67	-0.11	2.01	1.42
HI-Environment	0.018	0.21	-0.04	0.06	0.10
HI-Water	0.49	0.63	-0.07	0.88	0.55
HI-Sanitation	-0.07	-0.19	-0.27	0.07	-0.07
HI-Food	0.30	0.31	0.01	0.50	0.33
HI-Personal	0.38	0.47	0.25	0.46	0.42
HW-after defecation	44%	61%	18%	61%	49%
HW-before eating	70%	30%	85%	60%	56%
HW-before cooking	50%	47%	26%	67%	49%
HW-after work	45%	27%	64%	31%	39%

Table 13: Farming practices among the study groups. Expo. = Exposure group = irrigation water quality ≥ 1,000 E. coli/100 ml; Cont. = Control group = irrigation water quality < 1,000 E. coli/100 ml; WW= Wastewater group = farmers utilizing wastewater for irrigation; SW = Surface water group = farmers utilizing surface water for irrigation; Variables "Walking in irrigation water" & "Getting clothes wet" are categorical; 0 = never, 1 = rarely, 2 = often, 3 = always

Category	**Variable**	**Expo.** (n=106)	**Cont.** (n=45)	**WW** (n=49)	**SW** (n=57)	**Total** (n=161)
Farm	**Farm Size** [bigha]	5.1	6.2	3.7	6.3	5.4
Farm Workers	**Number of Workers**	3.5	4.3	2.6	4.3	3.8
	Any Family Members	95%	73%	98%	93%	88%
	Husband/Wife	58%	69%	53%	63%	61%
	Children	38%	51%	30%	46%	42%
	Day Labor	38%	58%	2%	68%	44%
Machinery	**Use of Any Machinery**	74%	100%	43%	100%	83%
	Tractor	72%	100%	39%	100%	82%
	Thresher	11%	47%	8%	14%	23%
	Pump	33%	18%	8%	54%	28%
Fertilizer	**Chemical Fertilization**	92%	98%	100%	86%	94%
	No Protection during application	56%	62%	63%	49%	58%
Pesticides	**Pesticides**	92%	100%	92%	93%	94%
	No Protection during application	72%	66%	92%	56%	65%
Exposure	**Walking in Irrigation Water**	2.1	2.0	2.6	1.8	2.1
	Getting Clothes Wet	2.4	2.0	2.5	2.3	2.3
Prevention	**Change Clothes after work**	55%	13%	73%	38%	40%
	No Protection during irrigation	41%	62%	57%	26%	47%

The use of machinery is widespread with 83% of farmers utilizing some kind of machinery during agricultural work. A tractor is most commonly used (82%); primarily for field preparation. 23% utilize a thresher or harvester to ease harvesting, while 28% indicating using a pump, which is used to draw irrigation water. Fertilization is chiefly achieved through the application of chemical fertilizer (94%) with about 22% of farmers applying compost or manure for fertilization. The vast majority (92%) applies fertilizer using their hands with only 2% resorting to a shovel. The remaining 6% do not apply fertilizer to their field themselves, but employ day labors for fertilization. 58% of farmers to not wear any protection during fertilizer application, whilst 15 and 26% wear sandals or boots, respectively. None of the farmers indicated wearing gloves during fertilization. Similarly, 94% of farmers apply pesticides with only 35% wearing any protection during application.

Whilst exposure to fertilizer and pesticides are important to consider, for the purpose of this study, exposure to irrigation water forms a more important variable. On average, farmers indicated walking in irrigation water ‘often’, with 7% never walking in irrigation water, 16% indicated rarely, whilst 32 and 45% walk in irrigation water ‘often’ or ‘always’, respectively. In consequence, farmers indicated getting their cloth wet ‘often’ during work. However, only 40% of farmers change their clothes after working. Half of the population ‘always’ gets their cloth wet, whilst 34% indicated ‘often’. Only 7 and 9%, ‘never’ or ‘rarely’ get wet cloth during work, respectively. 47% of farmers do not wear any protective clothing during irrigation work, with 18% indicating wearing sandals and 32% wearing boots.

In table 13 the farming practices of the study groups are contrasted. The farm size and consequently the number of workers are smaller among the exposure group. The difference is more pronounced between the wastewater and surface water groups, with the surface water group having almost double the farm size of the wastewater group. It should be noted, however, that the very large farm sizes in area III are responsible for the higher average farm size among the surface water group. Engagement of family members is common among the entire sample population; however, the control group shows a significantly lower proportion of family members involved in farm work compared to the exposure group. Children are more commonly engaged in farm work among the control group, whilst the wastewater group shows the lowest proportion. Whilst hiring day labor is common among the control group as well as the surface water group, wastewater farmers do not employ day labors. This is important in regard to exposure, as wastewater farmers cultivate their fields almost exclusively with family members it can be assumed that the household is more exposed compared to farms where day labors do the majority of the work. The use of machinery is common among all groups, except the wastewater group, where less than half of the sample uses any kind of machinery. In the control and surface water group, all farmers use some kind of machinery, with the majority using tractors. The use of threshers or harvesters is only common among the control group.

Fertilizer and pesticide application are widespread among the entire sample, with the surface water group showing the lowest proportion of farmers applying chemical fertilizers. Interestingly the only group showing 100% chemical fertilization is the wastewater group, despite the apparent fertilization capacity of the irrigation water itself. The use of protective clothing during fertilization and pesticide application is not very common; especially among the wastewater group large proportions of the sample do not wear any protection. As protective clothing reduces potential exposure, it is important to control for its use in analysis. Although exposure to chemical fertilizers and pesticides has health implication on its own, these are not subject of this study. As fertilizer and pesticide exposure is not linked to diarrheal disease theses variables are not essential for the analysis.

Direct contact with irrigation water, on the other hand, forms an important variable in regard to the degree of exposure. Whilst the exposure and control group both walk in irrigation water 'often', showing a similar average value, a significant difference is observed between the wastewater and surface group. This indicates that wastewater farmers have more direct contact with their irrigation water compared to surface water farmers, thus also being more exposed. The likelihood of getting ones' clothes wet during irrigation work is more variable, with the exposure group more likely compared to the control group. Wastewater farmers most frequently report getting their clothes wet during work, further indicating additional exposure among the wastewater group. As wastewater farmers appear to have more direct contact with their irrigation water, it is important to control for this additional exposure to avoid an exaggerated effect size.

Whilst the majority of wastewater farmers indicated changing their clothes after work, only 38% of the surface water did so. Among the control group, changing clothes after work is highly uncommon, with merely 14% indicating doing so. It must be noted, however, that the need to change clothes is also lower among the control group, as they are less likely to get their clothes wet during work and the quality of the irrigation water is better. Wearing protective clothing during irrigation work is only common among the surface water group (particularly in area III) with significant differences between the exposure and control group. Protective clothing during irrigation work potentially reduces exposure to irrigation water, it is thus important control for its use. Similarly, changing clothes after work can mitigate some of the additional exposure induced by walking in irrigation water and getting clothes wet, while avoiding cross-contamination between clothes, the home environment and other household members.

3.4 Conclusions

The study groups differ significantly in key variables affecting their risk of disease as well as their degree of exposure. Household size, the proportion of households with children and the number of children per household are lowest in the control group. Particularly the lower number of children is important, as they have the highest risk of diarrheal disease. In consequence, the larger child population of the exposure group may exaggerate the hypothesized elevated diarrheal incidence among the group. Therefore, controlling for household composition, particularly in regard to children, is essential for further analysis.

Access to safe drinking water and sanitation has been linked to the prevention of diarrheal disease; therefore, drinking water quality and lack of sanitation form important additional exposure variables. Ideally, these variables should be balanced among the study groups, ensuring that the differences observed stem from exposure to unsafe irrigation water rather than from a combination of exposure sources. Access to sanitation differs starkly between the research areas, with area III having almost total sanitation coverage and area II resorting exclusively to open defecation. A significant difference in sanitation coverage exists between exposure and control groups as well as wastewater and surface water groups.

Similarly, access to AMC-supplied drinking water is more common in the control group, thus the exposure group has a higher probability of receiving potentially contaminated drinking water. Water treatment is also more prevalent in the control group, further strengthening the assumption that consumption of unsafe drinking water is higher among the exposure group. In section 4.2, drinking water quality results are presented and correlated with the drinking water variables to understand the impact of exposure to unsafe irrigation water on drinking water quality and in-household water contamination. In a further analysis, the measured bacterial densities of drinking water need to be controlled to allow the estimation of the direct impact of wastewater irrigation on diarrheal disease.

Hygiene behavior forms a key confounding variable, as it can mediate the adverse effects of exposure on the one hand, but can also contribute to cross-contamination thus becoming an exposure source in its own right on the other hand. The complexity of hygiene behavior is further complicated by its inherent measuring bias. The hygiene index used in this study overcomes the potential of reporting bias through recording of observations. As a result, the hygiene index is a reflection of the hygienic situation merely indicating hygiene behavior. A low score in the personal category, for example, reflects unclean hands and clothing indicating inadequate hand hygiene. Considering this, the lower hygiene index scores among the exposure group indicate poorer hygiene behavior among the group. However, as the hygiene index measures the outcome of hygiene behavior, it is also possible that hygiene behavior is similar between the groups, but due to the higher exposure the final hygiene situation is worse among the exposure group. Nonetheless, the hygiene situation influences the disease outcome; it is therefore, essential to control for the effects of hygiene in an analysis.

Farming practices influence the degree of exposure to irrigation water, i.e. wearing protective clothing, avoiding direct contact with irrigation water and using machinery potentially reduce exposure. The engagement of family members in cultivation increases the exposure level of the household, as more individuals come into direct contact with irrigation water, whilst hiring of day labors may reduce exposure. Farming practices in this regard are largely unbalanced between the study groups, indicating higher exposure to irrigation water among the exposure group.

Overall, the description of the sample population highlights the heterogeneity of the study groups with significant differences in key characteristics influencing the degree of exposure. The exposure group shows higher exposure in regard to all variables, implying significant disease risk. However, the unbalanced study groups complicate the isolation of the effect size of exposure to unsafe irrigation water. It is therefore necessary to stratify the sample for analysis to avoid estimation of a compound effect of a multitude of exposure sources. Propensity score matching is also applied to achieve balanced groups in the regression analysis allowing the calculation of the average treatment effect of irrigation with unsafe water. However, the complexity of interactions must also be considered, as wastewater use may also influence other variables, such as drinking water quality, that in turn affect the incidence of disease. Therefore, the total effect of wastewater use is expected to be beyond its direct impact on disease, including its indirect effects mediated by drinking water, hygiene and sanitation.

4 Results

In the following chapter the results of the research study will be presented. It is divided into four sub-chapters: Irrigation Water Quality, In-Household Water Quality, Incidence of Disease, and The Impact of Wastewater Irrigation on Farmer's Children. The first sub-chapter (4.1) highlights the degree of irrigation water contamination of the irrigation water sources (ground, surface and waste) as well as differentiating the farming systems and preventive behaviors employed among the research groups. The sub-chapter addresses the second sub-question, assessing the hypothesis that wastewater users employ additionally preventive and hygiene behaviors compared to surface water irrigators.

In sub-chapter 4.2 drinking water contamination is assessed both at the point-of-source (PoS) and at the point-of-use (PoU), highlighting the degree of in-household water contamination among the sample population. The focus of the sub-chapter lies on the second sub-question, exploring the impact of irrigation water source and quality on the degree of drinking water contamination. Thus, also contributing to answering the secondary research question: how does the effect of wastewater irrigation compare to the impact of drinking water, sanitation and hygiene (WASH).

The next sub-chapter (4.3) forms the key analytical chapter addressing both the primary (What is the effect of wastewater irrigation on the incidence of diarrhea among urban farming households in Ahmedabad, India?) and secondary research question. The focus of the chapter is on the incidence of diarrhea disease, highlighting the differences between the research groups and calculating the average treatment effects (ATEs) of irrigation water quality, drinking water quality, hygiene and access to sanitation.

The final sub-chapter (4.4) forms an excursus focusing exclusively on children. In the chapter, the third sub-question is answered, comparing the nutritional status of children between the research groups and assessing its correlation to the incidence of diarrhea. Most importantly the influence of irrigation water quality and wastewater use on the nutritional status of children as well as incidence of disease is assessed.

4.1 Irrigation Water Quality:

Irrigation water quality forms the key exposure variable of this research study. It is assumed that the quality of irrigation water is dependent upon its source, with low contamination of groundwater and high contamination of wastewater. However, as untreated sewage is released into surface waterways, it is expected that surface water also contains high pathogen densities. The irrigation water quality of the different sources is, therefore, compared and classified according to the WHO irrigation water standard. Furthermore, the farming system and preventive behaviors of the groups are differentiated, it is hypothesized that wastewater users employ additional preventive behaviors to compensate for the high degree of contamination. Thus, the effect of wastewater irrigation on household hygiene is assessed.

4.1.1 *E. Coli* concentrations of Irrigation Water

The degree of irrigation water contamination is high among all exposure groups. Surprisingly, even groundwater used for irrigation shows high *E. coli* concentrations during the winter and summer. Figure 33 presents a box plot of the contamination level of irrigation water stratified by the three research groups. A clear gradient is observed, with the groundwater group showing the lowest contamination and the wastewater group showing the highest. The expected high *E. coli* concentrations of the surface water group indicate the frequent release of untreated sewage into surface waterways, thus also rendering surface water unsuitable for unrestricted irrigation.

The 1989 WHO water guideline states that less than 1,000 fecal coliforms per 100 ml are recommended for unrestricted irrigation (WHO, 1989; WHO, 2001). In 2006 the revised guidelines define health-based targets in regard to wastewater use, indicating that less than 10^{-6} DALYs (Disability Adjusted Life

Years) should be induced by the use of wastewater (WHO, 2006). According to the report this can be translated to less then 1,000–10,000 *E. coli* per 100 ml. For the purpose of this paper, less than 1,000 *E. coli* per 100 ml are considered suitable for *unrestricted* irrigation, while *E. coli* concentrations in excess of 10,000 CFU per 100 ml are classified as unsuitable for irrigation.

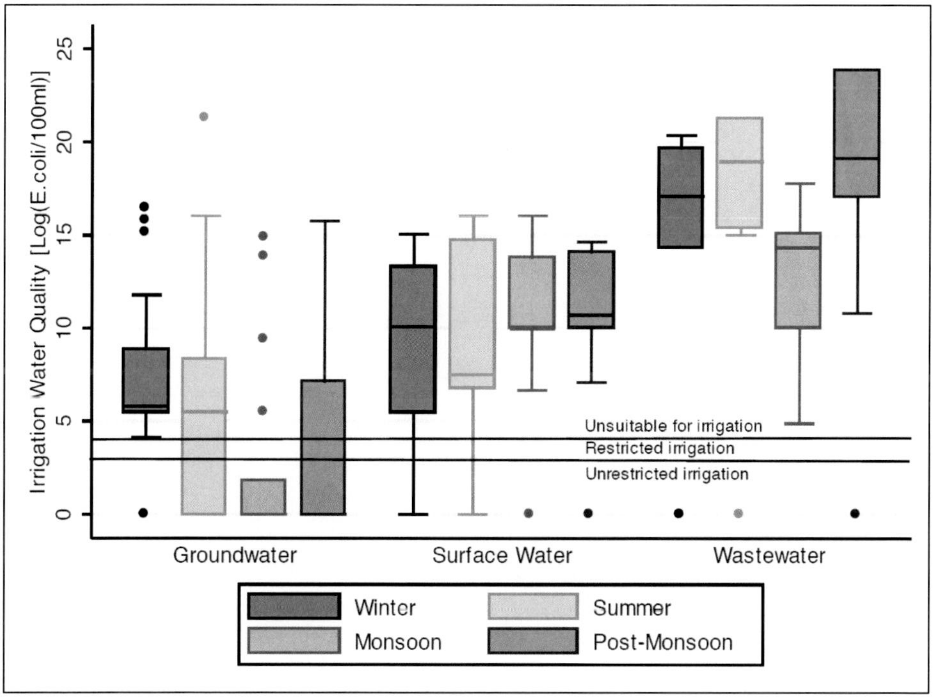

Figure 33: *E. coli* concentration of irrigation water by irrigation water source. Lines = 3 Log(E. coli/100 ml) (1,000 E. coli/100 ml) & 4 Log(E. coli/100 ml) (10,000 E. coli/100 ml) Irrigation Water Quality ≥ 10,000 E. coli/100 ml = unsuitable for irrigation; Irrigation Water Quality ≥ 1,000 E. coli/ 100 ml & < 10,000 E. coli/100 ml = restricted irrigation; Irrigation Water Quality < 1,000 E. coli/ 100 ml = unrestricted irrigation; Dots = outliers, top/bottom bars = max/min, box = quartile range (top = Q2; bottom = Q3), line = median

The average *E. coli* concentrations of the three study groups render all sources unsuitable for irrigation, with the average contamination of groundwater amounting to 3.04 x 10^4 *E. coli* per 100 ml and surface and wastewater to 9.28 x 10^5 and 4.02 x 10^9 *E. coli* per 100 ml, respectively. Groundwater clearly shows the lowest pathogen concentrations particularly during and after the monsoon. Nonetheless, the average water quality exceeds the permissible level for unrestricted irrigation throughout all rounds, except during the monsoon (see table 14).

Table 14: Irrigation water quality by irrigation water source. IW = Irrigation Water; GW = Groundwater; SW = Surface Water; WW = Wastewater

	Sampling Period				
IW Source	**Winter** [*E.coli* / 100 ml]	**Summer** [*E.coli* / 100 ml]	**Monsoon** [*E.coli* / 100 ml]	**Post-Monsoon** [*E.coli* / 100 ml]	**Average** [*E.coli* / 100 ml]
GW	$1.71x10^4$ (n=33)	$7.93x10^4$ (n=23)	$1.86x10^2$ (n=21)	$4.12x10^3$ (n=26)	$3.04x10^4$ (n=39)
SW	$7.59x10^5$ (n=38)	$1.18x10^6$ (n=32)	$1.72x10^6$ (n=44)	$5.78x10^5$ (n=45)	$9.28x10^5$ (n=48)
WW	$1.91x10^8$ (n=34)	$5.30x10^8$ (n=39)	$7.04x10^6$ (n=33)	$1.02x10^{10}$ (n=43)	$4.02x10^9$ (n=49)

However, ground water samples collected from the control area (area I) show lower average *E. coli* concentrations compared to ground water samples drawn from the exposure areas. When only groundwater samples from the control group are aggregated, the water is suitable for *unrestricted* irrigation with an average *E. coli* concentration of 411 CFU per 100 ml. Only during the winter one borewell produced water with high pathogen densities, yet still rendering the water suitable for *restricted* irrigation. The t-test presented in table 15 highlights significant differences in ground water quality, with samples from the exposure areas showing higher contamination than those from the control area. Whilst the water from the control group is mostly suitable for *unrestricted* irrigation throughout the year, groundwater samples from exposure groups are highly contamination with an average *E. coli* concentration amounting to 1.07×10^5 CFU per 100 ml. The unrestricted irrigation water standard is only met during the monsoon months, whilst ground water samples from the post-monsoon round are still suitable for *restricted* irrigation. During the winter and summer, water contamination exceeds the permissible level, thus classifying the water as *unsuitable* for irrigation. It is therefore, indicated that the use of water with high pathogen densities for irrigation affects the groundwater quality in the area. In consequence, farmers utilizing ground water in the exposure area are still exposed to unsafe irrigation water throughout the year, as irrigation is practiced primarily during the summer and winter and halted during the monsoon and post-monsoon months. Additionally, segregating the exposure groups reveals higher groundwater *E. coli* concentrations in the wastewater area (1.14×10^5 CFU/100 ml) compared to the surface water group (7.00×10^4 CFU/100 ml), however the difference is not significant.

The *E. coli* concentration of wastewater is highest during all rounds, exceeding the recommended water quality for restricted irrigation many-fold. The lowest concentrations are found during the monsoon month, as the heavy rain dilutes the wastewater. The peak of contamination occurs after the monsoon, with a decline in concentration during winter and a further peak during summer. During the hot summers less water is available, suggesting that wastewater is less diluted and thus contains higher pathogen concentration. Surface water contamination, however, follows a different temporal trend. The highest *E. coli* concentrations are observed during and after the monsoon with a low point during the summer. The high contamination during the monsoon appears counterintuitive at first glance as the heavy monsoon rain dilutes wastewater flowing into the river. However, the river and canal banks serve as open defecation site for the farming community; as the river grows during the monsoon these fecal matters are washed into the surface water. Therefore, suggesting that high surface water contamination is also linked to open defecation, particularly during the monsoon.

Table 15: Difference in groundwater quality between exposure groups. Control = area I; Expo. = Exposure = area II-IV. * $p < 0.1$; ** $p < 0.05$; *** $p < 0.01$

	Winter [*E. coli* / 100 ml] (n=33)	Summer [*E. coli* / 100 ml] (n=23)	Monsoon [*E. coli* / 100 ml] (n=21)	Post-Monsoon [*E. coli* / 100 ml] (n=26)	Average [*E. coli* / 100 ml] (n=39)
Control	$1.49x10^3$ (n=25)	$2.63x10^2$ (n=15)	$1.09x10^1$ (n=18)	$7.62x10^{-1}$ (n=21)	$4.11x10^2$ (n=28)
Expo.	$6.59x10^4$ (n=8)	$2.28x10^5$ (n=8)	$1.23x10^2$ (n=3)	$2.14x10^3$ (n=5)	$1.07x10^5$ (n=11)
T-Test	**-4.86**	**-2.05**	**-5.02**	**- 3.80**	**-3.01**

The three research groups capture the continuum of irrigation water quality, with the control group irrigating with water classified as safe for *unrestricted* irrigation, whilst the exposed groups irrigate with water *unsuitable* for even restricted irrigation. It is expected that the use of unsafe irrigation water will have a direct adverse effect on the health of the farmer and his family. It is assumed that farmers irrigating with wastewater have a certain awareness of possible adverse health effects and will thus adapt preventive behaviors. Surface water farmers, on the other hand, whilst also facing high pathogen concentrations in their irrigation water, may be less aware of the high contamination and consequent health threat. It is therefore expected that farmers of the wastewater group practice additional preventive behaviors compared to the control as well as the surface water group.

4.1.2 Farming System

The entire sample population utilizes a furrow irrigation system, except for rice cultivation, where flood irrigation is utilized uniformly. The range of farm sizes is large reaching from 0.5 bigha (approx. 0.1 ha) to 100 bigha (approx. 16 ha), with an average size of 5.3 bigha (approx. 0.8 ha). The farms are categorized according to their size; small farms are less than 3 bigha (0.5 ha), medium farms are ranged between 3 – 12 bigha (0.5 – 2 ha) and large farms exceed 12 bigha (2 ha). The average farm size of the control and surface water group is similar with 6.1 and 6.3 bigha (approx. 1 ha), respectively. The wastewater group has a significantly smaller average farm size of 3.8 bigha (0.6 ha). Only 6% of wastewater farmers have a large farm, whilst 27% of farms in the control group are large. 41% of the surface water farms are classified as large. Smaller farms are common throughout all groups with 40% of farms in the control group, 32% of surface water farms and 43% of wastewater farms. Similarly, medium size farms are prevalent in all groups, with about one third of the control and surface water farms and 50% of wastewater farms being classified as medium sized.

Crop selection is also relatively uniform, although a wide variety of crops are cultivated. The majority of farmers grow a mix of grains, vegetables and herbs. Millets, wheat, sorghum and rice form the primary grains cultivated. Both root and leafy vegetables are grown, including radish, spinach, eggplant and cauliflower. Additionally, herbs such as methi (fenugreek) and coriander are commonly cultivated. The ornamental flower marigold is commonly cultivated in the wastewater area, with 52% of wastewater farmers including the ornamental plant in their crop mix. It must be noted that farmers in the control and wastewater group cultivate grains and vegetables, whist farmers in the surface water group grow either grains or vegetables. Surface water farmers with larger farm sizes usually grow grains, whilst vegetable cultivation is common on smaller farms.

The use of machinery is widespread with the entire sample utilizing some type of machinery. Field preparation with tractors is the most common use of machinery, with 80% of the control group, 75% of the surface water group and 45% of the wastewater group utilizing tractors. Threshers and harvesters are only commonly used in the control group, where about one third of farmers use machinery to aid during harvest. In the surface and wastewater group 10 and 7% use threshers, respectively.

The involvement of family members in agricultural work is common, particularly in the wastewater group 92% of farmers work alongside family members. Whilst 70% of surface water farmers and 60% of control farmers engage family members in fieldwork. The average number of individuals involved in farm work is similar between the control and surface water group, 4.3 individuals, respectively. The wastewater farms are operated with 2.6 people on average. The smaller farm size in the wastewater area explains the lower worker requirement in the area. Employing laborers is uncommon among the wastewater group with just 2% hiring day laborers during harvest. In the control and surface water area, 45 and 51% of farmers employ day laborers, respectively.

The use of chemical fertilizers and pesticides is common among the sample population; surprisingly 94% of wastewater farmers apply chemical fertilizers despite the high nutrient content of the irrigation water. 78% of the control group utilizes chemical fertilizers and 63% of the surface water group. The use of compost and manure is only common among the control group, where 30% engage in the practice. The entire control group, 93% of the surface water group and 92% of the wastewater group apply pesticides to their crops.

Although the farm sizes differ among the sample population, the general farming system is similar across the sample. Nonetheless, it appears that wastewater farmers are aware of the potential health risks induced by eating their produce. Whilst 86% of the control group and 94% of the surface water group indicated eating some proportion of their harvest themselves, only 6% of wastewater farmers eat their own produce. It is therefore assumed that wastewater farmers engage in additional preventive behaviors to reduce the adverse health impact of working with wastewater.

4.1.3 Preventive Behavior

Protective clothing forms the first layer of protection against infection during irrigation with unsafe water. Half the control group wears some kind of protective clothing, whilst 67% of the exposure group does so. The exposure group is 50 percent less likely to wear no protective clothing (OR: 0.500), however, wastewater farmers are five times more likely to wear no protective clothing compared to the surface water exposure group (OR: 4.822). Breaking-up the exposure group shows that wastewater farmers and control farmers are equally likely to wear protective clothing, while the majority of surface water farmers (81%) wear protective clothing. The segregation of the exposure groups reveals that wastewater farmers are 23% more likely to work without any protective clothing (OR: 1.229) compared to the control group. Interestingly, the choice of protective wear appears more adequate in the exposure group, which is almost 28 times more likely to wear boots compared to the control group (OR: 27.69). Among the control group, wearing sandals is the primary form of protective clothing. However, 40% of the surface water group indicated wearing boots, consequently wastewater farmers are 28% less likely to wear boots compared to surface water farmers (OR: 0.72), the OR however fails to reach significance. The results indicate that the wastewater group is more likely to wear adequate preventive clothing compared to the control group, however, wastewater farmers do not show superior preventive behavior compared to surface water farmers. This implies that either surface water farmers are more aware of the potential health risks arising from their irrigation water, or the wastewater group is less willing to adopt preventive measures (see Table 16).

Another preventive approach is minimizing exposure, for example through avoidance of direct contact with the irrigation water. Yet the exposed population is 28% more likely to walk in their irrigation water (OR: 1.283), with all of the wastewater farmers indicating that they walk in their irrigation water. Consequently, it is unsurprising that the exposure group is 27% more likely to report getting their clothes wet during irrigation work (OR: 1.267). Segregating the exposure group shows that the wastewater group is 60% more likely to report wet clothes compared to the surface water group. Getting dirty hands during work is common among the entire sample, with no significant difference observed between the exposure and the control group. However, when segregating the exposure group, it appears that wastewater farmers are 3.5 times more likely to have dirty hands after working compared to the surface water group. The variable set has revealed that the exposure group does not take extra precautions to minimize exposure to irrigation water; on the contrary, the data indicates that the wastewater group in particular is more likely to contaminate their clothes and hands during work.

Adequate hygiene behavior forms the key preventive measure; particularly hand washing with soap is essential to halt the spread of pathogens. About 40% of the sample population indicated changing their clothes after work, which is appropriate when considering the frequent contamination of the clothes during work. The exposure group is over eight times more likely to change their clothes after work compared to the control group, while the wastewater group shows four times higher odds in comparison to the surface water group. In fact, none of the farmers in the control group reported changing their clothes after work, implying that the clothes are not considered dirty after work in the control group.

The majority of farmers wash their hands after work (82%); however, only about 60% indicate utilizing soap for washing their hands. The exposure group is almost three times more likely to wash their hands with soap after work (OR: 2.818), with the wastewater group about ten times more likely than the surface water group (OR: 10.181). Similarly, taking a bath after work is more common among the exposure group (OR: 3.125); with wastewater farmers having two times higher odds compared to the surface water group (OR: 2.208). Table 17 summarizes the odds ratios for the critical hand washing times, significant differences were found between the exposure and control group as well as the wastewater and surface group, indicating that the irrigation water choice influences hand hygiene behavior. Additional to being more likely to take adequate hygiene measures after work, the exposure group is also more likely to wash their hands before eating and cooking. Whilst wastewater farmers show a higher tendency to wash their hands before eating, they are less likely to wash them before cooking when compared to the surface water group. This may be linked to a higher proportion of women involved in farm work in the surface water group.

Table 16: Use of protective clothing among the exposure groups; Exposure Group = Irrigation water Quality ≥ 1,000 E. coli/100 ml (control= < 1,000 E. coli/100 ml), Wastewater Group = Utilizing wastewater for irrigation (control = groundwater irrigation), Surface Water Group = Utilizing surface water for irrigation. * $p < 0.1$; ** $p < 0.05$; *** $p < 0.01$

Exposure - Control	**Odds Ratio**	**CI 95%**	
No Protective Clothing (n=187)	**0.500****	0.254	0.988
Wastewater - Control			
Wearing Boots (n=110)	**27.686*****	3.903	11.76
Wastewater – Surface water			
No Protective Clothing (n=129)	**4.822*****	2.156	11.434
Wearing Boots (n=129)	0.721	0.321	1.598

Nonetheless, hygiene after work as well as hand hygiene linked to food is more prevalent among the exposure group, indicating an awareness of the contamination of the irrigation water among both wastewater and surface water farmers. Thus, supporting the hypothesis that exposure to unsafe irrigation water can lead to preventive compensation through hygiene. However, hand washing after defecation, shows an inverse trend, highlighting that the exposure group is 50% less likely to exhibit adequate hand hygiene after defecation. Furthermore, wastewater farmers are least likely to wash their hands after defecation, 86% less likely than the surface water group. It appears that heightened hand washing behavior linked to agricultural work may lead to the neglect of other critical hand washing times.

Table 17: Odds ratios (OR) of hand hygiene at critical times.
* p < 0.1; ** p < 0.05; *** p < 0.01

	Exposure - Control			**Wastewater – Surface Water**		
Wash Hands	OR	CI 95%		OR	CI 95%	
Before eating	**5.394***** (n=180)	2.579	11.44	**3.820***** (n=124)	1.429	11.32
Before cooking	1.191 (n=182)	0.604	2.352	**0.172***** (n=126)	0.072	0.406
After defecation	**0.501**** (n=182)	0.250	0.998	**0.143***** (n=126)	0.054	0.358
After work	**2.818***** (n=135)	1.233	6.493	**10.181***** (n=95)	3.184	37.65
Take bath after work	**3.125***** (n=134)	1.367	7.206	**2.208*** (n=93)	0.834	5.986

As self-reported hygiene behavior is prone to reporting bias, the five categories of the hygiene index, environment, sanitation, water, food and personal, measure the outcome of household hygiene behavior. The average hygiene index scores of the sample groups are presented in table 18. Significant differences are found both between the exposure and control as well as the wastewater and surface water groups. Household hygiene is superior in the control group, thus indicating that exposure to unsafe irrigation water does not lead to heightened preventive behavior on the household level. The average hygiene index score in the wastewater region is far lower compared to the surface water group, further disproving the hypothesis. Breaking down the hygiene index reveals further differences between the exposure and control group. Initially it is important to highlight that the sanitation and water categories reflect the infrastructure situation of the household, which are largely out of the control of the households. The environment and personal categories are much more variable throughout the research period and reflect the contamination of the living environment and the hands and clothing, respectively. Adequate food storage as well as food waste disposal are reflected in the food category, which is not directly influenced by the irrigation water source.

The categorical score of each hygiene category is converted into a binary variable reflecting adequate hygiene in the respective category. This allows for the calculation of the odds of exhibiting good hygiene, as presented in table 19. The exposure group is about 40% less likely to exhibit good overall hygiene, which is reflected by lower odds of exhibiting good hygiene in all categories, except the water category. The strongest effect is observed in the environment category where the exposure group is over 80% less likely to demonstrate good hygiene behavior. This result is further pronounced in the comparison of the exposure groups, with wastewater farmers having 97% lower odds of exhibiting good environmental hygiene. Thus, a transferal of contaminants from the work environment into the home environment is indicated. This is strengthened by the personal category, indicating that the exposure group is 40% less likely to demonstrate good personal hygiene and the wastewater group is almost 80% less likely than the surface water group. In the food category, the exposure group shows 40% lower odds of good hygiene compared to the control group, whilst the wastewater group is 99% less likely to have good food hygiene compared to the surface water irrigators. The only exception to the trend is observed in the water category, where the exposure group has 20% higher odds of good hygiene. Yet, the positive effect is only observed in the surface water group, as the wastewater group is 95% less likely to exhibit good water-related hygiene. The higher odds of exhibiting good sanitary hygiene among the wastewater group, is caused by the complete lack of sanitation facilities in area II. Overall, the results clearly indicate an adverse impact of irrigation water source on households' hygienic situation.

Table 18: Comparison of mean hygiene index scores among exposure groups. * $p < 0.1$; ** $p < 0.05$; *** $p < 0.01$

Exposure - Control	**Mean**	**CI 95%**		**T-Test**
Control (n=1264)	1.422	1.287	1.557	**5.117*** **
Exposed (n=2839)	1.014	0.929	1.100	
Wastewater – Surface Water	**Mean**	**CI 95%**		**T-Test**
Surface Water (n=1682)	1.898	1.785	2.011	**27.591*** **
Wastewater (n=1157)	-0.270	-0.357	-0.183	

Although exposure to unsafe irrigation water results in the adaptation of some preventive measures, the overall household hygiene level is inferior among the exposure group. Whilst preventive clothing is more common in the wastewater group, exposure is also higher, which is reflected by a higher proportion of wastewater farmers reporting walking in irrigation water and contaminating their clothes with irrigation water. The strongest effect is observed in hand washing behavior, with significantly higher odds of washing hands with soap after work among the exposure groups. This preventive behavior reflects a certain awareness of the contamination of irrigation water and the associated disease risk. However, the apparent higher odds of adequate hand hygiene after work is not reflected in the personal category of the hygiene index. It is thus indicated that contamination of hands and clothing is significantly higher among the exposure group. This may be caused by the over-reporting of hand washing behavior, inadequate hand washing technique or utilization of contaminated water for hand hygiene. Additionally, neglect of other critical hand wash times (especially after defecation) among the exposure group and the wastewater group in particular, may also contribute to the low personal hygiene scores. It appears that the exposure group adopts some preventive hygiene practices at the expense of other essential hygiene behaviors. This results in an overall adverse effect on household hygiene, thus leading to the rejection of the hypothesis. It must be noted, however, that the hygiene index measures the outcome of hygiene behavior, thus merely suggesting inferior hygiene behavior among the exposure group. Nonetheless, the environment and personal categories of the hygiene index clearly indicate a transfer of pathogens from the work to the home environment.

Table 19: Odds ratios of good hygiene behavior among exposure groups. HI = Hygiene Index Components; Hygiene Index = sum of components. * $p < 0.1$; ** $p < 0.05$; *** $p < 0.01$

	Exposure – Control		**Wastewater – Surface Water**	
	Odds Ratio	CI 95%	Odds Ratio	CI 95%
HI-Environment	**0.183***** (n=4117)	0.154 0.217	**0.027***** (n=2847)	0.010 0.601
HI-Sanitation	**0.400***** (n=4148)	0.341 0.464	**1.442***** (n=2866)	1.234 1.685
HI-Water	**1.219***** (n=4120)	1.055 1.409	**0.052***** (n=2849)	0.042 0.653
HI-Food	**0.627***** (n=4120)	0.547 0.719	**0.007***** (n=2850)	0.004 0.012
HI-Personal	**0.592***** (n=4119)	0.517 0.679	**0.212***** (n=2849)	0.180 0.251
HI-Index	**0.593***** (n=4103)	0.518 0.679	**0.114***** (n=2839)	0.094 0.138

4.1.4 Impact of Irrigation Water on Household Hygiene Outcome

It was hypothesized that wastewater farmers adopt additional preventive behaviors; however, the data has illustrated the contrary. The bivariate analysis of the hygiene index shows significantly worse hygiene outcomes among the exposure groups and the wastewater group in particular. These hygiene outcomes are affected by a variety of factors, including hygiene behaviors as well as the degree of exposure. Households with low exposure levels may require less frequent hygiene behavior to achieve good hygiene outcomes, whilst high exposure levels can lead to adverse hygiene outcomes despite practicing frequent hygiene behavior. To assess to what extent unsafe irrigation water adversely impacts household hygiene outcomes, an ordinary least square linear regression is conducted. The hygiene outcome forms the dependent variable and is quantified by the continuous hygiene index score. The primary independent variable is the continuous irrigation water quality in *E. coli* per 100 ml. It should be noted that a logarithmic transformation was applied to the irrigation water quality, due to the high bacterial counts of some samples. Additionally, variables reflecting exposure level and preventive behaviors are included in the regression, such as walking in irrigation water, getting clothes dirty, wearing protective clothing and hand hygiene. The regular control variables, access to sanitation, socio-economic status and education level, are also included in the regression.

The regression shows high correlations between most variables and the hygiene index score (see table 20). Interestingly the majority of critical hand washing times (after defecation, before eating and before cooking) do not show significant correlations, further strengthening the assumption that hand washing behavior was over-reported. The only hand washing time to reach significance is after work, which is positively correlated with the hygiene index scores, thus indicating that hand hygiene after work induces better household hygiene outcomes. The likelihood of getting hands dirty during work fails to reach a significant correlation. The remaining exposure and preventive factors all show significant correlations in the expected direction. The frequency of walking in irrigation water and getting clothes wet during work has adverse impacts on the hygiene index score, whilst wearing boots and changing clothes after work are associated with higher hygiene index scores. Households that own the land they cultivate as well as those that do not work along side family members are also correlated to better hygiene outcomes.

Table 20: Linear regression – impacts on the hygiene index score.
* p < 0.1; ** p < 0.05; *** p < 0.01

Category	Variable	Coef.	95% CI	
Irrigation Water	**Irrigation Water Quality (Log)**	**-0.21*** **	-0.36	-0.01
	Wastewater Use	**-1.27*** **	-1.55	-1.00
Handwashing	**HW-after defecation**	-0.16	-0.35	0.04
	HW-before eating	-0.09	-0.25	0.08
	HW-before cooking	0.03	-0.14	0.20
	HW-after work	**0.26*** **	0.11	0.41
Degree of Exposure	**No Family Members Working**	**0.50*** **	0.13	0.88
	Dirty Hands	-0.07	-0.25	0.12
	Wet Clothes	**-0.20*** **	-0.30	-0.10
	Walk in irrigation water	**-0.13*** **	-0.22	0.03
Prevention / Mitigation	**Wearing Boots**	**0.23** **	-0.01	0.46
	Change Clothes after work	**0.60*** **	0.41	0.79
Demographic Controls	**Farm Size Category**	**-0.30*** **	-0.45	-0.14
	Access to Sanitation	**1.79*** **	1.54	2.04
	Socio-Economic Status	**0.27*** **	0.18	0.37
	Max. Education Level	**0.05*** **	0.02	0.07
	Landowner	**1.03*** **	0.77	1.30
	No Animals	**0.27*** **	0.10	0.44
	R-squared	0.60		
	N	1878		

The degree of irrigation water contamination, quantified by the log transformation of the *E. coli* concentration per 100 ml, is linked to lower hygiene scores regardless of the source of irrigation water. Additionally, being exposed to wastewater irrigation is also associated with lower hygiene index scores. It is therefore indicated that exposure to unsafe irrigation water adversely impacts household hygiene outcomes. Nonetheless, adequate preventive behavior has significant beneficial effects that may balance the adverse impact of unsafe irrigation water. However, the exposed population does not adopt additional preventive behaviors, on the contrary, direct contact with irrigation water is more common among the exposed population.

To estimate the average treatment effect (ATE) of irrigation water quality on the hygiene index score, propensity score matching is conduced. The propensity score is calculated for the dependent variable, irrigation water quality, using the same independent variables from the regression. After matching the sample according to the propensity scores the sample achieves balanced across the independent variables, thus controlling for the confounding effects of these. The ATE is estimated at -2.05, indicating that for each log-unit increase in irrigation water contamination the hygiene index score is reduced by 2 points. Therefore, it can be concluded that the use of unsafe irrigation water causes adverse impacts on the household hygiene outcomes. This finding further supports the assumption that pathogens are transferred from the work to the home environment. Additionally, the evidence does not show superior preventive behaviors among the exposure group.

4.1.5 Resumé

The irrigation water quality results have revealed that both the wastewater and surface water group utilize water that is not suitable for irrigation, according to the international standard. Nevertheless, wastewater samples show significantly higher *E. coli* concentrations compared to surface water samples. The lowest contamination was found in groundwater samples; however, groundwater contamination is significantly higher in the exposure areas (area II–IV) compared to the control area (area I). The majority of groundwater samples from exposure areas do not meet the international standard for unrestricted irrigation, thus implying groundwater contamination induced by the use of unsafe irrigation water. The uncontrolled discharge of untreated wastewater into surface waterways therefore exposes down-stream farmers to unsafe irrigation, which in turn may adversely impact the groundwater quality of the area. The resulting health risks are numerous, ranging from the direct contact to unsafe irrigation water via indirect contact to drinking water and food contamination.

The primary hypothesis of this chapter needs to be rejected, as wastewater farmers do not engage in superior preventive behaviors compared to either the surface water or the control group. Although the prevalence of farmers wearing boots, as protective clothing is higher among the wastewater group, they are also more likely to walk in irrigation water and get their cloth wet during work. Additionally, reported hand hygiene behavior, particularly after work, is significantly higher among the exposure groups. However, the apparent additional focus on hand hygiene after work comes at the expense of other critical hand washing times, namely after defecation. It is therefore indicated that the exposure population does perceive some additional need for preventive behaviors, these, however, induce the neglect of other hygiene behaviors. As self-reported hygiene behavior is prone to reporting bias, the focus of the analysis was placed on household hygiene outcomes.

The hygiene index score indicates hygiene behavior through measuring hygiene outcomes. The exposed population and the wastewater group in particular have lower hygiene index scores compared to the control group. This finding is consistent throughout all hygiene categories with the exception of the water category, which reflects in-household water storage behavior. Particularly the environment and personal hygiene categories indicate a transfer of pathogens from the work to the home environment. Utilizing wastewater for irrigation, without consideration of the measured water quality, also highlights an adverse effect on the hygiene index score. Therefore, being located in the exposure area has adverse impacts on household hygiene outcome, even if safe irrigation water is used. Nonetheless, the degree of irrigation water contamination affects the hygiene index score directly, with the average treatment effect estimating a 2-point reduction in the hygiene index score for each log unit increase in contamination. The evidence therefore highlights that exposure to unsafe irrigation water adversely affects household hygiene. This further supports the assumption that pathogens are transferred from the work to the home environment, thus exposing the entire household to health risks associated with wastewater irrigation.

4.2 In-Household Water Quality

Access to improved drinking water sources, is prioritized by the WHO in their strategy against diarrhea. Ensuring the provision of safe drinking water is highly important, therefore drinking water treatment is undertaken centrally by the AMC. However, evidence from previous studies suggest that point-of-use (PoU) water treatment is more important than point-of-source (PoS) treatment, as water contamination also occurs during collection, transport and storage. One of the research areas (area II) is not serviced by the AMC, thus no water treatment or monitoring occurs. Initially, the source water contamination between AMC and non-AMC supplied water is compared. Secondly, the difference between PoS water quality and PoU water quality is determined to indicate the prevalence and degree of in-household water contamination among the sample population. Lastly, the determinants of in-household water contamination are quantified, focusing on the effects of irrigation water quality, access to sanitation and hygiene on the degree of water contamination occurring in the household.

4.2.1 Supplied Drinking Water Quality

The microbiological analysis has shown that the majority of samples exceed the permissible bacteria load thus rejecting the assumption that AMC supplied water largely meets the international drinking water standard. Figure 34 illustrates the *E. coli* concentrations for each research area over the four collection phases.

The box plot highlights a high degree of water contamination in all areas with the highest contamination clearly found in area III (canal exposure group). The large range found in the area indicates a high degree of variation in contamination levels between households, while the high median scores demonstrate high drinking water contamination throughout the entire community.

High quantity of outliers (represented by dots in the diagram) found in area I and IV point to the presence of small disadvantaged groups in the areas, where water quality is significantly worse than the community average. Overall, area I, II and IV appear to exhibit similar water quality with median scores at par throughout all rounds. The peak of contamination occurs during the monsoon, where not only the median score increases but also the range. This is particularly pronounced in area IV, where the range during the monsoon includes all values.

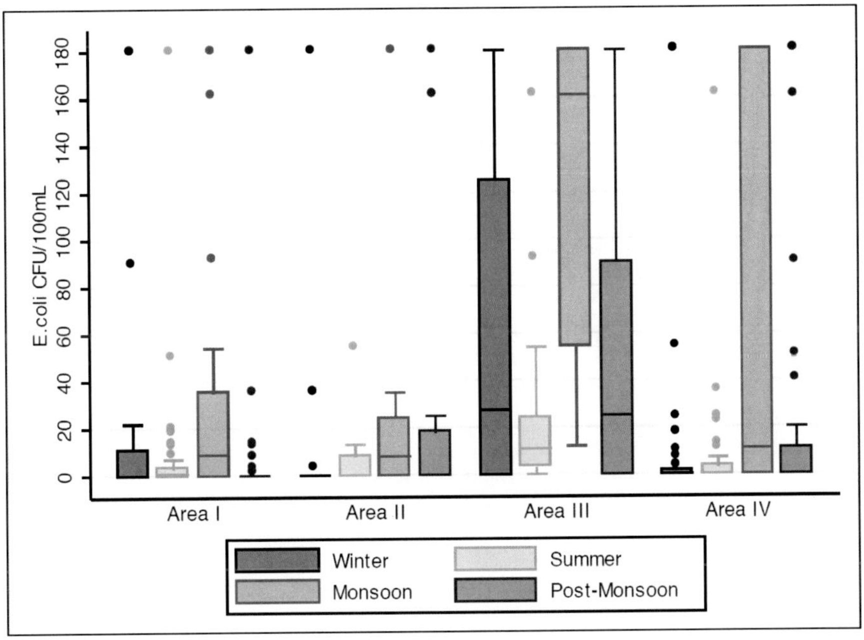

Figure 34: *E. coli* concentration in drinking water by area. Dots = outliers, top/bottom bars = max/min, box = quartile range (top = Q2; bottom = Q3), line = median

When looking at the average water quality, the difference between area I, area II and area IV are small, while area III shows significantly higher *E. coli* concentrations throughout all rounds. Nonetheless, the WHO drinking water standard of less than 1 *E. coli* per 100 ml is exceeded many fold in all areas and rounds. These results are surprising, as despite AMC's regular monitoring it appears that mean drinking water contamination renders the water not potable throughout the entire year. More surprising, water in area II, although also unsafe for drinking, appears to have lower contamination levels compared to the other areas despite not being serviced by the AMC.

Considering the large range of scores, the entire spectrum of 0 to 180 *E. coli*/100 ml was found in most areas and rounds, and the high average contamination level it becomes clear that large proportions of the sample population are exposed to unsafe drinking water. Figure 35 illustrates the percentage of the sample meeting the drinking water standard. Here it must be noted that only samples that do not exceed 10 thermotolerant coliforms and 1 *E. coli* per 100 ml are classified as meeting the drinking water standard.

The extreme water contamination in area III becomes more apparent, as not only are high *E. coli* densities found on average but also almost the entire community is exposed to unsafe drinking water throughout the year. Interestingly, area II and IV have about the same percentage of people receiving safe drinking water throughout the sampling period; only during the winter are significantly less people exposed to unsafe drinking water in area II. The control group (area I) does not exhibit the highest proportion of safe drinking water with the exception of the post-monsoon round. Interestingly, the peak occurs during the post-monsoon only for area I, whilst the peak for area II and IV are during the winter. The low point is observed during the monsoon, where only about one quarter of the population has access to safe drinking water.

Overall, the proportion of people with access to safe drinking water is similar in area I, II and IV. Due to the extreme conditions of area III, only about 5% of the village population has access to safe drinking water, the area is excluded from the following analysis. It appears that AMC supplied water does not have superior quality, in fact area II exhibits better water quality during some rounds. Table 21 shows the t-tests performed to compare AMC supplied water quality with non-AMC water supply. Area I and IV are grouped to reflect AMC water and are compared to area II, representing non-AMC water.

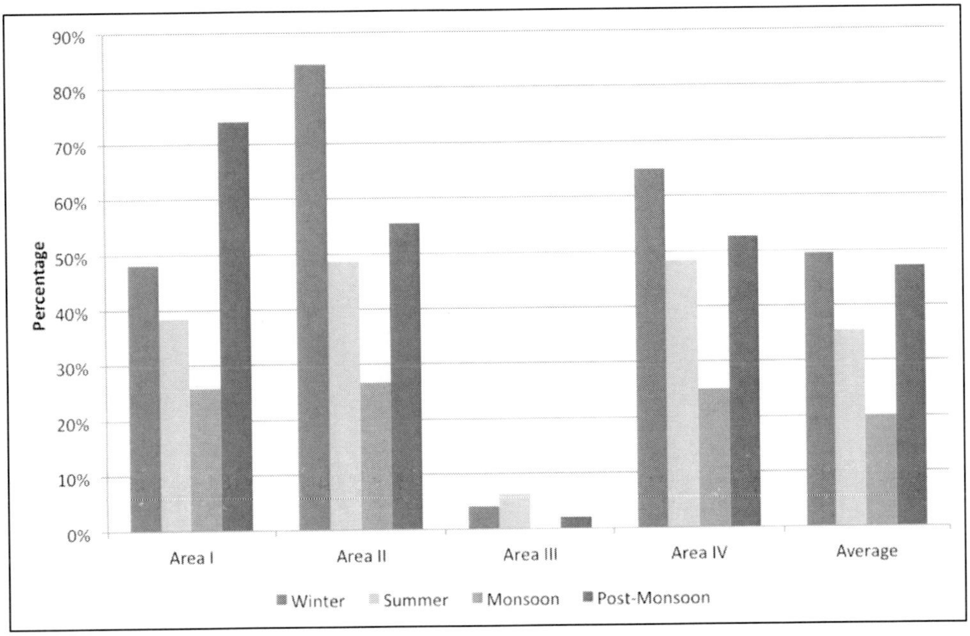

Figure 35: Percentage of households meeting the drinking water standard.

Table 21: Comparison of AMC-supplied and non-AMC supplied water. Meet Std. = Meeting (drinking water) Standard is defined by the WHO guidelines as < 1 E. coli/100 ml and < 10 coliforms/100 ml. * < 0.1 ** < 0.05 *** < 0.01

	Winter		**Summer**		**Monsoon**		**Post-Monsoon**	
	Mean *E.coli* [100 ml]	Meet Std. [%]	Mean *E.coli* [100 ml]	Meet Std. [%]	Mean *E.coli* [100 ml]	Meet Std. [%]	Mean *E.coli* [100 ml]	Meet Std. [%]
AMC water	32	56	8	42	46	24	19	60
	(n = 114)		(n = 110)		(n = 110)		(n = 111)	
Non-AMC water	9	80	7	43	26	20	27	50
	(n = 38)		(n = 35)		(n = 30)		(n = 36)	
T-test	-1.47		-0.26		-1.50		0.74	

4.2.2 Risk Factors for In-Household Water Quality Deterioration

Differences in Source and Storage Water Quality

In order to determine whether storage water quality further deteriorates from the source water, the mean bacteria concentrations of source (PoS) and storage (PoU) are compared using t-tests (see table 22).

The data clearly illustrates a significant increase in contamination level between source and storage water. The direction of the relationship stays robust throughout the research period. The only outlier is found in winter, where no significant difference was observed. Nonetheless, the results support the rejection of the null hypothesis. Furthermore, the direction of the difference confirms the hypothesis that drinking water is further contaminated inside the household. Consequently, the percentage of people having safe PoU drinking water is even lower compared to those receiving safe source water. During the post-monsoon 20% of households have safe stored drinking water; in winter the percentage peaks at 31%. During the summer only 17% of stored water meets the international standard and the low point of 6% was reached during the monsoon.

Table 22: Comparison of mean source and storage water quality.
* < 0.1 ** < 0.05 *** < 0.01

	Winter	**Summer**	**Monsoon**	**Post-Monsoon**
	E.coli [100 ml]	*E.coli* [100 ml]	*E.coli* [100 ml]	*E.coli* [100 ml]
Source	28	12	62	29
Storage	37	29	88	53
T-test	-1.27 (n= 195)	**-4.24**** (n= 180)	**-3.71**** (n= 172)	**-3.86**** (n= 191)

Assessing the level of in-house contamination requires the calculation of the mean difference between source and storage water. The following table (23) illustrates this difference through an area break-up.

Overall, the results indicate that storage water is more contaminated than source water with the exception of area III during the monsoon, where an improvement in water quality is observed. The degree of in-household water contamination differs between the areas; it is therefore necessary to compare the research groups. Area I forms the control area, whilst area II, III and IV are the exposure areas. The exposure areas are subdivided into the surface water group (area II and III) and the wastewater group (area IV).

Table 23: Mean difference between source and storage water by area. Δ E. coli = Storage Water E. coli/100 ml – Source Water E. coli/100 ml.

	Winter	**Summer**	**Monsoon**	**Post-Monsoon**
	Δ *E.coli* [100 ml]	Δ *E.coli* [100 ml]	Δ *E.coli* [100 ml]	Δ *E.coli* [100 ml]
Area I	2 (n = 54)	0 (n = 48)	28 (n = 54)	33 (n = 53)
Area II	11 (n = 38)	25 (n = 35)	40 (n = 27)	12 (n = 36)
Area III	20 (n = 46)	30 (n = 44)	-16 (n = 40)	9 (n = 46)
Area IV	4 (n = 57)	12 (n = 51)	50 (n = 51)	34 (n = 56)
Average	9 (n = 195)	17 (n = 180)	26 (n = 172)	24 (n = 191)

The data presented in table 24 indicates no significant difference in the average degree of in-household water contamination between the research groups. Remarkably, the degree of water contamination is not always lowest in the control group, particularly during the monsoon and post-monsoon higher differences between source and storage water quality were observed. Only during the summer, does the control group have significantly lower in-household water contamination compared to the exposure group. The break-up of the exposure groups also reveals no significant difference in the average degree of in-household water contamination between waste and surface water users. The only significant difference was observed during the monsoon, highlighting that the wastewater group has higher in-household water contamination compared to the surface water group. A large nominal difference favoring the wastewater group is found during the winter, however significance was not reached. Overall, the data indicates no significant difference in the degree of in-household water contamination; however, the temporal variations appear to be correlated to group allocation. Whilst the control group shows the lowest level of in-household contamination during the summer, the wastewater group's low point is during the winter and the surface water group has the lowest contamination during the monsoon.

Table 24: Degree of in-household water contamination among the research groups. * < 0.1 ** < 0.05 *** < 0.01

	Winter	**Summer**	**Monsoon**	**Post-Monsoon**	**Average**
	Δ *E. coli* [/100 ml]	Δ *E. coli* [/100 ml]	Δ *E. coli* [/100 ml]	Δ *E. coli* [/100 ml]	Δ *E. coli* [/100 ml]
Control	0.89 (n=64)	-0.66 (n=56)	34 (n=61)	28 (n=64)	16 (n=65)
Exposure	12 (n=128)	26 (n=119)	24 (n=108)	21 (n=123)	20 (n=131)
T-Test	-0.81 (n=192)	**-3.09*** ** (n=175)	0.62 (n=169)	0.49 (n=187)	-0.57 (n=196)
Waste-water	3.8 (n=52)	26 (n=47)	47 (n=46)	25 (n=50)	26 (n=53)
Surface	17 (n=76)	26 (n=72)	7.8 (n=62)	19 (n=73)	17 (n=78)
T-Test	-0.85 (n=128)	-0.05 (n=119)	**2.10** ** (n=108)	0.34 (n=123)	1.02 (n=131)

The t-tests have indicated that the mean difference between source and storage water is not significantly different between the groups. However, when transforming the continuous difference in *E. coli* per 100 ml into a binary variable, reflecting if in-household water contamination occurred, odds ratios can be calculated. The odds ratio of in-household water contamination between the exposure and control group does not reach significance. The OR of 1.68 (0.81–3.41), however, indicates higher likelihood among the exposure group. When comparing wastewater farmers with the groundwater group a highly significant odds ratio of 4.31 (1.42–15.6) is reached, thus indicating higher in-household contamination among farmers irrigating with wastewater. The odds ratio of the surface water compared to the ground water group did not reach significance. The insignificant OR of 1.11 (0.52–2.37) indicates slightly elevated odds of in-household water contamination among surface water irrigators. The four-fold increase in the odds of in-house contamination among wastewater farmers highlights that they are not only exposed to pathogens during their work but they are likely to transfer pathogens into their living environment and stored drinking water.

Sanitation & Hygiene

Access to sanitation also has an effect on the degree of in-household water contamination. The average level of contamination increase is significantly higher among households without access to sanitation (see table 25). Additionally, a temporal trend can be observed, with significant differences during the monsoon and post-monsoon and no significant difference during winter and summer. The significant differences found during the monsoon, post-monsoon and on average show higher in-households water contamination among households without access to sanitation. However, when calculating the odds ratio for in-household contamination based on access to sanitation significance was not reached. Nonetheless, the odds ratio of 0.60 (0.30–1.20) indicates reduced odds of in-house water contamination when sanitation facilities are available. The failure to reach significance implies the presence of a confounding factor, namely hygiene.

Table 25: Difference in source and storage water quality by sanitation.
* < 0.1 ** < 0.05 *** < 0.01

	Winter	Summer	Monsoon	Post-Monsoon	Average
	Δ *E. coli* [/100 ml]	Δ *E. coli* [/100 ml]	Δ *E. coli* [/100 ml]	Δ *E. coli* [/100 ml]	Δ *E. coli* [/100 ml]
No San.	1 (n=94)	17 (n=86)	41 (n=79)	34 (n=90)	24 (n=97)
San.	14 (n=101)	17 (n=91)	14 (n=93)	15 (n=100)	14 (n=102)
T-Test	-1.11	-0.01	**1.94****	**1.54****	**1.44****

Hand washing at critical times, such as after defecation, after work, before cooking and before eating impact the pathogen load entering the household, thus it is expected that these factors also influence the level of in-household water contamination. Table 26 illustrates the odds ratios for each of the critical hand washing times. Surprisingly only one of the four critical hand washing times reached significance (before cooking), illustrating that the odds of in-house contamination are reduced by 51% in households indicating hand washing before cooking. Hand washing after defecation also shows a reduction of the odds, reflecting the expected result. Failure to wash hands after defecation potentially results in high pathogen densities on the hands, which in turn transfer pathogens throughout the living environment. Although the result is in line with the expectation, it must be viewed with caution, as significance was not reached. The remaining two critical hand washing times have produced counterintuitive results, indicating that the odds of contamination increase when hand washing is practiced. The increased odds for people washing their hands after work may be related to the nature of the work. People working on wastewater-irrigated farms are more likely to wash their hands after work; additionally, hand washing after work often occurs on the farm with potentially contaminated water. The increased odds for people indicating washing their hands before eating is suspected to be an artifact, created through the over-reporting of hand washing behavior.

Reliance on self-reported hand washing behavior is prone to reporting bias, thus the observational spot-check method was used to quantify the hygiene index. Each component of the index was transformed into a binary variable to allow for the calculation of the odds ratio. Low scores were assigned ‘0’, whilst high scores were classified as ‘1’. Particular emphasis was paid to the environment and personal component, as high contamination of the environment likely leads to the transfer of pathogens into the water storage container. Low scores in the personal category indicate hand contamination, which may lead to pathogen transfer during water withdrawal.

Table 26: Odds ratio of in-household water contamination by handwashing.
* < 0.1 ** < 0.05 *** < 0.01

Hand washing	N [exposed/unexposed]	Odds Ratio	95% CI	
After defecation	97/103	0.60	0.30	1.20
After work	112/87	1.33	0.66	2.66
Before cooking	95/109	**0.49***	0.24	0.98
Before eating	110/86	1.47	0.73	2.96

All components of the hygiene index indicate a preventive effect on in-household water contamination (table 27). However, the sanitation and personal component, as well as the hygiene index as a whole, did not reach significance. This is surprising as especially access to sanitation and personal hygiene are considered key risk factors for in-household water contamination. Both the environment and food categories reduce the odds of in-house contamination by about 50%. The influence of food hygiene on in-household water contamination is theoretically unclear. It is assumed that a higher degree of food hygiene, leads to cleaner surfaces in the household and thus contributes to the reduction of in-household water contamination. Additionally, good food hygiene should reduce cross-contamination between household members, thus also influencing water contamination. The strongest preventive effect is induced by the water category, which reflects the cleanliness of the water source as well as basic water storage behavior (particularly whether the storage container is covered or opened). The data highlights the importance of hygiene in the prevention of in-household water contamination. Additionally, the strong effect of the water category indicates the robustness of the spot-check method, while also pointing to inadequate water storage behavior as a key risk factor for in-household water contamination.

Table 27: Odds ratio of in-household water contamination by hygiene index.
* $p < 0.1$; ** $p < 0.05$; *** $p < 0.01$

Hygiene Category (n=204)	**Odds Ratio**	**95% CI**	
Environment	**0.49****	0.24	0.98
Sanitation	0.65	0.32	1.30
Water	**0.34*****	0.16	0.71
Food	**0.50****	0.24	1.00
Personal	0.59	0.29	1.17
Hygiene Index	0.59	0.29	1.17

Water Storage & Treatment

The majority of households store their drinking water in traditional clay vessels, called mataka (92%). The vessel has the unique ability to cool the water inside thus providing a key benefit during the hot summers. A small proportion of the sample utilizes plastic storage containers (6%) and the remainder resort to jerry cans, buckets or other vessels (2%). Whilst the type of storage vessel is rather uniform, the withdrawal method differs. 84% of households draw water by hand with the help of a cup, whilst 12% have an outflow valve for the storage container; the remaining 4% utilize a scoop. The direct contact between hands and water is highly likely when using a cup, thus forming a potential contamination point. In table 28 the difference of source and storage water quality stratified by the presence of an outflow valve is presented. 42% of the sample population filters their drinking water before consumption. However, only 10% utilize a modern reverse osmosis filter (RO), known as aquaguard®. The remaining 15% and 17% filter their water with a cloth or sieve, respectively. Boiling of water before consumption is not practiced among the sample, with only 1% of households engaged in the practice.

Table 28: Difference of source and storage water quality by outflow-valve.
* p < 0.1; ** p < 0.05; *** p < 0.01

	Winter Δ *E. coli* [/100 ml]	Summer Δ *E. coli* [/100 ml]	Monsoon Δ *E. coli* [/100 ml]	Post-Monsoon Δ *E. coli* [/100 ml]	Average Δ *E. coli* [/100 ml]
No Outflow	7 (n=172)	20 (n=155)	32 (n=153)	27 (n=167)	22 (n=176)
Outflow	13 (n=23)	0 (n=22)	-21 (n=19)	3 (n=23)	-2 (n=23)
T-Test	-0.30	**1.59****	**2.38****	1.24	**2.22****

The possession of an outflow valve strongly hampers the degree in-household water contamination (see table 28). Particularly during the monsoon, a highly significant difference is observed, where households with an outflow valve appear to improve their water quality. The only exception is found during the winter, where households without outflow valve have lower in-household contamination, however significance was not reached. The data suggests that a significant proportion of water contamination occurs during the withdrawal of water, particularly through the contact between hands and water. Odds ratios were calculated for both the use of an outflow valve and the use of a cup. Both calculations produced highly significant results, with odds ratios of 0.30 (0.11–0.82) and 2.11 (0.91–4.75), respectively. The presence of an outflow valve reduces the odds of in-household water contamination by 70%, while the utilization of a cup doubles the odds of contamination. It must be noted, however, that reductions in water contamination, as suggested during the monsoon and on average may be linked to the water treatment system. Aquaguard® systems often include a storage vessel with outflow valve. Thus, the beneficial effect of the outflow valve may be influenced by collinearity with the use of RO.

Table 29 illustrates the odds ratios for the different methods of water treatment. The composite variable, consisting of any type of treatment utilized, indicates a 50% reduction of the odds of in-household water contamination. The break-up of the different methods, however, reveals that both plastic sieve and cloth do not produce significant improvements. Interestingly the implied trend points to increased odds of contamination when employing either of these methods. Without adequate cleaning and maintenance, pathogens and dirt may accumulate in such filters leading to increased contamination. The insignificant results additionally infer the low effectiveness of such filtration. The modern RO system is clearly the most effective mechanism for the prevention of in-household contamination. The highly significant result indicates a nearly 90% reduced odds of contamination. However, the high costs of such modern filters coupled with the need for maintenance render the widespread adoption, particularly among low-income groups, unfeasible without government or institutional support.

Table 29: Odds ratios of in-household water contamination by treatment. RO = reverse osmosis filter. * $p < 0.01$; ** $p < 0.05$; *** $p < 0.01$

Variable	**n** [treated/untreated]	**Odds Ratio**	**95% CI**	
Sieve	36/168	1.43	0.56	4.13
Cloth	32/172	1.49	0.55	4.71
RO	22/182	**0.11*** **	0.04	0.32
Any Treatment	92/112	**0.50** **	0.25	1.00

Regression Analysis

Thus far stratification has been limited to a single variable, however, given the complexity of interaction in the water, sanitation, hygiene nexus it is necessary to control for a multitude of factors to avoid confounding effects. The first regression is a linear model utilizing the continuous outcome variable (difference in *E. coli* concentration between source and storage water). The independent variables consist of the sanitation and hygiene variables; critical hand washing times, water storage variables and research group allocation as well as demographic variables (socio-economic status, education level and the proportion of children in the household). As the analysis is conducted on the household level, the household size is applied as frequency weight. The second model is a logistic regression (showing odds ratios), thus requiring the depended variable, in-household water contamination, in binary form. To create the binary variable, the cumulative difference between source and storage water quality are calculated. If the increased contamination exceeds 10 thermotolerant coliforms per 100 ml or 1 *E. coli* per 100 ml the household is classified as having in-household water contamination. The independent variables are the same for both models. The independent variables are summarized in table 30.

The bivariate analysis has indicated a preventive effect of the hygiene categories: environment, water and food. The use of an outflow valve as well as reverse osmosis water filters is also linked to lower odds of in-household water contamination, whilst water withdrawal with a cup increases the odds. Although the mean difference between source and storage water quality is not significantly different between the control and exposure group, significantly higher odds of in-household water contamination are indicated among the wastewater group. The regression analysis, presented in table 31, confirms the correlations of the strongest preventive variable (RO) as well as the adverse impact of exposure to wastewater irrigation. However, some counterintuitive results are also produced.

The OLS model assesses the correlation between the independent variables and the degree of water quality decrease, whilst the logistic regression analyses the variables influence on the likelihood of in-household water contamination. Access to sanitation is instinctively associated with hygiene and health advantages, however, a positive correlation to the degree of water contamination was found. Therefore, it is indicated that the difference between source and storage water quality is larger among households with access to sanitation. In the logistic regression, a non-significant odds ratio of 1.00 was calculated, highlighting that access to sanitation does not impact the likelihood of in-household water contamination directly. Households with access to sanitation have their facilities on-plot, often situated in close proximity to the water source and water storage area. This may result in the increased degree of water contamination found in the OLS model. However, this result should be viewed with caution as only weak significance was reached. Overall, it is indicated that access to sanitation does not influence the likelihood of in-household water contamination, thus the source of contamination lays elsewhere.

Table 30: Independent variables utilized in regression analysis. HI = Hygiene Index category; HW = Hand Washing; RO = reverse osmosis filter

Category	Variable	n	Mean	Std. Dev.	Type
Exposure	Wastewater	204	0.26	0.44	Binary
	Access to Sanitation	204	.50	0.50	Binary
Hygiene Index	HI-Environment	204	0.43	0.50	Binary
	HI-Water	204	0.49	0.50	Binary
	HI-Food	204	0.49	0.50	Binary
	HI-Personal	204	0.50	0.50	Binary
	Hygiene Index	204	6.9	7.9	Categorical
Hand Washing	HW-after defecation	200	0.49	0.50	Binary
	HW-before eating	196	0.56	0.50	Binary
	HW-before	204	0.47	0.50	Binary
	HW-after work	199	0.56	0.50	Binary
Treatment	RO	204	0.11	0.31	Binary
Water Storage and Withdrawal	Outflow	204	0.11	0.32	Binary
	Cup	204	0.81	0.39	Binary
	Storage Covered	204	1.80	0.58	Categorical
	Storage Volume	204	23	19	Absolute
Demographic Controls	Proportion of Children	204	0.21	0.20	Absolute
	Socio-Economic Status	199	2.96	1.43	Categorical
	Education HH-Head	204	4.99	4.43	Absolute

The components of the hygiene index have indicated preventive effects in the bivariate analysis; however, in the regression analysis the food hygiene variable has significant adverse effects. In the OLS model only food hygiene is significantly correlated to the degree of water contamination, indicating that better food hygiene is associated with increased in-household water contamination. This is a counterintuitive result, which is theoretically unsound. It is assumed that measuring error and observation bias may have resulted in elevated food hygiene levels leading to misclassification of households. The hygiene index as a whole shows a significant negative correlation to the degree of water contamination, thus confirming that good hygiene behavior reduces water contamination. Both the environment and water variable did not produce significant results in either model, while personal hygiene is the only hygiene variable to reach significance in the logistic regression. The personal hygiene variable proxies the cleanliness of the hands, thus a correlation to water contamination is expected. As water withdrawal is predominantly undertaken with a cup, contact between hands and drinking water are inevitable. The results indicate a 41% reduction in the odds of in-household water contamination when good personal hygiene is exhibited. Although the hygiene index as a whole did not reach significance in the logistic regression, a preventive effect of good personal hygiene behavior was confirmed. Considering that the personal hygiene variable proxies hand contamination (or the absence thereof) it can be assumed that water contamination occurs through the contact between hands and water during storage, transport or withdrawal.

Hand hygiene at four critical times (after defecation, before cooking, before eating and after work) was assessed, however the results are counterintuitive. In the OLS model two of the four critical hand wash times show highly significant correlations, before cooking and after working. However, the direction of the relation of both variables is positive, implying that practicing hand hygiene results in increased water contamination. It is therefore assumed that the self-reported hand washing behavior was over-reported, leading to misclassification. Additionally, the adequacy of hand washing technique was not assessed, thus individuals may wash their hands at the critical times, however with low efficiency. The presence of soap was confirmed in 94% of households but whether they utilize it for hand washing is uncertain. A degree of reporting bias must be assumed, thus rendering the results questionable. A preventive effect of hand washing behavior could not be confirmed.

The withdrawal method is suspected to form a key point of in-household water contamination. The bivariate analysis has indicated a preventive effect of utilizing an outflow valve, while resorting to a cup, results in increased odds of water contamination. This was not confirmed in the regression analysis; both variables show negative correlations with the degree of water contamination, however only utilization of a cup produces significant results. Both variables fail to reach significance in the logistic regression. The withdrawal method, therefore, does not have an adverse affect on the likelihood of in-household water contamination. The strong preventive effect of the outflow valve found in the bivariate analysis may be caused by colinearity with the RO variable. As RO systems usually include a storage container with an outflow valve, the preventive effect found in the bivariate analysis is expected to be an indirect effect of the water filtration system.

The most pronounced effect is water treatment with modern RO systems. A highly significant correlation is found in both models. The bivariate analysis has already suggested a 90% reduction of the odds of in-house contamination when utilizing RO. The effect is estimated to be even larger when controlling for various other factors reaching a 94% reduction of the odds. The strength of the relationship clearly indicates RO water treatment to be the most effective mechanism to prevent in-house water contamination. In fact, households with RO filters usually reduce the water contamination level between source and storage.

Covering the water storage container forms an important barrier to substances entering the water. Both models indicate a preventive effect of covering the water storage container, however, significance is only reached in OLS. It thus appears that covering the water storage container reduces the degree of water contamination but does not significantly influence the likelihood of water contamination. Nonetheless, the data confirms that covering the water storage container is an important component of safe water storage behavior.

Table 31: Linear regressions – difference between source and storage water quality. Dependent variable = 'In-Household water contamination'; independent variables are outlined in table 30. Model 1 is a linear regression model showing coefficients (OLS); Model 2 is a logistic regression showing odds ratios. * p < 0.1; ** p < 0.05; *** p < 0.01

Category	Variable	Model 1:	Model 2:
Exposure	Wastewater Group	**16.17*** **	**2.51*** **
	Access to Sanitation	**10.1** **	1.00
Hygiene Index	HI-Environment	0.19	1.01
	HI-Water	1.05	1.10
	HI-Food	**17.8*** **	0.92
	HI-Personal	-7.85	**0.59***
	Hygiene Index	**-0.83***	1.01
Hand Washing	HW-after defecation	-0.36	0.96
	HW-before eating	-4.59	1.00
	HW-before cooking	**10.2*** **	**1.34***
	HW-after work	**12.13*** **	1.16
Treatment	RO	**-45.3*** **	**0.06*** **
Water Storage and Withdrawal	Outflow	-7.71	1.79
	Cup	**-12.63***	1.48
	Storage Covered	**-7.31*** **	0.82
	Storage Volume	**0.51*** **	**1.03*** **
Demographic Controls	Proportion of Children	**27.23*** **	1.27
	Socio-Economic Status	-1.11	1.13
	Education HH-Head	-0.45	**1.04***
	R-squared	0.20	0.22
	N	1251	1251

The quantity of water stored is strongly correlated to water contamination, the more water is stored the higher the degree and likelihood of in-household water contamination. Highly significant correlations were found in both models, indicating a clear, yet small adverse effect. It is assumed that larger storage containers are used for longer periods, thus allowing more time for contamination and bacterial growth to occur. Only few pathogens added to the water in the morning may reproduce to a substantial bacterial load throughout the day given that conditions are favorable for bacterial growth.

Among the demographic control variables, the proportion of children in the household produced a highly significant correlation in OLS. The degree of in-household water contamination is strongly increased when higher proportions of children live in the household. It is assumed that children are less cautious during water withdrawal, potentially transferring higher pathogen loads to the water storage vessel. Interestingly, significance was not reached in the logistic regression. The education level of the head of household is weakly correlated to the likelihood of water contamination with an odds ratio of 1.04. The social-economic status is not significantly correlated in either model. It appears that neither education level nor social-economic status have significant impact on in-household water contamination.

Exposure to wastewater irrigation produced the most pronounced adverse effect. Highly significant correlations were found in both the OLS and the logistic regression model. The odds of in-household water contamination are increased 2.5-fold among households exposed to wastewater irrigation. This highlights that the effects of wastewater irrigation is not limited to the farm but intrude into the home environment. A transfer of pathogens from wastewater into stored drinking water is therefore indicated. Exposure to high pathogen loads during work elevates the likelihood of transferal of these pathogens onto hands and clothes, which in turn introduce pathogens into the living environment, potentially contaminating food, water and surfaces.

Average Treatment Effects

The regression analysis has identified one highly significant preventive effect (RO) and one highly significant adverse effect (wastewater use). Additionally, personal hygiene shows a preventive effect, although only with weak significance. The effect of access to sanitation is unclear with weak indication of an adverse effect. The average treatment effect (ATE) of each of these variables is calculated to confirm the direction and strength of the relationships. Causal inference is problematic in observational data, as treatment allocation is not random. To overcome this problem propensity-score matching is utilized to balance variables across the sample.

The set of independent variables of the regression analysis are also used for the calculation of the individual propensity scores. Treated and control households are matched according to their propensity score, with both the treated and the control household having the same (or very similar) propensity score. Testing that the mean scores of each independent variable are not significantly different between treated and control cases ensures the balancing of the matched sample across each block of propensity scores. Consequently, cases with similar propensity scores also exhibit similar characteristics across the control variables, thus differences in the outcome variable are induced by the exposure/treatment variable. The same set of independent variables was used for the calculation of all propensity scores, with the exception of the RO treatment variable. The apparent colinearity between RO and outflow resulted in the failure of the propensity score estimation. Therefore, the outflow variable was dropped from the propensity score calculation for RO. Across all propensity score estimations the quadratic transformation of the hygiene index caused the balancing property to be unsatisfactory. As a result, the hygiene index was applied in its original format to ensure balance across all variables.

The estimation of the average treatment effect confirms the adverse effect of exposure to wastewater irrigation on the degree of in-household water contamination. The ATE indicates that wastewater farmers add about 18 *E. coli*/100 ml to their drinking water during storage. Confirming that pathogens are transferred from the irrigation water to the stored drinking water of the household.

Table 32: Treatment effects of key variables on in-household water contamination. ATE = Average Treatment Effect. RO = reverse osmosis filter

Variable	n	ATE	Mean Bias
Wastewater	119	**18.15**	16.2
Personal Hygiene	194	**- 14.73**	14.1
Access to Sanitation	163	**- 10.41**	19.2
Cup	153	**8.54**	50.5
RO	98	**- 10.20**	18.1

Personal hygiene has the largest preventive ATE, indicating that the difference between source and storage water quality is 14 *E. coli*/100 ml lower among households with good personal hygiene. The hands form an important vehicle for transmission, the data suggests that contact between hands and water during withdrawal from the storage vessel form a key point of in-household water contamination. This is further supported by the cup variable, which shows an adverse average treatment effect. The ATE however showed a high bias, as balancing was imperfect for the cup variable. As the majority of households use a cup for water withdrawal the number of control cases is low. Due to the high bias the effect sizes should be viewed with caution, nonetheless the expected direction of the relationship is confirmed. When utilizing a cup for water withdrawal contact between hands and water is inevitable over the long-term, thus contributing to the contamination of drinking water. Additionally, households use a single designated cup, usually positioned on top or nearby the storage vessel, for water withdrawal. Therefore, all household members handle the same cup multiple times throughout the day. This leads to the potential accumulation of pathogens on the cup, which are then transferred to the water during withdrawal. Personal hygiene, particularly the cleanliness of the hands, in combination with the method of water withdrawal, forms the key determinants of in-household water contamination. Utilizing adequate water withdrawal methods that avoid contact between hands and stored water should reduce in-household water contamination significantly. Unfortunately, the ATE of utilizing an outflow valve could not be estimated due to the low occurrence among the sample population.

Although the preventive effect of RO was confirmed, the effect size was overestimated in the regression model. The ATE is 2.5 times lower compared to the unmatched estimate. Nonetheless, in-household water treatment proves to be an effective mechanism to reduce in-household water contamination. Intriguingly, the effect size of RO is lower than the one of personal hygiene, thus indicating that good personal hygiene is the most important preventive mechanism for in-household water contamination.

The regression analysis has indicated that access to sanitation has adverse effects on water contamination, the ATE, however, reveals a preventive effect.

This falls in line with the theoretical foundations of the F-diagram. Households with access to sanitation remove feces from their environment, thus reducing the transfer of pathogens and consequently the degree of in-household water contamination. It can be deduced that practicing open defecation forms an exposure source leading to higher water contamination. However, the effect size of exposure to wastewater irrigation is larger, highlighting that in-household water contamination is not only depended upon access to sanitation, personal hygiene and water withdrawal method, but utilizing wastewater for irrigation forms a key exposure source.

4.2.3 Resumé

Water contamination occurring in the households is widespread among the sample population. During the peak of water contamination, i.e. during the monsoon months, only 6% of households have safe drinking water at the PoU, and even during the winter, where contamination is lowest, only a mere 31% have safe PoU water. The series of t-tests reveals significant differences between PoS and PoU water quality throughout all sampling rounds, indicating the continual occurrence of in-household water contamination. This supports the view of recent systematic reviews that highlight the relative importance of PoU water quality in regard to drinking water treatment. Treatment of the source water is less effective in the combat against fecal-oral diseases as significant recontamination occurs in-household.

The source water contamination of the sample population is alarmingly high, which is surprising, as a drinking water monitoring system is employed by the AMC. It appears that the system in place is not effective in the outer areas of the city. The AMC regularly samples drinking water from the village borewells and accordingly determines that safe drinking water is supplied. However, households do not access the borewell directly, but instead pipelines transport the water to a central water tank from where it is distributed to each household via a further pipeline system. As the AMC monitors water quality at the well, contamination points along the distribution system are suspected. The pipeline system could have cracks or other leakages causing contamination. As the water supply is intermittent only providing water twice a day for a few hours, water is stored in a central village water tank before distribution to the households. The cleanliness and regular maintenance of the water tank is therefore important for the provision of safe water.

The data confirms that access to sanitation and adequate personal hygiene form key barriers to in-household water contamination. This finding is consistent with the expected transmission pathway, where access to sanitation and personal hygiene are primary barriers. Water treatment at the PoU forms an effective secondary barrier as highlighted by the preventive effect of the reverse osmosis filters. Water withdrawal was also identified as a key point of contamination. Using a cup to draw water from the storage vessel leads to potential contact between hands and water and thus water contamination. It is suspected that employing adequate water withdrawal methods that avoid direct contact between hands and water would lead to reductions in the in-household water contamination. The effect of utilizing an outflow valve could not be estimated, but the bivariate analysis indicated a preventive effect.

The key finding is the significant impact of exposure to wastewater irrigation on the degree of in-household water contamination. This clearly indicates a transfer of pathogens from the work to the home environment. Therefore, the risks of utilizing wastewater for irrigation are not limited to individuals involved in farming activities, but extend to the entire household. As in-household water contamination is directly affected by exposure to wastewater, it can be deduced that pathogens are also transferred between household members as well as between surfaces. The high average treatment effect renders wastewater irrigation a more important source of in-household contamination than open defecation. It is therefore indicated that effective barriers are required for wastewater irrigation, similar to the necessity of ensuring access to sanitation.

4.3 Incidence of Diarrheal Disease

The incidence of diarrhea is linked to various determinants, including the WASH (Water, Sanitation and Hygiene) factors. In the previous sub-chapters, it was demonstrated that irrigation water quality adversely impacts drinking water quality and hygiene, suggesting interconnections between irrigation water quality and WASH. In this sub-chapter the effects of irrigation water quality, as well as of WASH variables, on the diarrhea incidence are explored. Initially stratification is used to produce incidence rate ratios to indicate the direction of the bivariate correlations. A set of regression models is then used to confirm the findings of the bivariate analysis and identify the key determinants of diarrhea incidence. Ultimately, propensity-score matching is performed for the identified determinants, leading to the comparison of average treatment effects of irrigation water quality and the WASH variables.

4.3.1 Diarrheal Incidences

The incidence of diarrheal disease of the entire sample was 11.5 episodes per 1,000 person-weeks throughout the 12-month interval. The groundwater group (area I) shows the lowest incidence rate (7.93 episodes per 1,000 person-weeks), while the exposure groups show similarly elevated diarrhea incidence, with the wastewater (area IV) and surface water group (area II & III) having 13.1 and 13.4 episodes per 1,000 person-weeks, respectively (see table 33). Comparing the incidence rate of the control and exposure group (combining surface and wastewater farmers) produces a highly significant incidence rate ratio of 1.68, indicating near 70% higher diarrhea incidence among the exposure group. However, when utilizing irrigation water quality to classify between safe and unsafe irrigation water (utilizing 1,000 *E. coli* per 100 ml as standard) the incidence rate ratio (significant at 10%) amounts to 1.18, while using the 10,000 *E. coli* per 100 ml cut-off fails to reach significance. The odds ratios paint a similar picture, indicating that households in the exposure group (area II–IV) are twice as likely to suffer from diarrhea, while households exposed to unsafe irrigation water have a 45% increase in the odds of diarrhea disease. It is therefore, indicated that the exposure groups are subjected to other exposure sources additional to their irrigation water that may explain the increased incidence of diarrhea in these areas.

Table 33: Diarrhea incidence among the research groups. IR = Incidence Rate per 1,000 person-weeks; IRR = Incidence Rate Ratio; OR = Odds Ratio; # {total person-weeks}; + classified by 1,000 E. coli/100 ml threshold; Exposure group allocation according to irrigation water source. * $p < 0.1$; ** $p < 0.05$; *** $p < 0.01$

	IR	IRR	CI 95%		OR	CI 95%	
Exposure Group	13.3	**1.68*** ** {54224}#	1.37	2.06	**2.19*** ** (n=4171)	1.75	2.77
Control Group	7.9						
Safe Irrig. Water+	12.2	**1.18*** {30802}#	0.95	1.49	**1.45*** ** (n=2412)	1.11	1.91
Unsafe Irrig. Water+	14.5						

One of the surface water groups (area II) resorts exclusively to open defecation and in the wastewater group (area IV) only 37% have access to sanitation, while in the control group nearly 70% utilize sanitation facilities. Widespread open defecation exposes the community to pathogens, which may contribute to the elevated diarrhea incidence in the area. Households with access to sanitation have a lower diarrhea incidence compared to those resorting to open defecation, with incidence rates of 10.0 and 13.2 per 1,000 person-weeks, respectively. The incidence rate ratio is significant at 0.1% indicating 25 percent point lower diarrhea incidence among households with sanitation. The odds ratio shows a 20% decrease in the likelihood of suffering from diarrhea among households with sanitation. However, when comparing exposure to unsafe and safe irrigation water stratified by sanitation, significant differences in the incidence rate ratios and the odds ratio were only observed among the exposed population (see table 34). It appears that access to sanitation forms a preventive factor in the exposure group (*E. coli* ≥ 1,000 CFU/100 ml), while no difference was observed in the control group (*E. coli* < 1,000 CFU/100 ml). The relatively high sanitation coverage in the control area may be responsible for the failure of a clear preventive effect induced by access to sanitation. A preventive community effect may be present when sanitation coverage reaches a certain threshold, as lower volumes of fecal matter are released indiscriminately into the environment, potentially reducing cross-contamination within the community. Nonetheless, a preventive effect of access to sanitation is confirmed within the entire sample and the exposure group in particular.

Table 34: Diarrhea incidence stratified by access to sanitation. IR = Incidence Rate per 1,000 person-weeks; IRR = Incidence Rate Ratio; OR = Odds Ratio; # {total person-weeks}. Exposure group allocation according to irrigation water source. * p < 0.1; ** p < 0.05; *** p < 0.01

Variable		IR	IRR	CI 95%		OR	CI 95%	
Sanitation {31124}#		10.0	**0.76*** **	0.65	0.88	**0.82**** (n=3873)	0.69	0.98
No Sanitation {26798}#		13.2						
By exposure group								
Exposure	**San** {19230}#	11.4	**0.75*** **	0.63	0.90	**0.84*** (n=2877)	0.68	1.04
	No San	15.2						
Control	**San** {8546}#	7.84	0.97	0.67	1.42	1.07 (n=1294)	0.70	1.64
	No San	8.06						

Drinking water contamination is common among the entire sample; however, the degree of in-household water contamination is higher among the exposure group (recall chapter 4.2). It is expected that exposure to unsafe drinking water has direct adverse effects on the incidence of diarrhea, as water quality is inferior in the exposure group it is important to assess the impact of drinking water quality on the incidence of diarrhea. Segregating the sample by those with access to safe PoU drinking water and those with unsafe drinking water, a significant difference is observed with an incidence rate ratio of 1.29 (see table 35). Whilst households with safe drinking water have a diarrhea incidence of 9.47 per 1,000 person-weeks, the population exposed to unsafe drinking water shows an incidence of 12.3 per 1,000 person-weeks. The calculation of the odds ratio reveals a 30 percent increase in the odds of suffering from diarrhea when exposed to unsafe drinking water at the point-of-use. When utilizing source water (PoS) contamination, rather than PoU quality, no significant difference is found in the incidence rate ratio. However, the odds ratio indicates a 17 percent increase when exposed to unsafe source water. Therefore, indicating that safety of PoU water quality is more important that those of the drinking water source, as in-household water contamination can render previously safe source water unsafe at PoU.

When further stratifying the sample by exposure group (or irrigation water classification) significance is reached only for PoU water among the exposure group and only for PoS in the control area. Interestingly, it appears that households exposed to surface or wastewater irrigation do not suffer additional risk from exposure to unsafe PoS water, while in the control group a near 60 percent increase in the odds of diarrhea are observed when exposed to unsafe drinking water at the source. PoU water on the other hand, appears to only affect the exposure group, where unsafe PoU water is linked to a 25% percent higher diarrhea incidence (the odds ratio, however, fails to reach significance). Among the control group PoU water quality does not induce significant impact on the incidence of diarrhea, thus implying that PoS water quality is of higher importance in the control group, whilst PoU water adversely affects the exposure groups.

Table 35: Diarrhea incidence stratified by drinking water quality. IR = Incidence Rate per 1,000 person-weeks; IRR = Incidence Rate Ratio; OR = Odds Ratio; # {total person-weeks}; PoU = Point-of-Use (Storage Water); PoS = Point-of-Source (Source Water); Safe PoU/PoS = E. coli/100 ml < 1. * p < 0.1; ** p < 0.05; *** p < 0.01

Variable		IR	IRR	CI 95%		OR	CI 95%	
Safe PoU {11610}#		9.47	**1.29********	1.05	1.60	**1.33**** (n=4324)	1.05	1.68
Unsafe PoU {44760}#		12.2						
Safe PoS {22490}#		10.9	1.06	0.90	1.25	**1.17*** (n=4295)	0.97	1.41
Unsafe PoS {33192}#		11.6						
PoU stratified by Exposure								
Exposed	**Safe PoU** {6908}#	11.3	**1.24***	0.97	1.59	1.15 (n=2795)	0.87	1.53
	Unsafe PoU {31106}#	14.0						
Control	**Safe PoU** {3882}#	7.73	1.06	0.69	1.66	1.11 (n=1248)	0.69	1.53
	Unsafe PoU {10904}#	8.16						
PoS stratified by Exposure								
Exposed	**Safe PoS** {13780}#	13.9	0.92	0.77	1.11	0.99 (n=2746)	0.81	1.24
	Unsafe PoS {23334}#	12.8						
Control	**Safe PoS** {7028}#	6.40	**1.39***	0.95	2.07	**1.58**** (n=1267)	1.01	2.47
	Unsafe PoS {7960}#	8.92						

The results have clearly shown that the exposure groups suffer from significantly more episodes of diarrhea compared to the control group. It is therefore, indicated that the utilization of unsafe irrigation water has an adverse effect on the health status of the farmer and his family. However, it was also highlighted that other factors, particularly sanitation and drinking water quality adversely impact health status. As these factors are not balanced between groups and exposure to unsafe irrigation water influences some of these factors, it is necessary to control them to avoid confounding effects. The impact of hygiene is of particular concern, as exposure to unsafe irrigation water induces adverse effects on household hygiene outcomes (recall chapter 4.1). It is therefore, necessary to control for access to sanitation, drinking water quality and hygiene to estimate the average treatment effects of irrigation water quality on the incidence of diarrheal disease.

4.3.2 Correlations between WASH, Irrigation Water Quality and Diarrheal Incidence

The bivariate analysis has shown that the incidence of diarrhea is higher among the population exposed to unsafe irrigation, while also emphasizing that drinking water quality, access to sanitation and household hygiene directly influence the odds of diarrheal disease. A regression analysis is therefore conducted to assess the correlations between the variables and diarrhea incidence, while controlling for the effect of the remaining independent variables. The incidence of diarrhea per 1,000 person-weeks forms the dependent variable, while the set of exposure factors (irrigation water quality, PoU water quality, eating own produce), preventive behaviors (hygiene index, hand-washing, access to sanitation) and demographic control variables (socio-economic status, education level, proportion of children, landownership) form the independent variables. As analysis is conducted on the household level, the number of household members is applied as frequency weight.

Three regression models are tested, each utilizing the same set of depended and independent variables. The models differ only in the quantification of the primary exposure variable: irrigation water. In the first model, group allocation to exposure or control form primary independent variable. Households utilizing unsafe irrigation water sources (*E. coli* $\geq$ 1,000/100 ml) are classified as exposed, while those utilizing safe irrigation water (*E. coli* < 1,000/100 ml) form the control group. In second model households are not classified according to irrigation water quality, but irrigation water source. Farmers utilizing wastewater for irrigation are classified to the exposure group, whilst surface water farmers form the control group. Therefore, assessing the difference between the two exposure groups. The third model uses a continuous independent variable, the *E. coli* concentration per 100 ml of irrigation water. As the *E. coli* counts are very high, especially in the exposure group, the natural log of the *E. coli* concentration is used to ease calculation. All three models are run as ordinary least square (OLS) as well as logistic regression showing odds ratios.

The set of independent variables remains constant across the three models. The WASH variables are of particular concern. PoU water quality is applied as a continuous variable (*E. coli*/100 ml), while access to sanitation is in binary format. Additionally, the proportion of the community with access to sanitation is applied. The environment, water, food and personal categories of the hygiene index are used as categorical variables, where adverse hygiene outcome are scored '-1' and beneficial outcomes '+1', whilst indifferent outcomes are categorized as '0'. Self-reported hand washing at the critical times is included in binary form, as well as the observed presence of soap in the household. The categorical variable 'socio-economic status' and the number of schooling years completed are used as demographic control variables, along with the proportion of children in the household. Additionally, the binary variables 'landownership' and 'eats own produce' are included.

Initially, it is important to note the correlations between the outcome and the exposure variables (see table 36). Households in the exposure groups (*E. coli* $\geq$ 1,000/100 ml) are 87% more likely to suffer from diarrhea compared to the control group, showing significant correlations in both the OLS and logistic model. The second model reveals a significant correlation between wastewater use and incidence of diarrhea, indicating 30% higher odds of disease compared to the surface water group (area II and III). Considering that in both exposure groups irrigation water quality is far beyond permissible levels, it appears that the additional irrigation water contamination in the wastewater group still induces additional health risks. The third model, using continuous irrigation water quality as exposure variable, shows a significant correlation between the measured irrigation water *E. coli* concentration and the disease outcome variable in the OLS regression. Thus, affirming a direct relationship between irrigation water quality and incidence of diarrheal disease. The logistic regression, however, reveals an insignificant odds ratio of 1.00. Nonetheless, the three models have consistently shown a correlation between irrigation water and diarrheal disease. Utilizing either wastewater or surface water for irrigation adversely impacts the odds of suffering from diarrhea. It is indicated that the degree of contamination is directly correlated to the incidence of disease, thus highlighting the importance of controlling wastewater irrigation in the combat against diarrhea.

The WASH variables, drinking water quality, access to sanitation and hygiene behavior show robust results throughout all models. Although drinking water quality is significantly correlated to the disease outcome in both the OLS and the logistic regression, the effect is very small (OR: 1.00). Therefore, indicating that unsafe drinking water at the point of use does not directly translate to higher odds of disease. However, the hygiene category, water, which is a reflection of the visual cleanliness of the water source as well as adequate water storage, is strongly correlated with the outcome in all models. Households with good water hygiene scores have about 35% lower odds of diarrhea. It thus appears that adequate water behavior is more important than the actual pathogen density of drinking water. Thus, underscoring a mediating effect of hygiene behavior on the disease outcome.

Table 36: Regression models – impact on the incidence of diarrhea. Model 1: dependent variable = exposure group allocation (E. coli/100 ml $\geq$ 1,000); Model 2: dependent variable = irrigation water source among exposed; wastewater irrigators form the exposure group and surface water users form the control; Model 3: dependent variable = continuous irrigation water quality (Log(E. coli/100 ml)); HI = Hygiene Index Component; HW = Handwashing. The set of independent variables is consistent in all models, each model is run as linear regression (OLS) and logistic regression showing odds ratios (OR). * $p < 0.1$; ** $p < 0.05$; *** $p < 0.01$

Model 1: Exposure-Control (n=19250)		OLS			Logistic		
		Coefficient	95% CI		OR	95% CI	
Exposure	**Exposure Group**	**6.03*** **	4.71	7.36	**1.87*** **	1.65	2.11
	POU Water Quality	**0.02*** **	0.01	0.02	**1.00*** **	1.00	1.00
	Access to Sanitation	**4.29*** **	2.66	5.93	1.03	0.90	1.17
	Proportion with San	**-3.11** **	-5.77	-0.44	0.98	0.78	1.23
Hygiene Index	**HI-Environment**	-0.60	-1.78	0.58	1.01	0.91	1.11
	HI-Water	**-3.28*** **	-3.99	-2.56	**0.65*** **	0.61	0.68
	HI-Food	**1.59*** **	0.27	2.91	**1.23*** **	1.10	1.38
	HI-Personal	**-2.16*** **	-3.07	-1.26	**0.91** **	0.85	0.98
Hand Washing	**HW-after defecation**	**-3.17*** **	-4.43	-1.90	**0.83*** **	0.75	0.92
	HW-before eating	**-3.41*** **	-4.54	-2.27	**0.78*** **	0.71	0.86
	HW-before cooking	**1.33*** **	0.25	2.42	**1.11** **	1.01	1.21
	HW-after work	**1.06** **	0.002	2.12	1.01	0.92	1.10
	Soap Shown	**-11.56*** **	-14.1	-9.01	**0.61*** **	0.50	0.74
Demographic Controls	**Eats own Produce**	**2.37*** **	0.83	3.92	**0.83*** **	0.71	0.92
	Landownership	**-3.09*** **	-4.77	-1.42	**0.83*** **	0.73	0.95
	Socio-Economic Status	**-0.89*** **	-1.51	-0.27	1.04	0.99	1.10
	Proportion of Children	**13.45*** **	10.56	16.34	**7.18*** **	5.60	9.20
	Max. Education Level	-0.15	-0.34	0.05	1.01	0.99	1.02
	R-squared	0.04			0.07		

Table continues on next page

Model 2: Wastewater-Surface Water (n=20751)		OLS			Logistic		
		Coefficient	95% CI		OR	95% CI	
Exposure	**Wastewater Group**	**2.00****	0.08	3.92	**1.31*****	1.12	1.53
	POU Water Quality	**0.02*****	0.01	0.02	**1.00*****	1.00	1.00
	Access to Sanitation	**4.01*****	2.43	5.60	1.03	0.91	1.00
	Proportion with San	**-3.68*****	-6.23	-1.23	0.92	0.74	1.15
Hygiene Index	**HI-Environment**	**-1.58*****	-2.69	-0.48	0.92*	0.83	1.01
	HI-Water	**-2.98*****	-3.66	-2.29	**0.64*****	0.61	0.68
	HI-Food	**3.16*****	1.94	4.38	**1.42*****	1.28	1.58
	HI-Personal	**-2.11*****	-2.95	-1.26	**0.92****	0.86	0.99
Hand Washing	**HW-after defecation**	**-4.07*****	-5.27	-2.87	**0.76*****	0.69	0.85
	HW-before eating	**-2.55*****	-3.62	-1.47	**0.85*****	0.78	0.94
	HW-before cooking	**1.33****	0.29	2.36	**1.15*****	1.06	1.26
	HW-after work	**1.33*****	0.33	2.34	1.03	0.95	1.12
	Soap Shown	**-9.91*****	-12.0	-7.81	**0.52*****	0.44	0.61
Demographic Controls	**Eats own Produce**	**2.13****	0.43	3.83	**0.84****	0.73	0.96
	Landownership	-1.41*	-2.99	0.17	0.99	0.87	1.13
	Socio-Economic Status	**-1.00*****	-1.62	-0.38	1.04	0.99	1.10
	Proportion of Children	**13.30*****	10.58	16.02	**7.14*****	5.63	9.06
	Max. Education Level	-0.46***	-0.64	0.28	**0.97*****	0.96	0.99
	R-squared	0.04			0.07		

Table continues on next page

Model 3: Irrigation Water Quality (n=12912)		OLS			Logistic		
		Coefficient	95% CI		OR	95% CI	
Exposure	**Log *E. coli* /100 ml**	**0.13****	0.01	0.26	1.00	0.99	1.01
	POU Water Quality	**0.01****	0.003	0.021	**1.00****	1.00	1.00
	Access to Sanitation	**4.33*****	2.24	6.42	1.13	0.98	1.32
	Proportion with San	-2.39	-6.17	1.40	**0.65*****	0.49	0.87
Hygiene Index	**HI-Environment**	**-1.62***	-3.18	-0.06	0.94	0.84	1.06
	HI-Water	**-3.09*****	-3.96	-2.23	**0.65*****	0.61	0.69
	HI-Food	**1.83****	0.13	3.54	**1.39*****	1.23	1.59
	HI-Personal	**-2.42*****	-3.56	-1.28	0.96	0.88	1.04
Hand Washing	**HW-after defecation**	**-4.38*****	-6.12	-2.63	**0.77*****	0.68	0.88
	HW-before eating	**-5.55*****	-7.12	-3.98	**0.65*****	0.58	0.73
	HW-before cooking	**3.57*****	2.08	5.06	**1.17*****	1.05	1.31
	HW-after work	**1.17***	-0.21	-2.55	1.03	0.93	1.15
	Soap Shown	-1.83	-5.66	1.99	0.79*	0.61	1.03
Demographic Controls	**Eats own Produce**	**3.00*****	0.81	5.19	**0.71*****	0.60	0.83
	Landownership	-0.70	-2.89	1.49	0.89	0.76	1.05
	Socio-Economic Status	**-1.28*****	-2.10	-0.45	1.00	0.94	1.06
	Proportion of Children	**21.67*****	17.89	25.45	**11.05*****	8.20	14.9
	Max. Education Level	0.07	-0.18	0.33	**1.04*****	1.02	1.06
	R-squared	0.04			0.06		

Access to sanitation produces interesting results with significant positive correlations throughout all OLS models. This indicates that households with access to sanitation experience an increased risk of diarrheal disease. This is highly surprising as the safe disposal of feces forms a key primary barrier to disease transmission. The proportion of the community with access to sanitation, on the other hand, reveals a significant negative correlation. This finding suggests that the health benefits of sanitation only fully manifest when a large proportion of the community has gained access, confirming the community effect suspected during bivariate analysis. Households with access to sanitation but situated in an area where open defecation is predominantly practiced are still exposed to fecal contamination in the community. Additionally, the mere presence of sanitation facilities in a household does not necessarily ensure its safe and hygienic use. Facilities, which are not cleaned and maintained regularly, may form an exposure source, thus contributing to cross-contamination and disease transmission. On the other side, households without sanitation but situated in a community with high sanitation coverage, may benefit from reduced fecal contamination of the village environment and the consequent reduction in cross-contamination. Hand washing after defecation, therefore, forms an essential transmission barrier regardless of access to sanitation. Households that wash their hands after defecation have about 20% lower odds of diarrheal disease. It is therefore indicated that mere access to sanitation is not sufficient to induce health benefits, but community-wide sanitation coupled with adequate hand hygiene behavior are required. This reflects the finding from the drinking water variable, as hygiene behaviors mediate the effects of exposure.

In the OLS regression, the four hygiene index categories show consistent significant correlations with diarrhea incidence, with the exception of the environment category, which fails to reach significance in the first model. Nonetheless, the direction of the relationship is robust throughout the three models. Higher environmental hygiene scores are associated with a slight reduction of the odds of diarrhea. More pronounced effects are found in the water and personal categories, which are linked to 35 and 8% reductions of the odds, respectively. Thus, emphasizing the preventive effect of adequate hygiene behavior. The food hygiene category, however, produces highly significant positive correlations with the incidence of diarrhea, suggesting a 20 to 40%

increase in the odds when more adequate food hygiene was observed. It thus appears that kitchen hygiene does not contribute to the prevention of diarrheal disease. This is supported by the variable 'hand washing before cooking', which also shows significant positive correlations in all models. The data suggests a 10% – 15% increase in the odds of diarrhea among households that indicated washing their hands before food preparation. This is highly counterintuitive, as hand washing before cooking reduces cross-contamination between hands and foods and consequently the spread to other household members. Over-reporting of the behavior, inadequate hand washing technique, or utilization of unsafe water may induce these counterintuitive results.

Landownership is highly correlated to diarrhea in model 1, however only weak significance is reached in model 2; and in model 3 the association is not significant. Nonetheless, it is noteworthy that landowners appear to have lower diarrhea incidence rates compared to households merely cultivating the land. Landowners usually employ workers to conduct most of the fieldwork, particularly tasks that have perceived health risks, such as fertilization, pesticide application or irrigation. In consequence, landowners are less exposed to the risk of agricultural work compared to households that are mere farmers.

Among the control variables, the proportion of children in the household stands out. As children are more prone to develop diarrhea it is unsurprising that the proportion of children in the household is highly correlated to the outcome. It is indicated that household with higher proportions of children are between 7 to 11 times more likely to suffer from diarrhea. The maximum education level of the household only shows a highly significant correlation in the logistic regression of model 2, however, only indicating a negligible reduction in the odds of diarrhea. Similarly, the socio-economic status of thc household, although highly significantly correlated in all models, suggests minor reductions in the odds among more affluent households. It is suggested that the control variables, with the exception 'proportion of children', only have slight impact on the incidence of diarrhea.

A strong effect of exposure to unsafe irrigation on diarrheal disease has been identified, yet the measured irrigation water quality appears less important than the choice of irrigation water source. The preventive effects of adequate hygiene behavior are highlighted, particularly the importance of hand washing after defecation and before eating. Additionally, it is illustrated that mere access to sanitation is insufficient to induce health benefits; in fact, it appears that sanitation facilities can act as exposure source. Only if large proportions of the community have access to sanitation and adequate hygiene behavior is preformed can the full health benefits manifest.

To estimate the average treatment effects of the key variables on the incidence of diarrhea, propensity score matching is undertaken. Initially, the propensity score is estimated utilizing the set of independent variables from the regression. Households of the exposure group are then matched to control households based upon the estimated propensity score. Unfortunately, balancing was not fully achieved, as reflected by the high bias of the results. The average treatment effect of access to sanitation could not be calculated as balancing was unsuccessful for key exposure variables.

As the balancing property was not fully achieved and the percentage bias is high, the results need to be viewed with caution and cannot inform causal inference. Nonetheless, a similar average treatment effect (ATE) was found for both irrigation and drinking water, indicating more than two additional diarrhea episodes per 1,000 person-weeks. Although the ATE has a high bias, it is suggested that exposure to unsafe irrigation water has similarly strong adverse health impacts as exposure to unsafe drinking water. Additionally, it should be noted that exposure to wastewater irrigation adversely impacts the degree of in-household water contamination, thus implying further indirect effects of exposure to wastewater on diarrheal disease incidence. The average treatment effect of the hygiene index illustrates the preventive effect of adequate household hygiene, suggesting a reduction of 4 episodes per 1,000 person-weeks among households classified as practicing adequate hygiene behavior. However, the considerably high bias of 176%, points to confounding effects of unobserved variables.

Nevertheless, the direction of the association has been robust throughout analysis, thus confirming the preventive effect of adequate hygiene.

Table 37: Average treatment effects on the incidence of diarrhea. Average treatment effect (ATE) was calculated after propensity score matching using the independent variables from table 36.

Variable	N	ATE	Bias [Percent]
Irrigation Water Quality	1950	**2.73**	35
PoU Water Quality	2010	**2.54**	43
Hygiene Index	703	**-4.02**	176

4.3.3 Resumé

The incidence of diarrhea is significantly higher among the exposed population, indicating an adverse health impact of exposure to unsafe irrigation water. Among the exposure groups, farmers utilizing wastewater experience additional health risks compared to the surface water group. The results of the analysis clearly illustrate a direct positive correlation between the irrigation water source and the incidence of diarrhea. The measured *E. coli* density of the irrigation water is also positively correlated to the disease outcome; however, the effect size is smaller thus implying that the choice of irrigation water source has a stronger impact on the disease risk compared to the actual degree of irrigation water contamination. Individual farmers with relatively low *E. coli* concentrations in their irrigation water may still be exposed due to high contamination of neighboring farms. Direct contact between farmers may lead to cross-contamination; additionally, farmers often need to cross neighboring farms to reach their own land. Thus, merely improving the irrigation water quality of individual farmers may not induce significant health gains, while ensuring that most of the community utilizes safe irrigation water reduces cross-contamination and should result in health benefits for the individual as well as on the community level. Further research is required to analyze and understand the effectiveness of improving irrigation water quality to reduce disease incidence, the data however indicates a significant health risk induced by the exposure to unsafe irrigation water.

The impact of unsafe PoU drinking water is similar to that of wastewater irrigation. This emphasizes the relative importance of unsafe irrigation water, as PoU water quality is considered a primary causal factor in the transmission of diarrheal disease. The correlation between the *E. coli* concentration in PoU water and incidence of disease, although significant, only showed negligible differences in the odds of disease. It is assumed that a certain degree of immunity exists in the community, explaining why high bacterial densities do not always lead to infection. Moreover, a strong preventive effect of adequate water hygiene is indicated, which may mediate the adverse health impact of exposure to unsafe drinking water. It is assumed that long-term exposure builds immunity and thus decreases disease risk. This may explain the absence of a clear dose-response relationship.

Access to sanitation forms the foundation in the combat against infectious diseases, and the safe disposal of feces is the primary barrier to exposure to fecal pathogens. However, the data robustly indicates a significant positive correlation between access to sanitation and incidence of disease. This finding apparently contradicts the main findings of previous studies that highlight the preventive effect of sanitation. It should be noted that most of these studies assess the impact of constructing sanitation facilities, usually comparing communities that received the intervention with those not receiving it. The variable 'proportion with sanitation' showed the expected preventive effect, thus suggesting that the health benefits of access to sanitation only fully manifest if large proportions of the community have access to sanitation. It appears that access to sanitation can form an exposure source if the facilities are not maintained and cleaned adequately. It is therefore indicated that community-wide access to sanitation should be sought, which is in line with the new sustainable development target 6 calling for total sanitation coverage. Furthermore, hand hygiene after defecation forms an effective primary barrier, with households engaging in the practice exhibiting significantly lower incidence of diarrhea. This is regardless of the place of defecation, and should therefore form a cornerstone in the prevention of fecal-oral diseases.

The results of this study confirm the preventive effect of hygiene behavior, particularly the hygiene index categories environment, water and personal, induce significant reductions in the incidence of diarrhea. The critical hand washing times after defecation and before eating are also identified as key preventive behavior. In section 4.1, the adverse impacts of wastewater irrigation on hygiene outcomes are demonstrated, thus suggesting further indirect effects of exposure to unsafe irrigation water on the incidence of disease. Whilst hygiene behavior is usually conceptualized as a preventive mechanism, in the context of hygiene outcomes it can also form an exposure source. Low environmental hygiene scores are characterized by the presence of feces, waste, flies and stagnant water, thus forming an exposure source and a potential point of cross-contamination. Households practicing adequate hygiene will remove such contamination and will thus receive higher environmental hygiene scores. Similarly, dirty hands, indicated by a low personal hygiene score, contribute to cross-contamination and thus increase exposure, whilst adequate hand hygiene results in high personal hygiene scores. Exposure to unsafe irrigation water can lead to lower environmental and personal hygiene scores through the transfer of pathogens from the work to the home environment, thus forming additional exposure sources. It is therefore suggested that exposure to unsafe irrigation water has additional indirect effects on the incidence of diarrhea. Nonetheless, adequate hygiene behavior has a strong preventive effect, particularly when hygiene outcomes are assessed. The data suggests that additional hygiene behavior is required in communities with high exposure to avoid adverse hygiene outcomes, mitigate disease risks and induce health benefits.

4.4 The Impact of Wastewater Irrigation on Farmers' Children

Children are particularly vulnerable to diarrhea, with children under the age of five forming the high-risk group. Thus far analysis has been conducted on the household level, nonetheless the number of children in the household has shown high correlation to the incidence of disease (recall chapter 4.3). In this chapter, the sample population is reduced to only include children under the age of twelve. As the nutritional status of children is linked to disease risk (Dewey & Mayers, 2011), it is expected that higher prevalence of malnutrition will be found among the exposed population, given that exposed households exhibit higher diarrhea incidence. First, the child sample population is described, highlighting the distribution of children across the research groups. Second, the prevalence of undernourishment is compared between the groups utilizing the indicators weight-for-age, height-for-age and weigh-for-height. Third, the association between nutritional status and the incidence of diarrhea is assessed; differentiating between children under-five and those aged five to twelve. Ultimately, the effect of irrigation water quality on the nutritional status of children is analyzed using a series of regression models.

4.4.1 The Child Sample Population

Among the sample households, 67% have children aged twelve or younger and 48% have children under the age of five. Households with children have 2.4 children on average, ranging between 1 and 9 children per household. In total 332 children under the age of twelve form the child sample population, 44% (n=145) of which are aged under five. Gender is split almost equally, with 56% of children being male. All children were called for anthropometric measurements, which were conducted on two occasions in each community. 73% (n=242) of children attended at least one of the measuring events and thus form the BMI sample population.

In total 174 children are allocated to the exposure group and the control group consists of 68 children. The largest absolute number of children is found in area III (n=70) and area IV (n=69). In the control area (area I), 50 children were included in the sample, whilst 53 children were sampled in area II. As most households in area II, III and IV utilize surface or wastewater for irrigation, it is unsurprising that the number of exposed children is higher compared to the number of children in the control group. Among the child sample, 48% have access to sanitation, reflecting the proportion with access among the entire sample population. Whilst 49% of children in the exposure group have access to sanitation, 43% of control children have access. However, 70% of children under age five resort to indiscriminate defecation, often in the courtyard of the household. The proportion of child open defecation is the same between the groups.

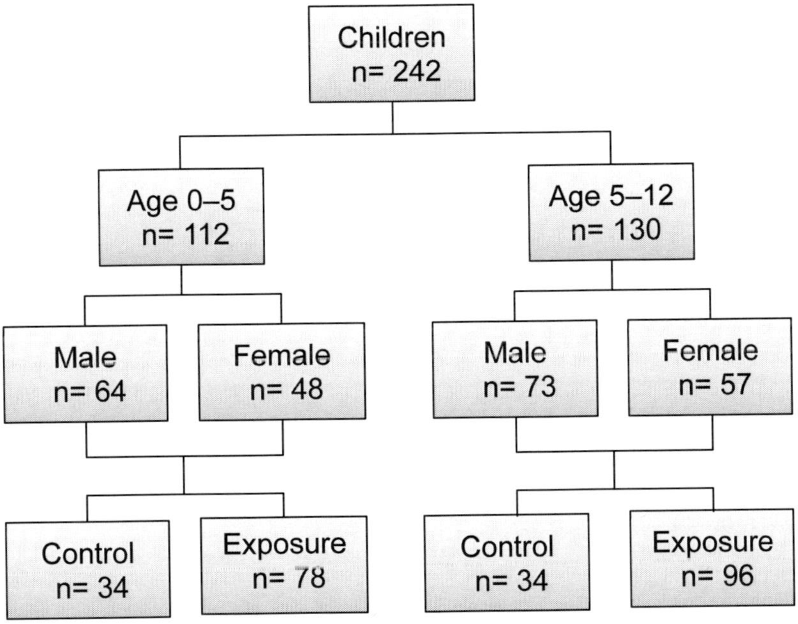

Figure 36: BMI sample population. n = sample size; the control group is made up of children from area I, whereas children of exposure group live in area II, III or IV.

4.4.2 Nutritional Status of Children

It is internationally recognized that the nutritional status of children is indicated by child growth performance. Children, who show low weight-for-age or height-for-age scores often suffer from malnutrition, which impairs child development and increases vulnerability to disease. Due to the adverse impact on nutrient absorption, induced by frequent disease episodes, a vicious cycle is created; where malnourished children have an increased susceptibility to disease and frequent disease episodes, which induce undernutrition and malabsorption and leads to malnutrition. Ensuring adequate child growth therefore lays the foundation for healthy child development.

Table 38: WHO cut-off values for public health significance of malnutrition. Adopted from WHO, 1995 in WHO, 2010.

Indicator	Prevalence Cut-Off Values for Public Health Significance	
Underweight < 2SD mean (weight-for-age)	< 10%: 10-19%: **20-29%:** **>=30%:**	Low prevalence Medium prevalence **High prevalence** **Very high prevalence**
Stunting < 2SD mean (height-for-age)	< 20%: 20-29%: **30-39%:** **>=40%:**	Low prevalence Medium prevalence **High prevalence** **Very high prevalence**
Wasting < 2SD mean (weight-for-height)	<5%: 5-9%: **10-14%:** **>= 15%:**	Acceptable Poor **Serious** **Critical**

The WHO utilizes child anthropometric measurements to define malnutrition. The key indicators used are: underweight, stunting and wasting. The deviation from the WHO Child Growth Standard median score was used for classification (WHO, 2010). Children whose weight-for-age lies more than two standard deviations below the median are underweight, whilst a deviation larger than three standard deviations indicate severe underweight. Underweight children are acutely undernourished and suffer increased mortality risk (ibid). Prolonged undernourishment can impair development and result in stunting. Stunting is defined by height/length-for-age and indicates growth retardation often resulting in higher susceptibility to disease (ibid). Stunting is an indication for chronic undernutrition and reflects nutritional deprivation since birth. Wasting, on the other hand, indicates acute undernutrition through deviation from the weight-for-height median. The relation between a child's physical growth (height) and weight reflects the long-term as well as acute nutritional status of the child. Children falling below two standard deviations suffer from malnutrition, impairing their immune system and thus increasing susceptibility to disease.

The WHO gages the public health significance of malnutrition in a particular population by the prevalence of the undernourishment (see table 38). Alternatively, the mean z-scores of the variables illustrate the relative shift of the normal distribution in the given population. Negative mean z-scores signify that the entire distribution is shifted downward, thus indicating that large proportions of the population are undernourished. The mean z-scores of the nutritional indicators are presented in table 39; the sample is stratified by age group and exposure group allocation.

The data clearly shows a downward shift of the normal distribution within the entire sample population. In both age groups, the weight-for-age indicator shows an average deviation larger than one standard deviation suggesting that the majority of the population is at least mildly underweight. The height-for-age variable, indicating stunting, also shows large negative average deviations. It appears that stunting is more common among the 0–5 age group suggesting that the proportion of the population suffering from chronic undernutrition reduces with age. As stunting is strongly associated with childhood mortality, the lower prevalence of stunting in the older age group may be caused by the lower chance of survival among the stunted population. The weight-for-height variable indicates wasting in the 0–5 age group and also shows a large downward deviation from the norm, high prevalence of acute malnutrition among children under-five is therefore suggested. Among the 5–12-year-old population, the BMI z-scores are used to indicate wasting. A large downward shift of the normal distribution is indicated, highlighting that the majority of children between five and twelve suffer from acute undernourishment.

Table 39: Mean z-scores of nutrition indicators. Calculation based on normal distributions available from WHO, 2010. Exposure group allocation if irrigation water ≥ 1,000 E. coli/100 ml

	Total Population (n=242)		**Age 0–5** (n=112)		**Age 5–12** (n=130)	
	Age 0–5 (n=112)	**Age 5–12** (n=130)	**Exposure** (n=78)	**Control** (n=34)	**Exposure** (n=96)	**Control** (n=34)
	Mean Z-score	Mean Z-score	Mean Z-score	Mean Z-score	Mean Z-score	Mean Z-score
under-weight	-1.31	-1.39	-1.029	-2.00	-1.36	-1.41
stunting	-1.05	-0.76	-0.89	-1.42	-0.93	-0.41
wasting	-1.11	/	-0.84	-1.74	/	/
BMI	-0.93	-1.57	-0.64	-1.58	-1.38	-2.26

Segregating the sample by exposure group allocation reveals significantly larger deviations among the control group. This suggests that the prevalence of children suffering from malnutrition is larger in the control group. In fact, among the 0–5 age group all nutritional variables indicate higher prevalence of undernourishment among the control group. The weight-for-age indicator is particularly noteworthy, as the mean z-score of -2 suggests that underweight children form the norm in the sample. In the 5–12 age-bracket a highly significant difference between control and exposure group is found for BMI. The mean z-score of the control group lies beyond the two standard deviations threshold, therefore highlighting that the majority of children aged five to twelve are classified as wasting. A high prevalence of acute malnutrition in the control population is therefore indicated. Whilst a high prevalence of undernourished children was expected, it is surprising that children from the control group exhibit poorer nutritional status compared to the exposure group. Analysis in the previous chapters, has demonstrated that exposure to unsafe irrigation water is associated with higher disease incidence (recall chapter 4.3). From the literature, it is assumed that children who suffer more frequently from diarrhea are more likely to be malnourished, leading to the assumption that children from the exposure group have lower nutritional status compared to those from the control group. However, the data does not confirm this assumption, as the prevalence of acute malnutrition is larger among the control group.

Table 40: Prevalence of underweight, stunting and wasting among research groups. Bold values indicate high or very high prevalence/ critical public health significance of malnutrition (see table 38).

	Total Population (n=236)		**Age 0–5** (n=112)		**Age 5–12** (n=124)	
	Age 0–5 (n=112)	**Age 5–12** (n=124)	**Exposure** (n=78)	**Control** (n=34)	**Exposure** (n=93)	**Control** (n=31)
	[%]	[%]	[%]	[%]	[%]	[%]
Under-weight	**35**	**25**	**29**	**47**	**24**	**29**
Severe Under-weight	12	15	8	**21**	11	**24**
Stunting	**35**	28	**35**	**35**	27	29
Severe Stunting	16	8	15	18	8	6
Wasting	**28**	**40**	**24**	**35**	**38**	**47**
Severe Wasting	**13**	0	10	**18**	0	0

The mean z-scores of the nutritional indicators have signified a large downward shift of the normal distribution. To assess the level public health significance, each child is categorized according to the z-score. Underweight, stunting and wasting are defined by z-scores below -2, whilst severe underweight, stunting and wasting is indicated by z-scores below -3. Table 40 illustrates the proportion of children suffering from low nutritional scores. Considering the WHO cut-off values to gage the public health significance of malnutrition in a particular population (recall table 38) highlights the degree of malnutrition experienced among the sample. All three indicators fall within the upper-end of the classification, with a very high prevalence of underweight children, high prevalence of stunting and critical levels of wasting. The wasting indicator in particular gives rise to concern, as the 'critical' threshold of 15% is surpassed many-fold. In the 0–5 age group the prevalence of 'severe wasting' almost reaches the 15% threshold, underscoring the extremely critical degree of acute malnutrition in the sample population.

Table 41: Odds ratios of exposure group allocation and nutrition indicators.
* p < 0.1; ** p < 0.05; *** p < 0.01

	Age 0–5 (n=112)			**Age 5–12** (n=130)		
	Odds Ratio	95% CI		Odds Ratio	95% CI	
Underweight	**0.47***	0.19	1.18	0.76	0.29	2.05
Severe Underweight	**0.32***	0.08	1.24	**0.42***	0.14	1.35
Stunting	0.97	0.39	2.50	0.89	0.35	2.39
Severe Stunting	0.85	0.26	3.05	1.45	0.27	14.73
Wasting	0.59	0.23	1.58	0.68	0.28	1.61
Severe Wasting	0.53	0.15	2.06	/	/	

The prevalence of all undernutrition indicators is higher among the control group, with the exception of stunting, where the prevalence is similar between exposure and control group. Despite lower prevalence of malnutrition among the exposure group, the prevalence level still indicates critical public health significance with high prevalence of underweight and stunting as well as surpassing the critical threshold of the wasting indicator. The odds ratios presented in table 41 signify lower odds of suffering from underweight, stunting and wasting among the exposure group. However, the large confidence intervals of the variables render the differences in the odds statistically insignificant, apart from the underweight indicator among the 0–5 age group. Although higher prevalence of malnutrition is observed in the control group, both the exposure and control group signify critical public health significance of the extent of malnutrition in the community. Therefore, inducing additional health risks for children from both groups.

4.4.3 Incidence of Diarrhea among Malnourished Children

The incidence of diarrhea of the entire sample population is 11.5 per 1,000 person-weeks. As children are more susceptible to diarrhea, it is not surprising that the incidence rate is significantly higher among the child population. Combining all children under age twelve produces an incidence rate of 24 diarrhea episodes per 1,000 person-weeks. Segregating the sample according to age group confirms that young children (under-age-five) suffer from more frequent diarrhea episodes compared to children aged five to twelve. Whilst children under five have a diarrhea incidence of 34 episodes per 1,000 person-weeks, older children only suffer from half as many episodes (16 episodes per 1,000 person-weeks), as indicated by a highly significant incidence rate ratio of 2.12.

Children, who suffered any number of episodes throughout the research period, are classified as ‘case’, whereas those reporting no diarrhea episodes form the control. Odds ratios are calculated for each nutritional indicator, where underweight, stunting and wasting form the exposure variables. In the 0–5 age group the odds ratio for the wasting variable could not be calculated, as 100% of wasting children suffered from diarrhea. The underweight and stunting variables produce results in inverse direction. While underweight children are 1.5 times more likely to experience diarrhea episodes, stunted children show significantly reduced odds of disease (see table 42). Interestingly only the stunting variable shows significant results. It must be noted however that the majority of children under age five suffered from diarrhea at least once, the number of controls is low (n=7), thus the results must be viewed with caution. The data suggests lower odds of diarrhea among children suffering from long-term nutrient deprivation, as measured by height-for-age. As this finding is theoretically unsound, it is expected that confounding effects, namely wastewater irrigation and WASH, influence the results.

Table 42: Odds ratios for diarrhea cases by nutrition indicators. Individuals reporting a single diarrhea episode during any of the 14-day intervals are classified as 'case'.
* $p < 0.1$; ** $p < 0.05$; *** $p < 0.01$

	Age 0–5 (n=112)			**Age 5–12** (n=126)		
	OR	95% CI		OR	95% CI	
Underweight	1.58	0.12	85.3	0.58	0.11	4.07
Stunting	**0.17***	0.003	2.14	1.12	0.19	11.9
Wasting	/	/		1.99	0.33	20.8

Among the five-to-twelve-year-old children both the stunting and wasting indicators follow the expected trend, while the underweight variable indicates a preventive effect. However, none of the three indicators reached significance. Children with low BMI z-scores (wasting) have almost double the odds of suffering from diarrhea, while the stunting indicator suggests an odds ratio of 1.12. The BMI is the ratio between weight and height in regard to age, therefore reflecting the acute effect of undernourishment (low weight-for-age) as well as the long-term impacts as measured by height-for-age. However, the 5–12 age-bracket exhibits a similar problem to the one found in the 0–5 age-group, the majority of children fell sick at least once throughout the reporting period (91%). Consequently, the number of control children aged five to twelve is low (n=11). It is therefore, necessary to examine the frequency of diarrhea episodes among malnourished children to estimate the full effect of malnutrition on disease risk.

Throughout the reporting period, children under age-five suffered a total of 4.3 diarrhea episodes on average. Segregating the sample by the nutrition indicators highlights the differences of the mean number of diarrhea episodes between malnourished and well-nourished children (see table 43). Whilst malnourished children suffer from about 5 diarrhea episodes on average, children falling into the normal range had 4 diarrhea episodes throughout the research period. However, the only significant difference of the mean number of diarrhea episodes is found between stunted children and those with normal height-for-age among the 0–5 age group. Almost all children under-age-five experience diarrhea at least once per year, malnourished children, however, suffer more frequent episodes. The findings are confirmed by the difference in incidence rates, however; only the stunting indicator produced a significant incidence rate ratio (see table 44). It is therefore suggested that chronic undernourishment, as indicated by stunting, has significant impact on the incidence of disease among children under-five.

Table 43: Mean number of diarrhea episodes by nutrition indicators. Diarrheal episodes were self-reported in bi-monthly intervals. Episodes of each interval were added, forming the annual number of episodes; the mean of the annual number of episodes is shown.
* p < 0.1; ** p < 0.05; *** p < 0.01

	Age 0–5 (n=112)			**Age 5–12** (n=130)		
	Mean	95% CI	T-Test	Mean	95% CI	T-Test
Under-weight	4.74	4.63 – 6.85 (n=38)	0.64	1.56	0.73 – 2.39 (n=33)	-0.58
Normal	4.03	2.84 – 5.21 (n=74)		2.36	0.76 – 3.95 (n=97)	
Stunting	5.26	3.31 – 7.20 (n=28)	**1.35***	1.68	0.88 – 2.47 (n=36)	-0.49
Normal	3.76	2.51 – 5.01 (n=74)		2.34	0.70 – 3.98 (n=94)	
Wasting	4.91	2.585– 5.20 (n=31)	0.75	1.42	0.96 – 3.35 (n=51)	-0.97
Normal	4.02	2.62 – 7.19 (n=81)		2.63	0.68 – 4.57 (n=79)	

The majority of older children (between the ages five and twelve) also exhibit at least one episode of diarrhea per year, with an average of 2.2 annual episodes. Whilst the odds ratios suggest higher odds of diarrhea among malnourished children, the mean number of episodes is lower in children with low nutritional status (see table 43). The incidence rates also reveal more diarrhea episodes per 1,000 person-week among well-nourished children (see table 44). However, the incidence rate ratios fail to reach significance. The null hypothesis is therefore accepted, indicating that diarrhea incidence among children aged five to twelve is not affected by the nutritional status of the child. As evidence from previous studies consistently indicates nutritional status as predictor for disease incidence, it is assumed that confounding factors, namely WASH factors, distort the effect of nutritional status among children between five and twelve.

Table 44: Diarrhea incidence rates by nutrition indicators. IR = Incidence Rate; IRR = Incidence Rate Ratio; # {total person-weeks}. * $p < 0.1$; ** $p < 0.05$; *** $p < 0.01$

	Age 0–5 (n=112)				**Age 5–12** (n=130)			
	IR	IRR	95% CI		IR	IRR	95% CI	
Underweight	36	1.07	0.77	1.47	13	0.76	0.43	1.27
Normal	33		{5014}#		17		{5853}#	
Stunting	40	**1.30***	0.94	1.78	15	0.95	0.58	1.52
Normal	31		{5014}#		16		{5853}#	
Wasting	38	1.19	0.84	1.66	14	0.84	0.54	1.31
Normal	32		{5014}#		17		{5853}#	

4.4.4 Impact of Undernourishment on the Incidence of Diarrhea

In the previous sub-chapters, it was demonstrated that exposure to unsafe irrigation water, as well as unsafe point-of-use (PoU) drinking water, access to sanitation and hygiene behavior influence households' disease risk. In the linear regression model, incidence of diarrhea forms the dependent variable and the nutrition indicators are primary independent variables. Additionally, the WASH variables, irrigation water quality, self-reported hand hygiene and demographic variables serve as control variables. Exposure to unsafe irrigation water is applied as binary variable, defined by irrigation water quality in excess of 1,000 *E. coli* per 100 ml. The PoU water quality is used in its continuous form (*E. coli*/100 ml). The hygiene index is a continuous composite variable of the hygiene components: environment, water, food, sanitation and personal. The self-reported hand hygiene variables are in binary format and reflect hand hygiene at critical times: after defecation, before eating, before cooking and after changing the child. It should be noted that the hand hygiene variables indicate the parent's rather than the child's hand hygiene behavior. Additionally, a categorical variable is used to reflect the number of times parents wash the hands of the young children with soap per day. The variable 'num wash – child' has five categories: (0) never, (1) 1-2 times, (2) 3-4 times, (3) 5-6 times and (4) > 7 times. The binary variable 'soap present' reflects the availability of soap in the household, whilst the variable 'soap child' indicates that the child knows where soap is located in the household. Access to sanitation is used in binary format, additionally the binary variable 'child open defecation' is applied, as many young children practice open defecation despite the household having access to sanitation. The variable 'child assist' is also in binary format and reflects whether young children are assisted during defecation. Additionally, the continuous variable 'number of meals' and the binary variable 'eat own produce' are included, along with the demographic controls; the continuous 'age' variable and the categorical 'socio-economic status'. The regression is conducted three times, once for the entire child sample population and once for each of the two age brackets, 0–5 year-olds and 5–12 year-olds.

Only two variables show significant correlations in all three regressions (see table 45). In the 5–12 age group merely three variables reached significance, whilst in the under-five age group eight variables are significantly correlated to the incidence of diarrhea. In the entire child sample population seven variables reached significance, among these are two of the nutrition indicators, which only show significant correlations for the entire child sample. The two nutrition indicators, stunting and wasting, produced significant correlations in the expected direction, while the underweight indicator suggests an inverse correlation. This reflects the findings of the bivariate analysis; acute undernourishment, as indicated by low weight-for-age, is a less important determinant of diarrhea incidence compared to the effects of chronic malnutrition as indicated by stunting. Comparing the two age groups shows larger coefficients among the 0–5 age-bracket, suggesting that the adverse effects of malnutrition on diarrhea incidence reduce with age. The failure to reach significance in the two age groups however, calls for caution when interpreting the results. Nonetheless, the significant correlations between stunting / wasting and diarrhea incidence highlights stark adverse health effects induced by undernourishment. Additionally, the 'age' variable consistently shows significant negative correlation throughout all three regressions indicating that the incidence of diarrhea reduces with age, while also suggesting that the adverse health effects persist beyond age-five.

The other variable that reached significance in all models is exposure to unsafe irrigation water. Remarkably the child diarrhea incidence is more affected by exposure to unsafe irrigation water than child nutritional status. This is surprising as children, particularly those aged under-five, do not work on the farm and are therefore not directly exposed to wastewater. The large effect of unsafe irrigation water on child health, therefore confirms that pathogens are transferred from the work to the home environment, exposing the entire household to fecal pathogens. The OLS shows larger coefficients among children aged-under-five, suggesting that young children are more susceptible to the adverse effect of unsafe irrigation water even when no direct contact with irrigation water occurs.

PoU drinking water quality does not reach significance in any of the models, thus suggesting that PoU water quality only has negligible impact on children's diarrhea incidence. Additionally, the coefficient size is around zero in all models further indicating no effect of unsafe PoU drinking water on the diarrhea incidence among children. It is highly surprising that drinking water contamination does not induce the expected adverse health impact in children. As suggested in the previous chapter, this may be linked to immunity. Children are exposed to unsafe drinking water from birth, which may lead to the development of immunity, in turn rendering children less susceptible to drinking water contamination. Regardless, the data calls for the acceptance of the null hypothesis, thus PoU water quality does not influence child diarrhea incidence.

The variable access to sanitation fails to reach significance in all three models. Interestingly in the entire child sample as well as the 5–12 age group, a positive correlation is suggested, similar to results of the previous sub-chapter. Thus, children from households with access to sanitation have higher diarrhea incidence compared to those resorting to open defecation. Therefore, indicating that sanitation facilities of the households can act as exposure source, especially if these are not well maintained. In the 0–5 age group however a preventive effect of access to sanitation is suggested. This is surprising, as young children usually do not utilize toilets but practice open defecation. It thus appears that sanitation facilities can act as exposure source especially for individuals frequently utilizing the facility. However, the adequate disposal of feces also results in a more hygienic living environment, which results in lower exposure to fecal matter for young children.

Interestingly contradicting correlations are found between the age groups for child open defecation. Whilst children under-five practicing open defecation are associated with higher diarrhea incidence, open defecation among children aged five to twelve appears to reduce the incidence. Young children usually defecate indiscriminately in the courtyard or in close proximity of the household, whilst older children practice open defecation in the surrounding fields. The place of open defecation may contribute to the inverse trend between younger and older children, as fecal contamination of the home environment, induced by young child open defecation, creates an exposure source and contributes to cross contamination. This is further supported by the 'child assist' variable, the only sanitation variable to reach significance. Children who are assisted by their parents or older siblings during defecation experience lower diarrhea incidence. The preventive effect is most pronounced for the 5–12 age group, although these older children are not necessarily assisted themselves, they benefit from the adequate disposal of the feces of their younger siblings. Therefore, assisting the child during defecation, through ensuring feces are disposed properly and the child's hands are washed afterward, is highly important to protect the health of the child. Indiscriminate open defecation of young children leads to large increase of the child's disease risk.

The hygiene indicators produced consistent results across both age groups; however, significance is only reached in the 0–5 age group. The direction of the correlations is generally in the expected direction with the exception of the hygiene index and the 'hand washing before cooking' variable. As already suggested in the previous sub-chapter, hand washing before cooking induces adverse effects on the incidence of diarrhea, which may be caused by the over-reporting of the practice, inadequate hand washing technique or the use of contaminated water for hand hygiene behavior. The hygiene index as a whole measures household hygiene outcomes, thus higher hygiene index scores indicate a more hygienic living environment, more adequate food and water storage as well as better personal hygiene. The significant positive correlation found in the 0–5 age group is therefore counterintuitive. Especially young children should benefit from a more hygienic home, as these often crawl on the ground; potentially sticking contaminated fingers or dirt into their mouths leading to potential consumption of pathogens. The data however suggests that better hygiene outcomes are linked to increased diarrhea incidence among young children. This finding shows a shortcoming of the hygiene index; as the index merely measures household hygiene, including the cleanliness of the home environment, the exposure sources of the community are omitted. Individuals are, however, not confined to their home environment but interact with the entire community. Therefore, young children who live in households with good hygiene index scores are potentially still exposed to fecal contamination and cross-contamination in the community. These children may be more susceptible to such community exposure sources if they live in a hygienic living environment, as immunity develops via exposure. Interestingly, the direction of the correlation, although insignificant, is in the expected direction among older children (aged five to twelve). The effect size is rather small; nonetheless, the data indicates that young children do not directly benefit from good household hygiene, while older children (as well as adults) experience the preventive effect of adequate hygiene.

Table 45: Linear regression – diarrhea incidence and nutrition indicators. Dependent variable = diarrhea incidence per 1,000 person-weeks. Unsafe IW = irrigation water ≥ 1,000 E. coli/100 ml; POU = Point-of-use; HW = Handwashing. * $p < 0.1$; ** $p < 0.05$; *** $p < 0.01$

Category	**Independent Variables**	**Total Sample** Coef. (Std. Err.)	**Age 0–5** Coef. (Std.Err.)	**Age 5–12** Coef. (Std. Err.)
Nutrition	**Underweight**	- 4.74 (6.48)	4.05 (10.1)	-10.38 (8.55)
	Stunting	**11.97*** (6.51)	10.59 (10.5)	9.79 (7.43)
	Wasting	**13.07**** (5.97)	14.36 (9.34)	8.00 (7.38)
Exposure	**Unsafe IW**	**26.37**** (11.2)	**36.07**** (16.6)	**31.34*** (16.0)
	PoU Quality	- 0.02 (0.66)	0.01 (0.11)	-0.03 (0.09)
Sanitation	**Access to sanitation**	1.03 (14.4)	-17.2 (20.6)	1.47 (23.7)
	Child open defecation	3.23 (12.99)	21.50 (21.05)	-16.73 (16.2)
	Child assist	-20.70 (13.21)	/	**-21.17*** (11.5)
Hygiene	**Hygiene Index**	5.29 (4.97)	**15.55**** (7.42)	-1.53 (7.47)
	HW – after defecation	-5.35 (7.99)	-7.67 (12.1)	-9.56 (11.3)
	HW – before eating	**-43.24***** (8.03)	**-65.5***** (13.2)	-15.45 (9.39)
	HW – before cooking	13.20 (8.06)	**24.3**** (11.6)	10.69 (13.0)
	HW – after child	-5.87 (8.06)	-2.72 (9.79)	-2.46 (8.61)
	Num wsh child	-0.89 (5.99)	-8.81 (9.39)	4.95 (9.69)
	Soap present	-21.05 (15.29)	**-35.52*** (20.74)	-23.43 (29.6)
	Soap child	-7.43 (7.93)	5.03 (11.0)	-18.71 (12.4)

Table continued from previous page

Demographic Controls	**Eat own produce**	**-38.63****** (10.97)	**-62.70****** (17.4)	-5.56 (14.8)
	Number meals	0.26 (4.89)	2.20 (7.97)	-3.88 (5.82)
	Age	**-4.26****** (0.95)	**-6.56*** (3.43)	**-3.67**** (1.62)
	Socio-economic status	**-10.40**** (4.07)	**-13.45**** (6.54)	-4.63 (5.71)
	R-square	0.50	0.57	0.56
	n	123	67	56

Whilst the hygiene outcomes, quantified by the hygiene index, produced inverse directions between the two age groups, the hand washing variables follow the same trend among the age groups. The presence of soap in the household forms a precondition for adequate hand hygiene behavior. It is therefore unsurprising that strong negative correlations are observed between the presence of soap and the incidence of diarrhea. Although the direction of the correlation is consistent throughout the age groups, significance is only reached among the 0–5 age-bracket. Interestingly, the variable 'soap child' only indicates a preventive effect among children aged five to twelve, whilst younger children, who know the location of soap, are associated with a slightly increased diarrhea incidence. Children aged below five usually do not wash their hands autonomously but are assisted by their parents or older siblings. Knowledge of the location of soap therefore does not reflect its use, especially among young children. The number of times child's hands are washed shows the opposite trend, with young children benefiting from increased number of hand wash times and older children exhibiting adverse effects. It is assumed that the reporting among older children is low, as many children aged between five and twelve will wash their hands independently, thus resulting in the counterintuitive result. The data highlights however that the number of times hands of young children are washed per day is negatively correlated to the incidence of diarrhea, emphasizing the strong preventive effect of frequent hand washing behavior.

Among the critical hand washing times, the most pronounced effect is observed for hand washing before eating. Although the correlation fails to reach significance in the 5–12 age group, the direction of the relationship is consistent. A strong preventive effect is indicated, with children under five benefiting more than older children. Hand washing after defecation did not produce significant results, however a preventive effect is suggested. As described above, hand washing before cooking produced consistent counterintuitive results, indicating increased diarrhea incidence when hand-washing behavior before cooking is practiced. Over-reporting of the practice, inadequate hand washing technique or the use of contaminated water for hand hygiene behavior may explain the theoretically unsound finding. The final critical hand washing time included in the regression analysis (after changing/cleaning child) did not produce significant results. Nonetheless a small preventive effect is suggested in both age groups. Overall, the coefficients of the hygiene variables are larger among children aged below five, suggesting that older children are less affected by the hygiene practices of their parents. Here it should be noted that the hand washing variables reflect the hygiene behavior of the parents rather than the children, thus younger children, who are more dependent on the parents, are also impacted more by their parents' hygiene behavior.

Among the control variables, 'eat own produce' stands out, indicating large reductions in diarrhea incidence among households eating parts of their harvest. Although the direction of the correlation is consistent across the age groups, significance was not reached for the 5–12 year-olds. Considering the potential contamination of food irrigated with unsafe irrigation water, this result is surprising. However, as noted before, all foods are cooked sorely before consumption and raw foods are eaten rarely. It is thus assumed that children eating their own produce have a more balanced diet, potentially leading to better nutrition and consequent health improvement. The coefficient is much lower among older children, thus suggesting that the health benefits of eating own produce reduce with age. As highlighted above, the 'age' variable is significantly correlated in both age groups, confirming the expected correlation between the incidence of diarrhea and age. The coefficient is smaller for older children, thus indicating that age becomes less important as children get older. As expected, the socio-economic status is negatively correlated to the diarrhea incidence, with children from more affluent households experience less diarrhea episodes compared to poorer households. However, among children aged between five and twelve the correlation does not reach significance and a much smaller coefficient is indicated. It is therefore suggested that the impact of socio-economic status is more pronounced in young children and reduces with age.

The linear regression has shown that malnutrition has adverse impact on the incidence of diarrhea among both children under-five and those aged five-to-twelve. However, various other independent variables also significantly impact diarrhea incidence. Particularly exposure to unsafe irrigation water as well as hygiene practices directly influences the incidence of diarrhea. In order to control for confounding effects and calculate the average treatment effect (ATE), the sample needs to be balanced across all independent variables. Propensity-score matching is used to balance the sample population. For each of the three nutrition indicators a propensity score is calculated based upon the independent variables of the OLS regression. Treated and control cases are then matched according to the estimated propensity-score ensuring that all independent variables are balanced between the treatment and control group. Consequently, individuals with the same propensity-score will also exhibit similar characteristics across the independent variables, thus ensuring that the differences between treated and control cases are induced by the treatment variable.

Despite the balancing property of the propensity-score being satisfied, the results are prone to bias. Comparing the mean scores of the independent variables after matching shows that all variables are balanced, except for wasting and stunting in the 5–12 age group as well as wasting for the entire population. Among children aged five to twelve, age and the number of meals are not balanced for wasting. However, both variables are unbalanced in favor of the control group, meaning that children in the control group a slightly older and consume more meals per day. In consequence, it can be assumed that the effect of wasting on diarrhea incidence in children aged five to twelve is overestimated. In the stunting variable, hand washing after defecation is not balanced among older children. As the control group shows lower prevalence of hand washing after defecation, it is assumed that the effect of stunting is underestimated. Hand washing after changing child is not balanced in the wasting variable among all children. The exposed population shows a slightly higher prevalence of this hand washing behavior, thus suggesting a slight underestimation of the effect. Although perfect balance was not achieved for all indicators, the balancing property is satisfied, thus implying the reliable estimation of the average treatment effects.

Table 46: Average treatment effects of nutrition indicators on the incidence of diarrhea. Average Treatment Effect (ATE) calculated after propensity score matching using the independent variables from the regression in table 45.

	Total Sample (n=139)		**Age 0–5** (n=83)		**Age 5–12** (n=58)	
	ATE	Bias [%]	ATE	Bias [%]	ATE	Bias [%]
Underweight	-6.00	91	-3.35	82	-7.41	106
Stunting	16.70	55	19.43	97	8.97	180
Wasting	13.45	75	20.67	100	4.81	118

In table 46 the ATEs are presented, confirming the findings from the regression analysis. Both stunted and wasting children show increased diarrhea incidence, with larger effects among the 0–5 age group. Whilst the ATE for stunting and wasting for children under-five is similar, indicating 20 additional diarrhea episodes per 1,000 person-weeks among malnourished children, wasting affects children between five and twelve more significantly than stunting. Stunted children between five and twelve, experience about 9 additional diarrhea episodes per 1,000 person-weeks, while those considered wasting suffer 15 additional episodes. It is thus indicated that, that height-for-age is less important in determining diarrhea than weight-for-height among children between five and twelve. In relation to the 0–5 age bracket, it appears that height-for-age reduces in significance with age, whilst weight-for-height remains a key predictor of diarrhea incidence. Therefore, weight-for-height is considered an age-robust indicator of malnutrition, whilst height-for-age is only reliable for children under-five.

The nutrition indicator, underweight produced counterintuitive results, suggesting lower diarrhea incidence among underweight children. The effect is more pronounced among children aged five to twelve, who exhibit a lower incidence of about 6 episodes per 1,000 person-weeks. Although the effect is smaller among young children, a reduction of 3 episodes per 1,000 person-weeks is still indicated. Low weight-for-age indicates acute undernourishment, which may be the result of insufficient food intake or hampered nutrient absorption. It is assumed that underweight children have reduced stool output, which may lead to less frequent reporting of diarrhea. Nonetheless, it appears that 'underweight' does not directly impact disease risk, it is therefore indicated to utilize weight-for-height as primary malnutrition indicator.

The results have demonstrated that malnourished children suffer from more frequent diarrhea episodes. It appears that weight-for-height forms the most robust indicator, as strong adverse effects are observed in both children under-five and those aged five to twelve. Additionally, age forms a key predictor for the risk of diarrhea, confirming young children as the high-risk group. Age is significantly correlated to the incidence of disease within both age-brackets, suggesting a continual decline in the frequency of diarrhea episodes, as children get older. As frequent episodes of diarrhea adversely impact the nutritional status of children and the nutritional status in turn affects the risk of disease, avoiding diarrhea at a young age induces lower disease risk throughout the child's life. The safe removal of child feces through parental assistance during defecation, coupled with frequent washing of the child's hands with soap and hand washing before eating are indicated as critically important preventive behaviors.

4.4.5 Impact of Exposure to Unsafe Irrigation Water on the Nutritional Status of Children

The bivariate analysis, see table 40 above, has suggested a higher prevalence of malnutrition in the control group. This implies that children from households exposed to unsafe irrigation have better nutritional status. The odds ratios, see table 41, confirm the direction of the association but fail to reach significance. It was demonstrated in the previous chapter (chapter 4.3) that irrigation water quality directly impacts the incidence of disease, thus leading to the expectation that children from exposed households have lower nutritional status compared to the control group. The prevalence of malnutrition, however, disproves the expectation. Therefore, a regression analysis is conducted to assess the correlation between exposure to unsafe irrigation water and the nutritional status. The dependent variable is the z-score of the nutrition indicators, weight-for-age (underweight), height-for-age (stunting), weight-for-height (wasting) and BMI-for-age. Therefore, four regression models are analyzed. The primary independent variable is the binary irrigation water classification into safe and unsafe irrigation water, where unsafe irrigation water exceeds 1,000 *E. coli* per 100 ml. Additionally, the set of independent control variables from the previous regression (see table 45) are also applied.

In all of the four regression models, exposure to unsafe irrigation water fails to reach a significant correlation with the nutritional indicators, thus leading to the conclusion that the null hypothesis is correct (see table 47). In fact, the majority of independent variables do not show significant correlation with the nutrition indicators. In the stunting model, only the variable 'number of times washing child's hands' is highly significantly correlated, suggesting that higher frequency of hand washing leads to higher height-for-age z-scores. The strongest correlation was found between child open defecation and the BMI z-score, highlighting that children practicing open defecation have significantly lower BMI z-scores. The age variable is also significantly correlated to the BMI z-score, indicating a slightly lower BMI scores among older children.

Table 47: Regression – nutritional status and exposure to unsafe irrigation water. UW = underweight; unsafe IW = irrigation water ≥ 1,000 E. coli/100 ml; POU = Point-of-use; HW = Handwashing. * $p < 0.1$; ** $p < 0.05$; *** $p < 0.01$

		UW	**Stunting**	**Wasting**	**BMI**
		Coef. (Std.Err)	Coef. (Std.Err)	Coef. (Std.Err)	Coef. (Std.Err)
Exposure	**Unsafe IW**	0.31 (0.61)	0.17 (0.86)	0.95 (0.90)	1.19 (0.79)
	PoU Quality	-0.002 (0.004)	**-0.01**** (0.005)	0.01 (0.01)	0.01 (0.01)
Sanitation	**Access to sanitation**	0.87 (0.79)	1.50 (1.12)	-1.11 (1.12)	-0.72 (1.03)
	Child open defecation	-1.09 (0.69)	0.44 (0.98)	0.24 (1.14)	**-2.23***** (0.90)
	Child assist	**-1.28*** (0.75)	**-2.06**** (1.02)	/	0.05 (0.94)
Hand Washing	**HW – before eating**	0.33 (0.46)	0.13 (0.63)	0.09 (0.73)	0.29 (0.58)
	HW – before cooking	-0.48 (0.44)	-1.04 (0.63)	0.51 (0.63)	0.28 (0.58)
	HW – after child	**0.79**** (0.36)	0.53 (0.31)	0.73 (0.53)	0.86* (0.48)
	Num wsh child	**0.64*** (0.31)	**1.49***** (0.49)	-0.74 (0.49)	-0.55 (0.41)
	Soap present	-0.07 (0.84)	0.25 (1.20)	-0.66 (1.16)	-0.85 (1.10)
	Soap child	0.51 (0.43)	0.23 (0.62)	0.43 (0.62)	0.38 (0.57)
Demographic Controls	**Eat own produce**	-0.29 (0.61)	0.39 (0.86)	-0.33 (0.97)	-0.77 (0.80)
	Number meals	0.07 (0.27)	-0.07 (0.38)	0.02 (0.45)	0.23 (0.35)
	Age	-0.06 (0.06)	-0.01 (0.07)	-0.31 (0.37)	**-0.16***** (0.07)
	SES	**-0.42*** (0.22)	-0.20 (0.32)	1.29 (2.62)	-0.28 (0.29)
	R-square	0.23	0.24	0.32	0.35
	n	118	123	67	123

The regressions were repeated utilizing the continuous irrigation water quality, as well as exposure group allocation, however no significant correlations were found. Additionally, the sample was stratified according to age group, yet none of the regressions produced significant correlations with the nutrition indicators. It can therefore be concluded that the null hypothesis is correct and thus exposure to unsafe irrigation water does not directly impact the nutritional status of children.

4.4.6 Resumé

The WHO has set cut-off points to assess the public health significance of malnutrition in a given country or community. This allows targeted interventions in areas that suffer the greatest burden and aid in the prioritization of communities to be targeted. The prevalence levels of the sample population in this study are worryingly high, suggesting very high prevalence of acute and chronic undernourishment, thus indicating a critical public health significance level. Slightly higher prevalence was observed in the control group; however, both exposure and control lie within the same public health significance level. The mean z-scores reveal that the normal distribution is shifted downwards by about one standard deviation, thus indicating that average children are already mildly undernourished. According to the WHO, even mild undernourishment is associated with increased mortality risk (WHO, 2010), therefore suggesting increased susceptibility to disease among the majority of the child sample population.

The adverse effect of exposure to unsafe irrigation water on the incidence of disease is demonstrated in section 4.3. The correlation was also confirmed in the child population, although young children do not work on the farm and therefore do not come into direct contact with irrigation water. It can therefore be confirmed that pathogens are transferred from the work to the home environment, thus exposing all household members to irrigation water. As a two-way causality between malnutrition and incidence of diarrhea is assumed, it is hypothesized that children from exposed households show higher prevalence of malnutrition. This hypothesis was, however, immediately rejected, as the control group showed slightly higher prevalence. Although the odds ratios indicate lower odds of malnutrition among the exposed population, the difference was not significant.

Even when controlling for potentially confounding factors, no significant correlation between exposure and malnutrition could be established thus leading to the acceptance of the null hypothesis indicating that exposure to unsafe irrigation does not directly affect child nutritional status. Consequently, it can be assumed that malnutrition is balanced between the groups, thus having no influence on the estimated treatment effect of exposure to unsafe irrigation water.

As the hypothesis was rejected, the assumption that malnutrition prevalence and disease incidence of the child population are correlated is questioned. The incidence rate of children aged under five signifies higher incidence among malnourished children, while malnourished children between the ages five and twelve show slightly lower incidence. However, none of the incidence rate ratios produced significant results. The regression analysis revealed highly significant correlations between various control variables and the incidence of disease, thus suggesting that confounding effects are responsible for the insignificant incidence rate ratios. The stunting and wasting nutritional indicators produced significant correlations with the incidence of disease in the entire child population, thus leading to the rejection of the null hypothesis. Surprisingly, the underweight indicator showed a negative correlation, suggesting lower diarrhea incidence among underweight children; however, the correlation did not reach significance. The calculation of the average treatment effect confirmed the direction of the association. It is assumed that children suffering from acute undernourishment have lower stool output, which may lead to lower reporting of diarrhea. Nonetheless, the two remaining nutrition indicators clearly show the adverse effect of malnutrition on the incidence of disease. It appears that the wasting indicator, reflecting weight-for-height, robustly indicates malnutrition across both age groups. The hypothesis that malnutrition is associated with higher disease incidence is therefore accepted.

Additionally, child open defecation was identified as a predictor of malnutrition, with children practicing open defecation, regardless of the availability of sanitation facilities, showing higher prevalence. The number of times parents wash their children's hands is also highly correlated to the prevalence of malnutrition. It thus appears that the place of defecation and frequency of hand washing are important predictors of the nutritional status in children. Especially young children should be assisted during defecation to ensure feces are disposed safely and hand hygiene is practiced.

5 Discussion

The sub-discipline 'medical geography' has transformed over the previous decades, adopting a more positive perspective of health by moving away from focusing on the distribution of disease towards understanding 'place' as a determinant of health (Kearns & Moon, 2002, Parr, 2002, Atkinson et al., 2015, Rosenberg, 2015). In line with the school of 'new public health', health is defined as more than the mere absence of disease, but encompasses mental health and well-being thus moving away from the dichotomous definition of health and disease towards a more continual scale of health status. Traditionally 'medical geography' has been concerned with the spatial distribution of disease and the identification of environmental determinants of disease (Atkinson et al., 2015). Over the past two decades, medical geographers have increasingly shifted the object of study towards well-being, inequity and social justice highlighting the processes and interrelations between place, health and healthcare (ibid). This shift has sparked academic discussion about the sub-discipline leading to its transformation into 'health geography'.

Despite the now widespread acceptance of the sub-discipline's new name (health geography or geographies of health), the academic debate about the direction of the sub-discipline persists. 'Heath geography' moves away from the medical frameworks and biomedical categorizations and focuses primarily on 'healthy' spatialities (Parr, 2002). The role of places and landscapes in shaping well-being is a particular focus of health geography, e.g. the concept of therapeutic landscapes (see Gebhard & Kistemann, 2016). Notably health geographers increasingly utilize qualitative research methods (Giesbrecht et al., 2014), focusing on the perceptions towards a particular place and the subjective feelings about the place and its components. Nonetheless, the more traditional medical geography approaches still form an important component of the sub-discipline. In developed countries, attention is predominantly given to non-communicable or chronic diseases, with obesity and the ageing of society forming popular themes (Rosenberg, 2015). In the developing country context, health inequalities and infectious diseases are chiefly studied. Generally, among disease-oriented health geography a few methodological approaches can be differentiated. The more traditional approaches of mapping distribution and spread of disease, public health approaches that focus on the social and political determinants of health, demographic approaches where the ageing society forms the central theme, and epidemiological approaches linking exposure sources to specific disease outcomes (Kwan, 2012).

Health geography inherently calls for interdisciplinarity, as the interactions between health, disease and their determinants are "far too complex to be fully deciphered by any single perspective" (Kwan, 2012:891). Despite the sub-discipline's interdisciplinary tradition and continued promotion of transdisciplinary approaches, an ongoing trend of subdividing the sub-discipline has been observed (Kearns & Moon, 2002, Kwan, 2012, Atkinson et al., 2015, Rosenberg, 2015). Although such categorizations may be useful to track the developments and research trends of the sub-discipline, as demonstrated by (Giesbrecht et al., 2014), the divisions hinder the evolution of a unified integrative framework of health geography. 'Place' has emerged as a health geography framework (Kearns & Moon, 2002), however, predominantly among qualitative health geographers and those concerned with well-being, therapeutic landscapes and sociocultural interactions. On the other side, disease-oriented health geographers still adhere to biomedical frameworks drawing on the medical, public health and epidemiological disciplines.

Health geography should avoid segregating itself into quantitative and qualitative or health and disease. Instead, an integrated interdisciplinary perspective should be adopted where social, political, economic and ecological systems are studied in regard to 'place shaping', as well as the microbiological, psychological and physiological processes causing health effects in a particular place. Places are shaped by a multitude of factors including its geographic, topographic, geological and hydrological features as well as the political, social, cultural and economic interactions. The holistic perspective of health, as adopted by health geography, should not induce a shift from disease prevention to health promotion but instead foster synergy between the health and disease perspectives.

Certainly, epidemiological and biomedical frameworks are necessary to understand the complex processes involved in the spread of disease and pathology. Similarly, the analysis of social, cultural and political interactions with place and health require the adaptation of sociological, political and anthropological frameworks, while economic frameworks are important in the study of healthcare provision and cost-effectiveness of interventions. Health geography's broad range of topics demands the adaptation of various frameworks and consequently encompasses a wide variety of methodological approaches, often interdisciplinary in nature. Nonetheless, a unified health geography framework could benefit the sub-discipline through the development of a more cohesive health geography identity. However, such a framework should not restrict the scope or undermine the interdisciplinary focus and the methodological diversity of health geography, but instead provide an overarching framework connecting the various themes of the sub-discipline. The 'place' framework could serve as such, as it is broad enough to allow thematic expansion of the sub-discipline, while also providing a common framing, putting place and place shaping at the heart of health geography (Figure 3).

Underlying the unified framework is the common understanding among health geographers that "place matters to health" (Andrews et al., 2012:1925). On the one hand, complex interactions between environmental, social, cultural, political and economic systems influence 'place shaping', thus influencing the physical features and socioeconomic characteristics of the place. On the other hand, these unique features and characteristics jointly shape the health status and disease risks of the inhabitants of the place. Health geography is thus the study of the complex interactions shaping 'place' and the influence of its interwoven characteristics and features on health. The scale of place can be individually defined and can be as large as cities, countries or even continents or as small as a community or a particular park, square or street. Following the holistic definition of health, it can be expected that some features of a place exert health benefits while others produce health risks, and that the aggregate health effects may differ between sub-groups of the place's inhabitants. Consequently, health geographic research identifies the underlying determinants of health in a particular place, aiming to minimize places that induce significant health risks while maximizing the health benefits of places. Therefore, policy-relevant and action-oriented health geography research needs to be promoted, as health geography can inform decision making in land usage, urban planning and landscape design to create a healthier society through building healthier places.

Urban agriculture is common in many metropolitan regions throughout the world and has been hailed as a strategy to tackle the challenges of poverty and food security. In the context of health geography, urban agriculture utilizes open spaces in the city and transforms these into places of food production. Urban agriculture shapes the place, not only through the physical alterations of the space (through field preparation, crop selection and the introduction of irrigation water) but also via psychological processes of place identity and ownership. However, urban agricultural places are also shaped by a multitude of environmental, economic, political, and social forces that are largely out of the control of the individual urban farmer. Usually the interactions between these forces determine the health effect of urban agriculture in a particular place. For example, the political attitude towards urban agriculture influences the availability of agricultural extension services, land-use rights and planned irrigation systems, whilst socio-economic forces may influence access to such services and the relative power of urban farmers to influence decision making.

Although many adverse health effects existing in agricultural urban places can be mitigated by an individual farmer's behavior, the underlying causes of water, air and soil contamination are connected with industrial processes, economic considerations, infrastructure capacity, urban planning and environmental protection standards. To urban authorities it may thus appear that urban agriculture poses significant health risks and that banning the practice would be the most sensible solution, as regulating industry and introducing environmental standards may adversely impact economic growth and development in the short term. However, in light of population growth, increasing pressure is placed upon already scarce resources. Larger populations have higher food requirements, thus relying on the agricultural sector to increase efficiency of food production to ensure food security. Irrigation is a key instrument for increasing food production, as it allows cultivation in more than one season and decreases reliance on variable rain patterns. Consequently, agriculture is the largest water user globally. As fresh water resources are, however, increasingly scarce the need to reuse water is urgent.

The growing urban agglomerations produce a continuous stream of wastewater, which causes challenges for the authorities of the urban centers of emerging economies. As a result, places in the city become hazardous through contaminated waterways, and inadequate disposal of waste and industrial emissions, which have negative impacts on the quality of life and health status of the inhabitants. In parallel, rapid urbanization causes not only densification of the agglomeration but also its spatial expansion, resulting in the encroachment into agricultural areas. In consequence, increasing food demands depend on increasingly scarce land and water resources. Banning urban agriculture therefore undermines the sustainability of food security in the metropolis. It is thus inevitable that as urbanization progresses, the extent of farming activities undertaken in or around urban areas will increase. The concept of urban agriculture is a strategy to formalize agriculture in metropolitan regions to ensure the planned recycling of the urban waste stream while minimizing the associated health hazards. Health geography can make important contributions to the development of urban agriculture strategies through the study of place and the processes shaping place essentially developing places where the health risks of urban agricultural activities are minimized to allow the benefits to be fully realized.

In the study area Ahmedabad, however, urban agriculture is undertaken unplanned, in fact the existence of farming activities was denied by the authorities. At the beginning of the study, the farmers from the wastewater area were hesitant to join as farming is prohibited in the area. As a result, key advantages conceptualized for urban agriculture are not realized in Ahmedabad. Utilization of the urban waste stream as inputs for production reduces the need to apply artificial fertilizers due to the high nutrient content of wastewater and organic waste. Yet in Ahmedabad, the vast majority of farmers utilize chemical fertilizers, highlighting the lacking awareness of the nutrient properties of their irrigation water. This is likely to cause over-fertilization, which may adversely affect the environment in the long term. Additionally, the reliance on diluted wastewater for irrigation, usually not known by the farmers, is widespread and practiced unplanned and unregulated. As a result, the disadvantages of urban agriculture in form of disease risks are manifested in Ahmedabad.

The presence of sewage outflow valves along the west bank of the River Sabarmati flowing through the city was observed during sample collection and forms a key characteristic shaping place in the area. As suggested in the literature, large volumes of untreated sewage are released into the surface waterways on a daily basis (UNESCO, 2003). Analysis of the irrigation water samples collected in this study confirms the suspected high degree of surface water contamination. As surface water forms the primary source of irrigation water in Ahmedabad (Palrecha et al., 2012), large proportions of the farming population are exposed to diluted wastewater that is not suitable for irrigation according to the international irrigation water standard. The full extent of surface water contamination and the consequent use of unsafe irrigation water in Ahmedabad was not assessed in this study. However, given the measured surface water contamination, it can be assumed that downstream farming communities are also exposed to diluted wastewater.

Introducing the concept of urban agriculture to the AMC appears essential given the extent and unplanned nature of wastewater irrigation. Urban agriculture as a concept forms a framework for policy interventions essentially addressing the challenges of agriculture in an urbanization world. Also, rural farmers applying traditional agricultural methods are increasingly affected by the challenges of urban agriculture, as they rely on surface water that may be contaminated by upstream urban areas. Furthermore, many rural farmers become peri-urban farmers as the cities grow and new urban centers emerge. Urban agriculture calls for the planned usage of the urban waste stream, thus requiring its integration into the municipal waste management strategy with an underlying set of regulations protecting human and environmental health without undermining the livelihoods of urban farmers. Particularly in the short term, regulating crop selection can form part of such strategy. Cultivation of fruit trees, energy or ornamental crops, as well as crops that do not grow in close proximity to the ground can reduce exposure and the risk of crop contamination. In addition, promoting simple on-farm treatment systems and monitoring their maintenance and effectiveness can be a decentralized solution to sewage treatment, reducing the discharge of untreated wastewater into waterways while simultaneously meeting irrigation and potentially even fertilization requirements. In the context of Ahmedabad, the full advantages of urban agriculture are not realized, whilst the negative effects manifest. Building awareness of the health risks among the farmers along with policies formalizing and regulating urban agriculture are the first steps needed to capitalize on the challenge of treatment capacity and wastewater discharge.

The F-diagram depicts 'access to sanitation' as the most important primary barrier highlighting that feces are transferred via multiple routes in the absence of sanitation (Wagner & Lanoix, 1958; Curtis et al., 2000). The element 'fields' is the closest reference to wastewater irrigation, indicating a possible transfer of pathogens from field to food to mouth. The findings of this study, however, emphasize a stronger interconnection between irrigation water quality and the WASH variables. In the F-diagram, 'sanitation' is simply conceived as the primary barrier. However, sanitation is essentially a series of barriers, all of which can be potentially compromised leading to the discharge of fecal pathogens. (Prüss et al., 2002) highlighted the adverse effects of poorly functioning sanitation pointing out potential ground- and surface water contamination. The results of the present study suggest a systematic failure of the primary barrier on the municipal level, leading to the reintroduction of fecal pathogens into the community through irrigation water. The adverse effects are potentially compounded by failure of primary barriers on the community and household level. The results confirm the initial conceptual framework, hypothesizing that irrigation water quality operates parallel to open defecation in disease transmission, both affecting drinking water quality, cleanliness of hands and surfaces and ultimately incidence of disease. Irrigation water is therefore an integral component of the WASH nexus.

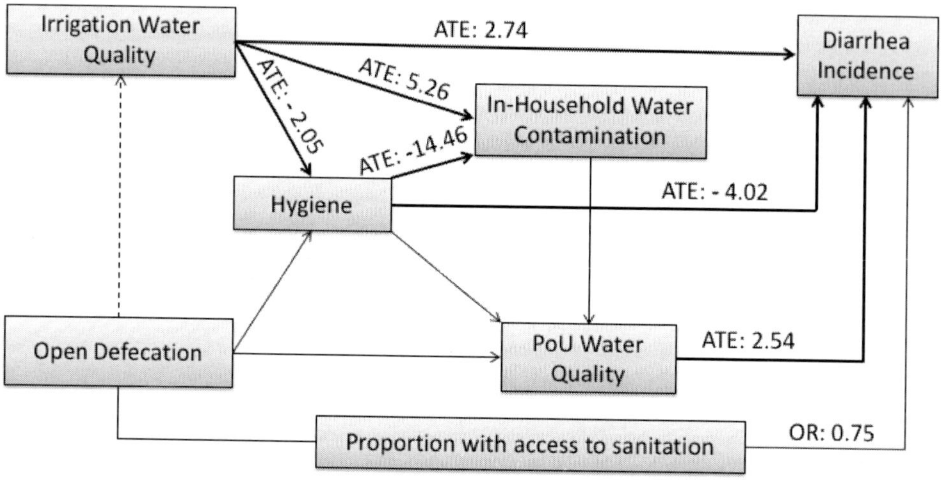

Figure 37: Impact of irrigation water quality on WASH variables and incidence of diarrhea. ATE = Average Treatment Effect; OR = Odds Ratio

The primary hypothesis of this research that irrigation water quality has direct adverse impacts on the incidence of diarrhea is confirmed. It is demonstrated that the adverse health effect is not limited to individuals working on the farm, but extends to the entire household. Even children under five are significantly affected by irrigation water quality despite their not coming into direct contact with the water. The data therefore strongly suggests a transfer of pathogens from the farm to the home environment. This is further supported by the direct association between irrigation water quality and in-household water contamination, which also illustrates the interconnection of irrigation water in the WASH nexus. In the urban agriculture literature, the health risks are divided into occupational (or farmer) and consumer risks (Mougeot, 2000), where occupational risks refer to chemical, biological, psycho-social and physical risks induced by agricultural work, while the consumer risks involve the chemical and biological risks of consuming urban produce (Lee-Smith & Prain, 2006). The results of this study, however, indicate an additional risk type, namely the community risk. It is demonstrated that wastewater irrigation adversely affects the entire household and not just the individuals engaged in agricultural work. This transfer of pathogens from the farm to the community and household environment leads to significant health risks that are often neglected in urban agriculture assessments. Emphasizing the community health risks of urban agriculture illustrates the indirect effects induced by pathogen transfer, which leads to cross-contamination, in-household water contamination and secondary infections. It is therefore necessary to extend the occupational and consumer risks by community risks, as individuals not engaged in urban agriculture still suffer from additional exposure due to the transfer of pathogens.

The secondary research question could not be completely answered due to the high colinearity between the factors, i.e. average treatment effects could not be calculated for all WASH factors. Figure 37 illustrates the key associations found in the study, where thick lines represent average treatment effects and thinner lines indicate significant correlations. The dotted line between open defecation and irrigation water quality was not assessed but is rather a product of theoretical considerations. The results demonstrate that drinking water and irrigation water quality have similar ATEs, thus partly confirming the hypothesis. The ATE of access to sanitation could not be calculated, but the data consistently indicates an adverse health effect among households with access to sanitation. Only when the proportion of the community with access to sanitation is considered do the preventive effects manifest. In consequence, the effect size of open defecation and irrigation water quality could not be compared. Nonetheless, both influence the level of fecal exposure and the degree of cross-contamination, leading to the acceptance of the hypothesis that the impact of unsafe irrigation water is at par with the established WASH factors. Moreover, the direct effects of irrigation water quality on both hygiene and in-household water contamination suggest further indirect effects of irrigation water quality on the incidence of disease. It is therefore suspected that the adverse effect of exposure to unsafe irrigation water is underestimated.

Sanitation is considered one of the most important mechanisms in the fight against diarrheal disease, forming the primary barrier to disease transmission (Curtis et al., 2000). The available evidence, as aggregated in several systematic reviews (see Clasen et al. (2010); Waddington et al. (2009) or Fewtrell et al., (2005) for example) consistently found protective effects of access to sanitation in the range of 20–40%. It should be noted, however, that the studies included in these systematic reviews are primarily intervention studies, comparing communities receiving improved sanitation with a non-intervention group. The data from this research is on the household level and demonstrates that households with access to sanitation do not experience the expected preventive effect, but on the contrary appear to exhibit additional health risks. The health benefits only manifest when considering the community level sanitation coverage, illustrating that the proportion of the community with access to sanitation is correlated to the preventive effect experienced by individual households. This finding underscores the need to achieve full sanitation coverage as formulated in the SDG goal 6: to achieve full sanitation coverage by 2030 thus ending open defecation (WHO, 2015). It should also be noted that mere access to sanitation does not induce health benefits but that adequate use and maintenance are a prerequisite.

The vast majority of the sample population utilized improved drinking water sources according to the JMP definition. Nonetheless, the microbiological analysis demonstrates alarmingly high levels of water contamination, with 50–80% of the sample population's PoS water not adhering to the international water standard. Despite the call of caution that "technology indicators do not provide information about the quality of the water provided or about its use" (UNICEF/WHO, 2000:4), the effectiveness of source-based improvements is questioned. A systematic review of Clasen et al. (2015) could not confirm that source-based improvements consistently reduce diarrheal incidence. The high drinking water contamination found among the 'improved' drinking water sources in this study clearly illustrates that source-based improvements do not necessarily lead to improved water quality. In consequence, drinking water treatment needs to be a central component of diarrhea prevention strategies.

Contributing to the debate about the relative importance of PoU and PoS water quality, in-household water contamination is identified as a central intersect in the WASH nexus affected by irrigation water quality, access to sanitation and hygiene, while inevitably impacting PoU water quality and in consequence diarrhea incidence. In the literature, it is highlighted that PoU water treatment is more effective in reducing diarrheal incidence than PoS treatment (Fewtrell et al.,

2005, Clasen et al., 2015). The results of this study show widespread in-household water contamination among the entire sample population emphasizing the relative importance of PoU water quality over PoS drinking water quality, as previously safe PoS water may be rendered unsafe at the PoU. Water withdrawal from the storage vessel is identified as the key point of in-household water contamination. Water is predominantly withdrawn with a cup, thus contact between hands and water is likely. Personal hygiene and hand hygiene in particular therefore form the key barrier to in-household water contamination. In line with Fewtrell et al. (2005) and Clasen et al. (2015), the high effectiveness of PoU water treatment is demonstrated, highlighting significant reductions of in-household water contamination among households using reverse-osmosis water filters. However, when comparing the average treatment effects of personal hygiene (-14.73) and PoU water treatment (-10.20), the relative importance of personal hygiene is highlighted. In the literature, PoU water treatment is portrayed as the most effective mechanism for diarrhea prevention, however usually in relation to PoS treatment. The results of this study illustrate that hygiene behavior has the largest effect size, thus leading to the conclusion that hygiene is the most important preventive instrument, which confirms the recommendations of Esrey et al. (1991), Fewtrell et al. (2005) and Waddington et al. (2009) to combine hardware interventions (construction of sanitation and water treatment systems) with software interventions (hygiene promotion).

As suggested in the literature, the nutritional status of children is directly associated with the incidence of diarrhea (Dewey & Mayers, 2011) leading to the hypothesis that exposure to unsafe irrigation water is linked to lower nutritional status due to the high incidence of disease among the exposed population. Higher prevalence of malnutrition was, however, observed in the control group. Ultimately, the null hypothesis is accepted, as the difference in nutritional status between the groups is not statistically significant leading to the conclusion that the nutritional status is balanced between the groups, thus not affecting the effect size of irrigation water quality on the incidence of disease.

The results of this research demonstrate that irrigation water quality directly impacts the incidence of disease. Fecal pathogens are transferred from irrigation water via hands, clothes and food into the home environment. The adverse health effects of wastewater use are consequently not limited to individuals working on the field but impact the entire household. The results also show that irrigation water quality is interwoven into the WASH nexus, both affected by and affecting the WASH variables. Although only the adverse effect of irrigation water quality on hygiene outcomes was assessed in this study, it is suspected that hygiene also serves as a mediator for the health impact of irrigation water quality. The reliance on unsafe irrigation water introduces fecal pathogens into the environment, leading to their spread along the pathways depicted in the F-diagram. Considering the widespread discharge of untreated sewage and its often-unknowing use for irrigation renders irrigated urban agriculture a key source of fecal contamination. It is therefore indicated that the water, sanitation and hygiene nexus should be expanded by agriculture in the combat against infectious diseases, essentially putting the 'A' in WASH.

Limitations

The key shortcoming of this study lies in the sampling design. As population registers of the individual research areas were unavailable, a true random sampling technique could not be employed. Given the low information initially available, snowball sampling was applied. Nonetheless, the resulting non-random sample provides a representative sample of the research areas, as the entire spatial extent of the village was covered and clustering of households was avoided. However, the individual research areas were selected purposively, thus the representative strength can be questioned. It can be assumed that certain characteristics, such as the degree of surface water contamination, are similar in other agricultural communities in Ahmedabad, but generalizing the results on the metropolitan level should be viewed with caution. Although the sample size is adequately large in the individual villages, it is small in relation to the population of Ahmedabad.

Measuring bias forms another limitation of this research, particularly in regard to disease incidence and hygiene. As the prospective health diary approach had to be abandoned, a certain degree of recall bias can be expected. The long follow-up period also gives rise to concerns regarding reporting fatigue and sensitization. The data collectors also introduced bias, as their personal relationship with the participants influenced their willingness to share sensitive information. The gender of the data collectors may also influence their relationship, and female data collectors were more frequently engaged with female participants while male collectors had better relations with the males of the households. However, in various training sessions, the data collectors were sensitized to these dynamics and were instructed to counteract such favorization.

Similarly, measuring hygiene is prone to reporting bias. Particularly the hand washing variables produced counterintuitive results during the analysis, indicating the over- or miss-reporting of hand hygiene practice. To offset the potential reporting bias, the hygiene spot-check method was additionally applied. While the focus on hygiene outcomes certainly avoided reporting bias, it introduced an observer bias. The subjective interpretations of the data collectors form the underlying cause of the bias. The individual data collectors may have had different interpretations about what constitutes dirty hands or clothes. In an attempt to limit this bias, extensive training was provided to the data collectors aiming to standardize the procedure and establish a common understanding of the individual hygiene factors.

References

Ahs, J. W., Tao, W., Löfgren, J. & Forsberg, B. C. (2010). Diarrheal Diseases in Low- and Middle-Income Countries: Incidence, Prevention and Management. *The Open Infectious Disease Journal*, 4, 113-124.

Amahmid, O., Asmama, S. & Bouhoum, K. (1999). The effect of waste water reuse in irrigation on the contamination level of food crops by Giardia cysts and Ascaris eggs. *Int J Food Microbiol*, 49, 19-26.

AMC (2006). City Development Plan Ahmedabad 2006 - 2012. Ahmedabad Municipal Corporation.

American Public Health Association (2008). *Control of communicable diseases manual: an official report of the American Public Health Association*. Washington, D.C.: American Public Health Association.

Andrews, G. J., Hall, E., Evans, B. & Colls, R. (2012). Moving beyond walkability: On the potential of health geography. *Social Science & Medicine*, 75, 1925-1932.

Athayde Júnior, G. B., Mara, D. D., Pearson, H. W. & Silba, S. A. (2000). Faecal coliform die-off in wastewater storage and treatment reservoirs. *Water Science & Technology*, 42, 139-147.

Atkinson, S., Evans, B., Woods, A. & Kearns, R. (2015). The medical and health in a critical medical humanities. *Journal of medical humanities*, 36, 71-81.

Baron, S. (1996). *Medical Microbiology 4th Edition*. Galveston: University of Texas.

Bartram, J. & Cairncross, S. (2010). Hygiene, Sanitation, and Water: Forgotten Foundations of Health. *PLoS Medicine*, 7, e1000367.

Bartram, J. & Hunter, P. (2015). Bradley Classification of disease transmission routes for water-related hazards. In Bartram, J., with Baum, R., Coclanis, P.A., Gute, D.M., Kay, D., McFadyen, S., Pond, K., Robertson, W. & Rouse, M.J. (eds.) Routledge Handbook of Water and Health, London: Routledge.

Bellows, A. C., Brown, K. & Smit, J. (2004). Health Benefits of Urban Agriculture. *Community Food Security Coalition*.

Beuchat, L. R. (1998). *Surface decontamination of fruits and vegetables eaten raw : a review*. Geneva: World Health Organization.

Bhatt, M. R. (2003). *The case of Ahmedabad, India, Understanding Slums – Case Studies for the Global Report of 2003*, London: University College London.

Bhutta, Z. A., Bird, S. M., Black, R. E., Brown, K. H., Gardner, J. M., Hidayat, A., Khatun, F., Martorell, R., Ninh, N. X., Penny, M. E., Rosado, J. L., Roy, S. K., Ruel, M., Sazawal, S. & Shankar, A. (2000). Therapeutic effects of oral zinc in acute and persistent diarrhea in children in developing countries: pooled analysis of randomized controlled trials. *Am J Clin Nutr*, 72, 1516-1522.

Biran, A., Rabie, T., Schmidt, W., Juvekar, S., Hirve, S. & Curtis, V. (2008). Comparing the performance of indicators of hand-washing practices in rural Indian households. *Trop Med Int Health*, 13, 278-85.

Birmingham, M. E., Lee, L. A., Ntakibirora, M., Bizimana, F. & Deming, M. S. (1997). A household survey of dysentery in Burundi: implications for the current pandemic in sub-Saharan Africa. *Bulletin of the World Health Organization*, 75, 45-53.

Bitton, G. (2005). *Microbial Indicators of Fecal Contamination: Application to Microbial Source Tracking*, Florida Stormwater Association.

Black, R. E. (1984). Diarrheal Diseases and Child Morbidity and Mortality. *Population and Development Review*, 10, 141-161.

Black, R. E., Morris, S. S. & Bryce, J. (2003). Where and why are 10 million children dying every year? *The Lancet*, 361, 2226-2234.

Bleker, J. (2014). Medizinische Geographie. in *Enzyklopädie der Neuzeit Online*, Brill. http://referenceworks.brillonline.com/entries/enzyklopaedie-der-neuzeit/medizinische-geographie-a2677000, on: 17 May 2015.

Boot, M. T. & Cairncross, S. (1993). *Actions speak : the study of hygiene behaviour in water and sanitation projects*. The Hague: International Research Centre (IRC).

Brown, K. H. & Jameton, A. L. (2000). Public health implications or urban agriculture. *J Public Health Policy*, 21, 20-39.

Bryan, F. L. (1974). *Wastewater Use in the Production of Food and Fiber -- Proceedings*, Oklahoma City: United States Enviornmental Protection Agency.

Buchanan, R. L., Smith, J. L. & Long, W. (2000). Microbial risk assessment: dose-response relations and risk characterization. *Int J Food Microbiol*, 58, 159-72.

Byass, P. & Hanlon, P. W. (1994). Daily morbidity records: recall and reliability. *Int J Epidemiol*, 23, 757-63.

Cairncross, S. (1987). *Developing World Water Vol. II*, London: Grosvenor Press.

Cairncross, S. & Cliff, J. L. (1987). Water use and health in Mueda, Mozambique. *Transactions of the Royal Society of Tropical Medicine and Hygiene*, 81, 51-54.

Cairncross, S. & Feachem, R. (1993). *Environmental health engineering in the tropics: an introductory text (2nd edition)*. Chichester: John Wiley & Sons.

Cairncross, S. & Shordt, K. (2004). It does last! Some findings from a multi-country study of hygiene sustainability. *Waterlines*, 22, 4-7.

Cairncross, S., Shordt, K., Zacharia, S. & Govindan, B. K. (2005). What causes sustainable changes in hygiene behaviour? A cross-sectional study from Kerala, India. *Social Science & Medicine*, 61, 2212-2220.

Chang, A. C., Pan, G., Page, A. L. & Asano, T. (2002). *Developing Human Health-related Chemical Guidelines for Reclaimed Waster and Sewage Sludge Applications in Agriculture*, Geneva: World Health Organization.

Chatterjee, A., Mahalanabis, D., Jalan, K. N., Maitra, T. K., Agarwal, S. K., Dutta, B., Khatua, S. P. & Bagchi, D. K. (1978). Oral rehydration in infantile diarrhoea. Controlled trial of a low sodium glucose electrolyte solution. *Archives of Disease in Childhood*, 53, 284-289.

Chen, L. C. & Scrimshaw, N. S. (1983). *Diarrhea and Malnutrition. Interactions, Mechanisms, and Interventions*. New York: Plenum Press.

Clasen, T. F., Alexander, K. T., Sinclair, D., Boisson, S., Peletz, R., Chang, H. H., Majorin, F. & Cairncross, S. (2015). Interventions to improve water quality for preventing diarrhoea. *Cochrane Database of Systematic Reviews*, 10.

Clasen, T. F., Bostoen, K., Schmidt, W.-P., Boisson, S., Fung, I. C. H., Jenkins, M. W., Scott, B., Sugden, S. & Cairncross, S. (2010). Interventions to improve disposal of human excreta for preventing diarrhoea. *Cochrane Database of Systematic Reviews*, 6.

Clay, E. (2002). *Food Security: Concepts and Measurement*, Rome: Food and Agriculture Organization of the United Nations.

Costa-Pierce, B. A., Desbonnet, A., Edwards, P. & Baker, D. (2005). *Urban Aquaculture*. Cambridge: CABI Publishing.

Curran, P. F. (1960). Na, Cl, and Water Transport by Rat Ileum in Vitro. *The Journal of General Physiology*, 43, 1137-1148.

Curtis, T. P., Mara, D. D. & Silva, S. A. (1992). Influence of pH, Oxygen, and Humic Substances on Ability of Sunlight To Damage Fecal Coliforms in Waste Stabilization Pond Water. *Applied and Environmental Microbiology*, 58, 1335-1343.

Curtis, V. & Cairncross, S. (2003). Effect of washing hands with soap on diarrhoea risk in the community: a systematic review. *The Lancet Infectious Diseases*, 3, 275-281.

Curtis, V., Cairncross, S. & Yonli, R. (2000). Review: Domestic hygiene and diarrhoea – pinpointing the problem. *Tropical Medicine & International Health*, 5, 22-32.

Curtis, V., Cousens, S., Mertens, T., Traore, E., Kanki, B. & Diallo, I. (1993). Structured observations of hygiene behaviours in Burkina Faso: validity, variability, and utility. *Bulletin of the World Health Organization*, 71, 23-32.

Curtis, V., Kanki, B., Cousens, S., Diallo, I., Kpozehouen, A., Sangaré, M. & Nikiema, M. (2001). Evidence of behaviour change following a hygiene promotion programme in Burkina Faso. *Bulletin of the World Health Organization*, 79, 518-527.

Curtis, V., Schmidt, W., Luby, S., Florez, R., Toure, O. & Biran, A. (2011). Hygiene: new hopes, new horizons. *Lancet Infect Dis*, 11, 312-21.

Dangour, A. D., Watson, L., Cumming, O., Boisson, S., Che, Y., Velleman, Y., Cavill, S., Allen, E. & Uauy, R. (2013). Interventions to improve water quality and supply, sanitation and hygiene practices, and their effects on the nutritional status of children. *Cochrane Database of Systematic Reviews*, 8.

De Zeeuw, H., Van Veenhuizen, R. & Dubbeling, M. (2011). The role of urban agriculture in building resilient cities in developing countries. *The Journal of Agricultural Science*, 149, 153-163.

Dewey, K. G. & Mayers, D. R. (2011). Early child growth: how do nutrition and infection interact? *Maternal & Child Nutrition*, 7, 129-142.

Drechsel, P. & Evans, A. E. V. (2010). Wastewater use in irrigated agriculture. *Irrigation and Drainage Systems*, 24, 1-3.

Drechsel, P., Scott, C. A., Raschid Sally, L., Redwood, M. & Bahri, A. (2010). *Wastewater irrigation and health: assessing and mitigating risk in low-income countries*. London: International Water Management Institue (IWMI); Earthscan; International Development Research Centre (IDRC).

Duruibe, J., Ogwuegbu, M. O. C. & Egwurugwu, J. N. (2007). Heavy metal pollution and human biotoxic effects. *International Journal for Physical Sciences*, 2, 112-118.

Eisenhart, C. & Wilson, P. W. (1943). Statistical Methods and Control in Bacteriology. *Bacteriological Reviews*, 7, 57-137.

Ejemot-Nwadiaro, R. I., Ehiri, J. E., Arikpo, D., Meremikwu, M. M. & Critchley, J. A. (2015). Hand washing promotion for preventing diarrhoea. *Cochrane Database of Systematic Reviews*, 9.

Ejemot-Nwadiaro, R. I., Ehiri, J. E., Meremikwu, M. M. & Critchley, J. A. (2008). Hand washing for preventing diarrhoea. *Cochrane Database of Systematic Reviews*, 1.

Ensink, J. H. J., van der Hoek, W., Matsuno, Y., Munir, S. & Aslam, M. R. (2002). *Use of untreated wastewater in peri-urban agriculture in Pakistan: risks and opportunities*, International Water Management Institute Report 64.

EPA (2002). Method 1680: Fecal Coliforms in Biosolids by Multiple-Tube Fermentation Procedures. *U.S. Enviornmental Protection Agency*.

Esrey, S. A., Feachem, R. G. & Hughes, J. M. (1985). Interventions for the control of diarrhoeal diseases among young children: improving water supplies and excreta disposal facilities. *Bulletin of the World Health Organization*, 63, 757-772.

Esrey, S. A., Potash, J. B., Roberts, L. & Shiff, C. (1991). Effects of improved water supply and sanitation on ascariasis, diarrhoea, dracunculiasis, hookworm infection, schistosomiasis, and trachoma. *Bulletin of the World Health Organization*, 69, 609-621.

Evans, B., Bartram, J., Hunter, P., Williams, A. R., Geere, J. A., Majuru, B., Bates, L., Fisher, M., Overbo, A. & Schmidt, W. P. (2013). *Public health and social benefits of at-house water supplies*, Leeds: University of Leeds.

FAO (2003). *Trade Reforms and Food Security: Conceptualizing the linkages*, Rome: Food and Agriculture Organization of the United Nations.

FAO (2014). *Growing Greener Cities in Latin America and the Caribbean: An FAO report on urban and peri-urban agriculture in the region*, Rome: Food and Agriculture Organization of the United Nations.

Farthing, M. J. G. (1994). Oral rehydration therapy. *Pharmacology & Therapeutics*, 64, 477-492.

Feachem, R. (1978). *Water, health and development. An interdisciplinary evaluation*. London: Trimed Books Ltd.

Feachem, R. G., Bradley, D. J., Garelick, H. & Mara, D. D. (1983). *Sanitation and disease: health aspects of excreta and wastewater management*, New York: John Wiley & Sons.

Fewtrell, L. & Colford, J. M. J. (2004). *Water, sanitation and hygiene: interventions and diarrhoea: a systematic review and meta-analysis*, Washington DC: World Bank.

Fewtrell, L., Kaufmann, R. B., Kay, D., Enanoria, W., Haller, L. & Colford, J. M. (2005). Water, sanitation, and hygiene interventions to reduce diarrhoea in less developed countries: a systematic review and meta-analysis. *The Lancet Infectious Diseases*, 5, 42-52.

Fischer Walker, C. L., Perin, J., Aryee, M. J., Boschi-Pinto, C. & Black, R. E. (2012). Diarrhea incidence in low- and middle-income countries in 1990 and 2010: a systematic review. *BMC Public Health*, 12, 220-227.

Freeman, M. C., Stocks, M. E., Cumming, O., Jeandron, A., Higgins, J. P. T., Wolf, J., Prüss-Ustün, A., Bonjour, S., Hunter, P. R., Fewtrell, L. & Curtis, V. (2014). Systematic review: Hygiene and health: systematic review of handwashing practices worldwide and update of health effects. *Tropical Medicine & International Health*, 19, 906-916.

Fry, S., Cousins, B. & Olivola, K. (2002). *Health of Children Living in Urban Sums in Asia and the Near East: Review of Existing Literature and Data*, Washington, DC: U.S. Agency for International Development.

Gebhard, U. & Kistemann, T. (eds.) (2016). *Landschaft Identität und Gesundheit – Zum Konzept der Therapeutischen Landschaften*. Wiesbaden: Springer VS.

Gerba, C. P., Rose, J. B. & Haas, C. N. (1996). Sensitive populations: who is at the greatest risk? *Int J Food Microbiol*, 30, 113-23.

Giesbrecht, M., Cinnamon, J., Fritz, C. & Johnston, R. (2014). Themes in geographies of health and health care research: Reflections from the 2012

Canadian Association of Geographers annual meeting. *The Canadian Geographer / Le Géographe canadien*, 58, 160-167.

Gilman, R. H., Marquis, G. S., Ventura, G., Campos, M., Spira, W. & Diaz, F. (1993). Water cost and availability: key determinants of family hygiene in a Peruvian shantytown. *American Journal of Public Health*, 83, 1554-1558.

Gleick, P. H. (1996). Basic Water Requirements for Human Activities: Meeting Basic Needs. *Water International*, 21, 83-92.

GoI (2011). *Urban Agglomerations/Cities having population 1 lakh and above*, New Delhi: Goverment of India.

Grandjean, A. C. (2005). *Nutrients in Drinking Water*, Geneva: World Health Organization.

Guerrant, R. L., Van Gilder, T., Steiner, T. S., Thielman, N. M., Slutsker, L., Tauxe, R. V., Hennessy, T., Griffin, P. M., DuPont, H., Sack, R. B., Tarr, P., Neill, M., Nachamkin, I., Reller, L. B., Osterholm, M. T., Bennish, M. L. & Pickering, L. K. (2001). Practice guidelines for the management of infectious diarrhea. *Clinical Infectious Diseases*, 32, 331-51.

Gupta, M. R. (1993). Rural-urban migration, informal sector and development policies: a theoretical analysis. *J Dev Econ*, 41, 137-51.

Hach (2012). *Method 8368 Most Probable Number (MPN) Method*. Hach Company.

Hamilton, A. J., Stagnitti, F., Xiong, X., Kreidl, S. L., Benke, K. K. & Maher, P. (2007). Wastewater Irrigation: The State of Play. *Vadose Zone Journal*, 6, 823-840.

Hanjra, M. A., Blackwell, J., Carr, G., Zhang, F. & Jackson, T. M. (2012). Wastewater irrigation and environmental health: implications for water governance and public policy. *Int J Hyg Environ Health*, 215, 255-69.

Harris, P. A., Taylor, R., Thielke, R., Payne, J., Gonzalez, N. & Conde, J. G. (2009). Research electronic data capture (REDCap)--a metadata-driven methodology and workflow process for providing translational research informatics support. *J Biomed Inform*, 42, 377-81.

Herbst, S. (2006). *Water, sanitation, hygiene and diarrheal diseases in the Aral Sea area (Khorezm, Uzbekistan)*. Göttingen: Cuvilier Verlag.

Holliday, M. A. & Segar, W. E. (1957). The Maintenance need for Water in Parenteral Fluid Therapy. *Pediatrics*, 19, 823-832.

Holt-Giménez, E., Patel, R. & Shattuck, A. (2009). *Food rebellions! : crisis and the hunger for justice*. Cape Town: Pambazuka Press.

Hoque, B. A. & Briend, A. (1991). A comparison of local handwashing agents in Bangladesh. *Journal of Tropical Medicine and Hygiene*, 94, 61-64.

Hoque, B. A., Juncker, T., Sack, R. B., Ali, M. & Aziz, K. M. (1996). Sustainability of a water, sanitation and hygiene education project in rural Bangladesh: a 5-year follow-up. *Bulletin of the World Health Organization*, 74, 431-437.

Hosmer, D. W. & Lemeshow, S. (2000). *Applied Logistic Regression*. New York: John Wiley & Sons.

Howard, G. & Bartram, J. (2003). *Domestic Water Quantity, Service, Level and Health*. Geneva: World Health Organization.

Jamil, M., Zia, M. S. & Qasim, M. (2010). Contamination of Agro-Ecosystem and Human Health Hazards from Wastewater used for Irrigation. *Journal of the Chemical Society of Pakistan*, 32, 370-378.

Kawata, K. (1978). Water and other environmental interventions--the minimum investment concept. *American Journal of Clinical Nutrition*, 31, 2114-23.

Kearns, R. & Moon, G. (2002). From medical to health geography: novelty, place and theory after a decade of change. *Progress in Human Geography*, 26, 605-625.

Keraita, B., Konradsen, F. & Drechsel, P. (2010). *Wastewater Irrigation and Health: Assessing and mitigating risk in low-income countries*. London: Earthscan Publications Ltd (10).

Khandker, S. R., Koolwal, G. B. & Samad, H. A. (2009). *Handbook of Impact Evaluations - Quantitative Methods and Practices*. Washington, DC: The World Bank.

Korth, M., Stewart, R., Langer, L., Madinga, N., Rebelo Da Silva, N., Zaranyika, H., van Rooyen, C. & de Wet, T. (2014). What are the impacts of urban agriculture programs on food security in low and middle-income countries: a systematic review. *Environmental Evidence*, 3, 21.

Krones, E. & Högenauer, C. (2012). Diarrhea in the immunocompromised patient. *Gastroenterol Clin North Am*, 41, 677-701.

Kundu, S. & Roy, S. D. (2012). Urbanisation and De-Sanitation: A De-Compositional Analysis by Taking a Case Study of Few Indian Cities. *Procedia - Social and Behavioral Sciences*, 37, 427-436.

Kwan, M. (2012). Geographies of Health. *Annals of the Association of American Geographers*, 102, 891-892.

Laidlaw, M. A. S., Mielke, H. W., Filippelli, G. M., Johnson, D. L. & Gonzales, C. R. (2005). Seasonality and Children's Blood Lead Levels: Developing a Predictive Model Using Climatic Variables and Blood Lead Data from Indianapolis, Indiana, Syracuse, New York, and New Orleans, Louisiana (USA). *Environmental Health Perspectives*, 113, 793-800.

Lazzerini, M. & Ronfani, L. (2013). Oral zinc for treating diarrhoea in children. *Cochrane Database of Systematic Reviews*, 1.

Leclerc, H., Schwartzbrod, L. & Dei-Cas, E. (2002). Microbial agents associated with waterborne diseases. *Crit Rev Microbiol*, 28, 371-409.

Lee-Smith, D. & Prain, G. (2006). Understanding the links between agriculture and health. *International Food Policy Research Institute*, 2020 Vision Focus Brief, 13, 1-2.

Luby, S. P., Halder, A. K., Huda, T., Unicomb, L. & Johnston, R. B. (2011). The Effect of Handwashing at Recommended Times with Water Alone and With Soap on Child Diarrhea in Rural Bangladesh: An Observational Study. *PLoS Medicine*, 8, e1001052.

Luby, S. P., Halder, A. K., Tronchet, C., Akhter, S., Bhuiya, A. & Johnston, R. B. (2009). Household characteristics associated with handwashing with soap in rural Bangladesh. *Am J Trop Med Hyg*, 81, 882-7.

Mahadevia, D. (2002). Communal Space over Life Space: Sage of Increasing Vulnerability in Ahmedabad. *Economic and Political Weekly*, 37, 4850-4858.

Mara, D. D. (2004). *Domestic wastewater treatment in developing countries*. London: Earthscan Publications Ltd.

Mehta, M. & Metha, D. (1993). *Urbanisation in Developing Countries: Basic Services & Community Participation*. New Delhi: Institute of Social Sciences & Concept Publishing Company

Mims, C., Nash, A. & Stephen, J. (2000). *Mims' Pathogenesis of Infectious Diseases 5th Edition*. London: Academic Press.

Moe, C. L., Sobsey, M. D., Samsa, G. P. & Mesolo, V. (1991). Bacterial indicators of risk of diarrhoeal disease from drinking-water in the Philippines. *Bulletin of the World Health Organization*, 69, 305-317.

Mougeot, L. J. A. (2000). *Urban Agriculture: Definition, Presence, Potentials and Risks, and Policy Challenges*, La Habana, Cuba: International Development Research Centre (IDRC).

Müller, O. & Krawinkel, M. (2005). Malnutrition and health in developing countries. *Canadian Medical Association Journal*, 173, 279.

Munos, M. K., Walker, C. L. F. & Black, R. E. (2010). The effect of oral rehydration solution and recommended home fluids on diarrhoea mortality. *Int J Epidemiol*, 39, i75-i87.

Nabulo, G., Oryem-Origa, H., Nasinyama, G. W., Cole, D. C. & Diamond, M. (2008). *Healthy city harvests: Generating evidence to guide policy on urban agriculture*. Lima, Peru: CIP/Urban Harvest; Makerere University Press.

Palrecha, A., Kapoor, D. & Malladi, T. (2012). Wastewater Irrigation in Gujarat: An exploratory study. *International Water Managemnet Institute*, 30.

Parr, H. (2002). Medical geography: diagnosing the body in medical and health geography, 1999–2000. *Progress in Human Geography*, 26, 240-251.

Prüss, A., Kay, D., Fewtrell, L. & Bartram, J. (2002). Estimating the burden of disease from water, sanitation, and hygiene at a global level. *Environmental Health Perspectives*, 110, 537-542.

Quigley, J. M. (2008). Urbanization, Agglomeration, and Economic Development. *Berkeley Program on Housing and Urban Policy*, 19.

Ravallion, M. (2002). On the urbanization of poverty. *Journal of Development Economics*, 68, 435-442.

Ray, C. N. (1997). How Polluted Is Ahmedabad City? Environmental Risk Assessment. *Economic and Political Weekly*, 32, 2508-2510.

Richardson, A. (1994). The health diary: an examination of its use as a data collection method. *Journal of Advanced Nursing*, 19, 782-791.

Rosenberg, M. (2015). Health geography II: 'Dividing' health geography. *Progress in Human Geography*, 40, 546-554.

Rothman, K. J. (2012). *Epidemiology – An Introduction*. Oxford: Oxford University Press.

Rothman, K. J., Greenland, S. & Lash, T. L. (2008). *Modern Epidemiology*. Philadelphia: Lippincott Williams & Wilkins.

Ruel, M. T. & Arimond, M. (2002). Spot-check Observational Method for Assessing Hygiene Practices: Review of Experience and Implications for Programmes. *Journal of Health, Population and Nutrition*, 20, 65-76.

Ruel, M. T., Garrett, J. L., Morris, S. S., Maxwell, D. G., Oshaug, A., Engle, P. L., Menon, P., Slack, A. & Haddad, L. J. (1998). Urban challenges to food and nutrition security: a review of food security, health, and caregiving in the cities. *International Food Policy Research Institute (IFPRI)*, 51.

Santamaría, J. & Toranzos, G. A. (2003). Enteric pathogens and soil: a short review. *International Microbiology*, 6, 5-9.

Schmidt, W.-P., Arnold, B. F., Boisson, S., Genser, B., Luby, S. P., Barreto, M. L., Clasen, T. & Cairncross, S. (2011). Epidemiological methods in diarrhoea studies—an update. *Int J Epidemiol*, 40, 1678-1692.

Shuval, H. & Fattal, B. (2003). *Handbook of Water and Wastewater Micobiology*. London: Academic Press

Smit, J., Ratta, A. & Nasr, J. (1996). *Urban Agriculture: Food, Jobs and Sustainable Cities*. New York: United Nations Development Programme Publication Series.

Snow, J. (1857). Cholera, and the water supply in the south districts of London. *British Medical Journal*, s4, 864 - 865.

Sobsey, M. D. (2015). Waterborne and water-washed disease. In Bartram, J., with Baum, R., Coclanis, P.A., Gute, D.M., Kay, D., McFadyen, S., Pond, K., Robertson, W. & Rouse, M.J. (eds.) *Routledge Handbook of Water and Health*, London: Routledge.

Srinivasan, J. T. & Reddy, V. R. (2009). Impact of irrigation water quality on human health: A case study in India. *Ecological Economics*, 68, 2800-2807.

StataCorp. (2011). *Stata Statistical Software: Release 12 StataCorp. LP.*, College Station, TX.

Swaroop, S. (1956). Estimation of bacterial density of water samples: Methods of attaining international comparability. *Bulletin of the World Health Organization*, 14, 1089-1107.

Tam, S. (2012). Coprology and Caste: The Status of Sewerage in Ahmedabad, India. Northwestern University, *Comparative-Historical Social Science (CHSS) Working Paper No 12-002.*

Taylor, D. L., Kahawita, T. M., Cairncross, S. & Ensink, J. H. J. (2015). The Impact of Water, Sanitation and Hygiene Interventions to Control Cholera: A Systematic Review. *PLoS One*, 10, e0135676.

Teunis, P. F. M., van der Heijden, O. G., van der Giessen, J. W. B. & Havelaar, A. H. (1996). *The dose-response relation in human volunteers for gastro-intestinal pathogens*, Bilthoven, NL: National Institue of Public Health and the Enviornment (RIVM).

Thompson, J. & Cairncross, S. (2002). Drawers of water: assessing domestic water use in Africa. *Bulletin of the World Health Organization*, 80, 61-62.

Tirado, M. C., Cohen, M. J., Aberman, N., Meerman, J. & Thompson, B. (2010). Addressing the challenges of climate change and biofuel production for food and nutrition security. *Food Research International*, 43, 1729-1744.

Trang, D. T., Van Der Hoek, W., Tuan, N. D., Cam, P. D., Viet, V. H., Luu, D. D., Konradsen, F. & Dalsgaard, A. (2007). Skin disease among farmers using wastewater in rice cultivation in Nam Dinh, Vietnam. *Tropical Medicine & International Health*, 12, 51-58.

UNESCO (2003). *Water for People, Water for Life*, United Nations/World Water Assessment Programme, Paris: UNESCO.

UNICEF/WHO (2000). *Global Water Supply and Sanitation Assessment 2000*, New York: United Nations Children's Fund & World Health Organization.

UNICEF/WHO (2004). *Clinical Management of Acute Diarrhoea*, New York/Geneva: The United Nations Children's Fund/World Health Organization.

UNICEF/WHO (2009). *Diarrhoea: Why children are still dying and what can be done*, New York: UNICEF/WHO.

Verbrugge, L. M. (1980). Health diaries. *Med Care*, 18, 73-95.

Waddington, H., Snilstveit, B., White, H. & Fewtrell, L. (2009). Water, sanitation and hygiene interventions to combat childhood diarrhoea in developing countries. *3ie Synthetic Reviews*, 1.

Wagner, E. G. & Lanoix, J. N. (1958). Excreta disposal for rural areas and small communities. *Monograph Series World Health Organization*, 39, 1-182.

WaterAid (2006). *Sanitation for All - Still a long way to go*, New Delhi: WaterAid India.

Webb, A. L., Stein, A. D., Ramakrishnan, U., Hertzberg, V. S., Urizar, M. & Martorell, R. (2006). A simple index to measure hygiene behaviours. *Int J Epidemiol*, 35, 1469-77.

White, G. F., Bradley, D. J. & White, A. U. (1972). *Drawers of water: domestic water use in East Africa*. Chicago: University of Chicago Press.

WHO (1958). *International Standards for Drinking-Water*, Geneva: World Health Organization.

WHO (1989). *Health Guidelines for the Use of Wastewater in Agriculture and Aquaculture*, Geneva: World Health Organization.

WHO (2001). *Water quality: Guidelines, standards and health*, London: IWA Publishing.

WHO (2002). *Reduced Osmolarity Oral Rehydration Salts (ORS) Formulation*, Geneva: World Health Organization.

WHO (2006). *Guidelines for the safe use of wastewater, excreta and greywater. Volume 2: Wastewater use in agriculture, Vol. 2*, Geneva: World Health Organization.

WHO (2010). *NLIS Country Profile Indicators Interpretation Guide*, Geneva: World Health Organization.

WHO (2011). *Guidelines for drinking-water quality, fourth edition*, Geneva: World Health Organization.

WHO (2013). *Diarrhoeal disease*. World Health Organization. http://www.who.int/mediacentre/factsheets/fs330/en/, on: 27 February 2014.

WHO (2015). *Health in 2015: from MDGs to SDGs*, Geneva: World Health Organization.

Wilson, J. M. & Chandler, G. N. (1993). Sustained improvements in hygiene behaviour amongst village women in Lombok, Indonesia. *Transactions of the Royal Society of Tropical Medicine and Hygiene*, 87, 615-616.

Wolf, J., Prüss-Ustün, A., Cumming, O., Bartram, J., Bonjour, S., Cairncross, S., Clasen, T., Colford, J. M., Curtis, V., De France, J., Fewtrell, L., Freeman, M. C., Gordon, B., Hunter, P. R., Jeandron, A., Johnston, R. B., Mäusezahl, D., Mathers, C., Neira, M. & Higgins, J. P. T. (2014). Systematic review: Assessing the impact of drinking water and sanitation on diarrhoeal disease in low- and middle-income settings: systematic review and meta-regression. *Tropical Medicine & International Health*, 19, 928-942.

Zhang, M., Lu, F., Miao, R. & Jin, Y. (2014). System Variable Analysis on Development Stages of Urban Agriculture in Large Cities. *Asian Agricultural Research*, 06.

GEOGRAPHISCHE GESUNDHEITSFORSCHUNG

GEOGRAPHIC HEALTH RESEARCH

herausgegeben von

Thomas Kistemann, Jürgen Schweikart

Bisher ist in dieser Schriftenreihe erschienen:

Volume 1:

Rechenburg, A. (2016) Vorkommen von *Campylobacter* spp. in Oberflächengewässern

Die hygienische Trinkwasseraufbereitung und Abwasserentsorgung in Deutschland haben stark zur Reduzierung der Gesundheitsgefährdung der Bevölkerung durch wasserübertragene Krankheitserreger beigetragen. Dennoch kann die Wasserqualität durch den Eintrag von Mikroorganismen aus Punkt- oder diffusen Quellen beeinträchtigt werden. Fäkalbürtige Bakterien der Gattung *Campylobacter* finden sich regelmäßig in Oberflächengewässern. Sie können bereits in geringen Konzentrationen v.a. bei Kindern Durchfallerkrankungen mit teilweise schweren Verläufen induzieren. Die Studie schließt die Lücke einer bisher ausstehenden Risikoevaluierung von räumlich differenzierten Einzugsgebieten, verschiedenen Abwasserbehandlungen und einer bevölkerungsbezogenen Gesundheitsgefährdung für diese Bakterien.

Fließgewässer in vier Einzugsgebieten wurden auf das Auftreten von *Campylobacter* und weiteren hygienisch-mikrobiologischen Indikatorparametern sowie chemisch-physikalischen Kenngrößen untersucht. Zusätzlich wurden Proben an sechs Kläranlagen und an zwei Entlastungsbauwerken während Mischwasserabschlägen nach Starkregenereignissen gewonnen. Die Ergebnisse zeigten deutliche Unterschiede der Campylobacterkonzentrationen je nach maßgeblicher Oberflächennutzung im Einzugsgebiet, Ausbaugrad der Kläranlagen und Wetterbedingungen. Daraus ergeben sich Konflikte und

Infektionsrisiken bei der Gewässernutzung zur Trinkwassergewinnung, zu Freizeitzwecken und als Tränken-/Bewässerungswasser. Die Studie leistet einen wichtigen Beitrag zur Beurteilung von Gesundheitsgefährdungen durch *Campylobacter* bei der Nutzung von Oberflächenwasser.

Volume 2:

Githniji, S. W. (2017): Human Ecology of Malaria in Kenya. A case study of Kisii Highlands

Malaria uses almost half of the clinical services in Africa, making its control one of the most important challenges in global public health. Interventions such as the use of insecticide treated nets (ITNs) for people at risk; appropriate antimalarial drugs for people with probable or confirmed malaria and indoor residual spraying (IRS) of insecticides have been at the forefront of global efforts to control the disease. While these measures are important, proven environmental measures that succeeded in eradicating malaria vectors in vast parts of Europe and the Americas in the early 20th century and even in some parts of Africa are largely lacking.

This study examined the associations of malaria incidences with micro-ecological, socio-demographic and behavioural aspects in a rural highland epidemic-prone zone in south western Kenya.

Location of houses on flat swampy areas, staying outdoors at night, presence ofoxen in the compound, sleeping in a house with open eaves and family size greater than four people were significantly associated with increased risk of malaria. On the other hand, having sufficient food supplies throughout the year and keeping medicine at home were significantly associated with reduced risk of malaria. These findings point to the need for holistic approaches that draw connections between behavioural, socioeconomic and micro-ecological factors in malaria control.

Volume 3:

Ueberschär, N. (2018): Access to and utilization of health care. Spatial disparities of health center utilization in Huye District (Rwanda)

While the access to primary health care services is recognized as an important factor, it is rather their utilization that is contributing to a better health status of the population. Therefore Rwanda puts a lot of effort in the enhancement of the spatial and the financial access to health care services and its utilization. Only few studies have been dealing with the geographical access to health care in Rwanda. Until now the administrative boundaries of the sectors are considered as catchment areas of health centers but available data give the impression that not all patients follow this presetting.

The present study was conducted with the scope to contribute to the discussion of analyzing access and utilization in the context of the geographies of health. The main objectives of this study have been to determine the actual catchment areas of health centers in Huye District (Southern Province, Rwanda) and to test different approaches for an improved estimation of catchment areas. To identify the actual catchment areas, utilization data of health centers was analyzed and used for the validation of the different approaches. The comparison of different methods used in the GIS will add to a better understanding of their application. Additionally the study hopes to contribute to the general health care improvement process in Rwanda.

Volume 4:

Schreiber, C. (2019): Antibiotikaresistenzen in Abwasser und Gewässern. Einträge, Vorkommen, Verbreitung und gesundheitliche Bedeutung antibiotikaresistenter Bakterien in der aquatischen Umwelt

Antibiotika finden in der Humanmedizin und Intensivtierhaltung heute breite Anwendung. Sie gelangen über natürliche Ausscheidung von Mensch und Tier sowie unsachgemäße. Entsorgung in die Umwelt. Wichtige Eintragspfade stellen somit Abwasser, Klärschlamm und Gülle dar. Fließgewässer bilden wegen ihrer räumlichen Ausdehnung, ihrer Laufstrecke und Nutzung als Vorfluter für Siedlungsabwasser und Oberflächenabfluss landwirtschaftlich genutzter Flächen das Umweltkompartiment mit der größten Raumwirkung. Mikroorganismenund Bakterien können Resistenzen gegen Antibiotika entwickeln, was zu Problemen bei der medizinischen Behandlung führt. Bislang ist nicht hinreichend geklärt, welche Bedeutung der Eintrag häuslichen Abwassers sowie die Resistenzweitergabe zwischen Organismen für dieEntwicklung von Resistenzen in der aquatischen Umwelt haben.

Die vorliegende Studie liefert hierzu einen Beitrag aus Sicht der geographischen Gesundheitsforschung. Ziel des Vorhabens war es, am Beispiel eines Kläranlageneinzugsgebietes ohne angeschlossenem Krankenhaus, dem zugehörigem Vorfluter sowie dessen von Abwasser unbeeinflussten Oberläufen, die Verbreitung erworbener bakterieller Antibiotika-Resistenzen durch kommunales Abwasser zu analysieren. Untersucht wurden die Krankheitserreger *Pseudomonas aeruginosa* und *Campylobacter* spp. und die nicht-pathogenen Gewässerbakterien der Familie Rhodospirillaceae. Versuche zum horizontalen Gentransfer der Umweltisolate und eine Erhebung des Risikoverhaltens der Bevölkerung im Kläranlageneinzugsgebiet bezüglich ihres Entsorgungsverhaltens von Arzneimittel und Therapietreue bei Anti-biotikaeinnahme ergänzen den methodischen Dreiklang, der im Sinne sozial-ökologischer Forschung auch die Triangulation der betrachteten Subjekte Umwelt, Mikroorganismen und Mensch spiegelt. Die Ergebnisse der Studienabschnitte münden in einer Risikoabschätzung.

Volume 5:

Völker, S. (2020): Stadtblaue Gesundheit. Aspekte menschlichen Wohlbefindens an urbanen Gewässern

Aquatische (blaue) Landschaften dienen dem Menschen schon seit Jahrhunderten als Gesundheitsressource, jedoch hat sich dieser Landschaftstyp erst in den vergangenen Jahren zu einem Thema der Gesundheitsforschung entwickelt. Während im städtischen Umfeld Wasser als wichtiges Gestaltungselement integriert („Stadtblau") wird, sind seine gesundheitlichen Wirkungen bisher nur wenig erforscht.

Das vorliegende Buch konzeptualisiert und analysiert umfassend die Komplexität menschlicher Interaktion mit Stadtblau. Unter Anwendung geographischer, soziologischer und psychologischer Forschungsmethoden wird ein interdisziplinäres, multi-dimensionales Abbild gesundheitswirksamer Prozesse in stadtblauen Räumen generiert. Ein anschließender qualitativer und quantitativer Vergleich mit Grünräumen kann zusätzlich raumspezifische, gesundheitliche Wirkungen aufdecken.

Die interdisziplinäre, triangulative Herangehensweise des Buches bildet die Grundlage für ein detailliertes Verständnis für die Bedeutung von Stadtblau für die Öffentliche Gesundheit und das menschliche Wohlbefinden.

Volume 6:

Kistemann,T. & Schweikart, J. (Hrsg.) (2022): Geographien der Gesundheit. Beiträge zum 50-jährigen Bestehen des Arbeitskreises Medizinische Geographie und Geographische Gesundheitsforschung in der DGfG

Vor 50 Jahren, im Jahr 1972, wurde auf Schloss Reisensburg in Günzburg an der Donau der Arbeitskreis mit dem Namen Medizinische Geographie im damaligen Zentralverband der deutschen Geographen gegründet. Damit wurde ein gemeinsamer Raum geschaffen, der es erleichterte, sich zu Themen an der Schnittstelle von Medizin und Geographie auszutauschen. Gleichzeitig war die Institutionalisierung ein wichtiger Meilenstein, um deutschsprachige Aktivitäten im internationalen Kontext besser sichtbar zu machen. Mit den Jahrzehnten erweiterten sich die Inhalte deutlich und immer wieder wurden aktuelle Forschungsfragen des dynamischen Fachgebietes integriert. Dies hatte zur Folge, dass der Name des Arbeitskreises mehrfach angepasst wurde.

Der vorliegende Sammelband spiegelt das breite Spektrum aktueller Themen des Arbeitskreises wider. Der erste Beitrag beleuchtet die Historie des Arbeitskreises von 1972-2022 sowie seine Perspektiven für die Zukunft. Es folgen Beiträge von Mitgliedern des Arbeitskreises, die das Themenspektrum sicherlich nicht vollständig, jedoch weitgehend repräsentativ wiedergeben. Die Beiträge reichen von der Krankheitsökologie über die Versorgungsforschung bis hin zu aktuellen Themen aus der postmedizinischen Geographie. Bei der Lektüre werden mehrerer Aspekte offenkundig: der interdisziplinäre Charakter der Beiträge, ihre Aktualität, die große methodische Vielfalt und die erhebliche praktische und gesellschaftliche Relevanz.